Writing about Theatre and Drama

Second Edition

Writing about Theatre and Drama

Second Edition

Suzanne Hudson
University of Colorado

WADSWORTH
CENGAGE Learning

Australia • Brazil • Japan • Korea • Mexico • Singapore • Spain • United Kingdom • United States

WADSWORTH
CENGAGE Learning

Writing about Theatre and Drama, Second Edition
Suzanne Hudson

Publisher: Holly J. Allen

Assistant Editor:
Darlene Amidon-Brent

Editorial Assistant: Sarah Allen

Marketing Manager: Mark Orr

Marketing Assistant:
Andrew Keay

Technology Project Manager:
Jeanette Wiseman

Advertising Project Manager:
Shemika Britt

Manager, Editorial Production
Edward Wade

Print Buyer: Barbara Britton

Permissions Editor:
Chelsea Junget

Cover Designer:
Brenda Duke Design

Cover photograph courtesy of
Cynthia Turnbull and
Hsing-lin Tracy Chung of
Denison University,
Granville, Ohio.

For product information and
technology assistance, contact us at **Cengage Learning
Customer & Sales Support, 1-800-354-9706**

For permission to use material from this text or product,
submit all requests online at **www.cengage.com/permissions**
Further permissions questions can be emailed to
permissionrequest@cengage.com

Library of Congress Control Number: 2004117706

ISBN-13: 978-0-534-62913-7

ISBN-10: 0-534-62913-X

Wadsworth
20 Davis Drive
Belmont, CA 94002
USA

Cengage Learning is a leading provider of customized learning solutions with office locations around the globe, including Singapore, the United Kingdom, Australia, Mexico, Brazil, and Japan. Locate your local office at **www.cengage.com/global**

Cengage Learning products are represented in Canada by Nelson Education, Ltd.

To learn more about Wadsworth, visit
www.cengage.com/wadsworth

Purchase any of our products at your local college store or at our preferred online store **www.CengageBrain.com**

Printed in the United States of America
3 4 5 6 7   16 15 14 13 12

FD221

Contents

Chapter Three

Chapter Four

Chapter Five

Preface

Although many composition texts cover the general topic of writing about literature, few address the particular needs of any one form of literature. The analysis of drama demands not only the basics of college-level composition, but also the critical skills of inquiry and inference relating to the foundations and structures of drama, the social and religious purposes of performance, and the interplay between actor and audience.

In combining composition and critical inquiry, *Writing about Theatre and Drama* meets the needs of both students who write about theatre and of instructors who want to read interesting, insightful student essays and research papers.

Writing about Theatre and Drama intends to demystify the process of producing such papers. It takes readers through every step from choosing a topic to citing sources, with emphasis on formulating and supporting a thesis. The principles and processes recommended in this book are classroom tested; every student essay in this book has resulted from their application. For this reason, the student essays are a highlight of *Writing about Theatre and Drama*.

Another highlight of *Writing about Theatre and Drama* is the diverse collection of professionally written samples. As students read prose that projects confidence and expertise, their own writing improves. Here, students can study the techniques and styles of writers who span the ages—from Aristotle to Susan Sontag—as they cover topics ranging from kabuki to queer theory.

Organized according to writing assignments, *Writing about Theatre and Drama* devotes a chapter each to writing short responses, analytical essays, argument essays, performance reviews, and research papers. Each chapter includes learning aids—critical thinking and writing exercises, topic suggestions, templates for planning essays, references to pertinent Web sites, illustrations from plays, and revision checklists. Students who use the guidance offered in this textbook are likely to produce sophisticated, organized, focused critical essays.

Anyone who compares this second edition to the first one, titled *How to Write about Theatre and Drama*, will notice extensive revisions apart from the changed title. This edition reflects lessons I have learned from my students at the University of Colorado who have used my textbook and proven some of my assumptions to be false, some of my instructions hasty. For example, this edition dedicates an early chapter to generating emotional responses to theatre and drama and to writing informal papers that reflect those responses—a necessary step in the process of composing more formal essays. My students have also convinced me that writing the performance review is more difficult than I had supposed and should not be presented as a less rigorous task than writing critical essays and research papers. Additionally, the style of writing in this edition is livelier and the projected attitude toward teaching composition more positive. I have grown, apparently, as both a writer and a teacher.

Along with improvements in the textbook suggested both consciously and unconsciously by my students, this second edition capitalizes on innumerable helpful suggestions made by experts in the fields of composition, rhetoric, and theatre: Lou Ann Wright, University of Wyoming; Don Marinelli, Carnegie Mellon University; Felicia Hardison Londre, University of Missouri—Kansas City; Charlotte Canning, University of Texas—Austin; Nate Bynum, Mississippi State University; Joan Harrington, Western Michigan University; Kent Lantaff, University of Miami; John Gronbeck-Tedesco, University of Kansas—Lawrence; Wendy Arons, University of Notre Dame; Don Eron, Molly LeClair, Judith Lavinsky, Juliet Wittman, and Joan Lord-Hall, University of Colorado. To Paul Levitt and Elissa Guralnick, thank you for teaching me how to teach composition.

I also thank my publisher and editors at Wadsworth, Cengage Learning for the opportunity to revise and improve upon the first edition of this textbook, as well as their expertise in organizational and technical considerations: Holly Allen, Sarah Allen, Edward Wade, Shona Burke, Mary Noel, Brenda Duke, Chelsea Junget, and Barbara Armentrout.

To the students who have allowed me to use their work—Benjamin Fisher, Denise Bush, Zachary Bush, Joe Darden, Rebecca Penkoff, Debra Blaine, Jordan Young, Kim Compton, and Chris Gluckman—you are in my extreme good graces.

Introduction

Voltaire, a French playwright, once said that attending the theatre is "the most divine pastime," a sentiment with which theatre students tend to agree. The pleasure of sitting in a quiet, dark place, suspending disbelief, and submitting to that curious but undeniable theatrical impulse is indeed divine. The theatre is personal and interactive in ways that television and movies can never be. Someone in the audience might be compelled to stand up, as according to legend one man did, and scream as Othello wraps his hands around Desdemona's throat, "She is innocent, Othello!" Attending the theatre is an immediate, not a canned, experience.

Theatregoing requires active participation. One must decide, for example, where to look, and how closely, for there is no camera to make such decisions for us. Theatregoing requires concentration as well. An actor might sneeze; a stagehand might stumble, but the theatregoer blocks out all distractions from the drama unfolding onstage.

Writing, like theatregoing, is an active, not a passive occupation. Writers must decide where to look and how closely. They too must block out distractions and concentrate on their ideas to prevent them from evaporating. Writing, like theatregoing, is not for the lazy.

Demanding as it is, writing reaps vast rewards. The act of writing sharpens our wits and bolsters our confidence in our persuasiveness. When we write well, our stock rises. People seek our advice and companionship. Since good writers are in short supply, an applicant's writing skills are often the deciding factor in hiring. More importantly, though, we are obligated to contribute to the study of humanity, and theatre mirrors the experience of being human more effectively, perhaps, than any other art form.

Writing about Theatre and Drama is designed to equip you with an understanding of the processes of discovery, development, and structure that will help you communicate your own unique perceptions. The book will spark fresh insights and show you how to validate and display them. Your most sophisticated ideas are best hung on the barest frames.

Chapter 1 aims both to arouse your emotional responses to drama and to help you recognize them. Chapter 2 guides you through basic principles and processes that apply to just about any writing challenge. Chapters 3 and 4, designed to convey the elusive concepts inherent in analysis and argument, will help you advance your own opinions. Chapter 5, with the assistance of some of the world's most engaging theatre critics, shows you how to write colorful, entertaining performance reviews. Chapter 6 demonstrates legitimate and effective uses of sources to corroborate your own ideas. Finally, a handbook summarizes conventions in usage, grammar and punctuation to help you polish that final draft.

Writing about Theatre and Drama exists for the benefit of students who hope to write well about plays as literature and plays in performance. It is useful to both undergraduates and graduate students who are expected to analyze their subjects, not merely describe them. But this book is also for anyone who loves a good intellectual stretch. Use this book if you love the theatre and want to claim some part of it for yourself.

Responding to Theatre and Drama

Responding Objectively	*Paraphrasing*
	Summarizing
A One-Act Play: *Trifles*	
Responding Subjectively	Questions to Guide Your
	Responses to Theatre
	and Drama
	Inferring
	Comparing or Contrasting
	Interpreting
	Evaluating
	Arguing
Writing Informally	

The performing arts evoke unique responses in us. When Arthur Miller's *Death of a Salesman* premiered, Brooks Atkinson wrote, "Arthur Miller has written a superb drama. From every point of view *Death of a Salesman*, which was acted at the Morosco last evening, is rich and memorable drama."[1] Having seen the same production, Frederick Morgan wrote, "The language is entirely undistinguished (their personages are continually grunting, groaning and vehemently repeating the tritest colloquialisms); the tone of the play can best be described as a sustained snivel."[2] Though our responses to art vary, sometimes wildly, they do matter. They characterize us both individually and as a culture. This chapter provides you with the opportunity to recognize your emotional responses to drama and to record them *informally*, an important step in the process of writing. Often, such informal responses grow into fuller, more formal critical essays.

Responding Objectively

Sometimes we react to drama swiftly and surely. Other times, we do not know what to think. If you have just read or seen in performance Amiri Baraka's *Dutchman*, for example, your response may be confusion. What on earth are Lula and Clay talking about? Why does she kill him?

At such times, we might try paraphrasing one of the couple's conversations or summarizing a scene. Using our own words can help us clarify the play's meaning. Then our reactions can emerge.

Paraphrasing

To **paraphrase** is to restate another's speech, either written or spoken, in your own words and style. Paraphrasing is an important academic skill; it allows you to develop and demonstrate your understanding of ideas. When you are paraphrasing for yourself only, there are no rules. You may shift points of view, interpret broadly or narrowly, and use interesting phrases from the original passage at will. But when paraphrasing for a listening or reading audience, certain conventions apply:

- You must completely recast the original passage. If your paraphrase resembles the original too closely, you have, perhaps unwittingly, committed an act of **plagiarism,** which is the illegitimate use of another's words. Simple substitution of synonyms or rearranging of word order is insufficient; you must use your own words, your own style, and your own sentence structure.

- Your paraphrase must accurately convey what the original passage *says*, not what you believe it *means*.

- Do not set paraphrased material in quotation marks.

- Maintain a consistent point of view; that is, do not shift from third person to second person, for example, or shift from an objective viewpoint to a subjective one.

- Your paraphrase must not be colored by your own ideas or opinions.

- When you are paraphrasing facts that are *widely available*, there is no need to cite or acknowledge your source. Still, you cannot copy another writer word for word, no matter how well-known the content.

- If the words you are paraphrasing convey factual information that is *not* widely available, you must provide a source citation.

- If you are paraphrasing someone's ideas, as opposed to facts, you must accompany the paraphrase with an *acknowledgment phrase*, such as "According to so and so . . ." or "As so and so has observed . . . ." You may also need a source citation at the end of your paraphrase, if the original source is not widely available.

Exercise 1-1

Read the following passage from Shakespeare's *Hamlet* and the paraphrases that follow. Which paraphrase of Polonius's advice to his son, Laertes, most completely fulfills the preceding guidelines for paraphrasing? Explain your choice and your rejection of the other paraphrases.

Polonius:
[. . .] Give thy thoughts no tongue,
Nor any unproportioned thought his act.
Be thou familiar but by no means vulgar.
The friends thou hast, and their adoption tried,
Grapple them to thy soul with hoops of steel,
But do not dull thy palm with entertainment
Of each new-hatched unfledged comrade. Beware
Of entrance to a quarrel, but being in,
Bear't that th'opposèd may beware of thee.
Give every man thine ear but few thy voice.
Take each man's censure, but reserve thy judgement.
Costly thy habit as thy purse can buy,
But not expressed in fancy; rich not gaudy;
For the apparel oft proclaims the man,
And they in France of the best rank and station
Are of all most select and generous chief in that.
Neither a borrower nor a lender be,
For loan oft loses both itself and friend,
And borrowing dulls the edge of husbandry.
This above all—to thine own self be true,
And it must follow, as the night the day,
Thou canst not then be false to any man. (1.3.59-80)

Paraphrase #1: Polonius tells Laertes to behave yourself while you're in France.

Paraphrase #2: Polonius tells Laertes not to "talk too much or be too familiar." He also warns Laertes to "hang with old friends, not make new friends; don't fight, but fight well; buy nice clothes; and don't lend friends money." Polonius's most important advice, however, is that to one's own self one should be true because, then, one can't be false to any man (1.3.59-80).

Paraphrase #3: Polonius offers Laertes the following advice: Don't say what you're thinking, and don't act without thinking. Be friendly, but not too friendly. Spend your time with your old, tried-and-true friends; don't spend too much money on entertainment with new friends, whose loyalties haven't yet been tested. Try not to get into fights, but if you find yourself in one, let your opponent know you're no pushover. Listen to everyone's point of view, but don't tell everyone yours. When other people judge you, take it gracefully, but don't be quick to judge others. Buy tasteful clothes; people often judge others by the way they're dressed, and the French know a good dresser when they see one. Don't borrow money, and don't lend it. Lending your friends money will cost you both your money and your friendship, and borrowing money makes you less conservative than you should be. Most importantly, be honest with yourself, and you'll be honest with others (1.3.59-80).

Exercise 1-2

Paraphrase the following passage from Shakespeare's *Othello*. The speaker is Emilia, Desdemona's maid.

Emilia:
But I do think it is their husbands' faults
If wives do fall. Say that they slack their duties,
And pour our treasures into foreign laps,
Or else break out in peevish jealousies,
Throwing restraint upon us; or say they strike us,
Or scant our former having in despite:
Why, we have galls; and though we have some grace,
Yet have we some revenge. Let husbands know
Their wives have sense like them. They see, and smell,
And have their palates both for sweet and sour,
As husbands have. What is it that they do
When they change us for others? Is it sport?
I think it is. And doth affection breed it?
I think it doth. Is't frailty that thus errs?
It is so, too. And have not we affections,
Desires for sport, and frailty, as men have?
Then let them use us well, else let them know
The ills we do, their ills instruct us so. (4.3.85-102)

Summarizing

Whereas a paraphrase offers a literal translation of the original passage, including most of its details, a **summary** offers the original passage's main idea, often without the supporting details. Therefore, a summary is usually shorter than a paraphrase. A summary of Emilia's speech in Exercise 1-2 might be that women are no different from men in their reasons or propensity for unfaithfulness. Otherwise, the criteria for summarizing are essentially the same as those for paraphrasing.

1-1 "To thine own self be true," says Polonius to his son, Laertes, in this 1995 production of *Hamlet* by the Colorado Shakespeare Festival at the University of Colorado, directed by Patrick Kelly. Photographer: Martin Natvig.

The following guidelines provide an efficient method for summarizing longer prose passages:

- First, read the passage carefully.
- Find the **thesis** (the statement of the whole passage's main point). Underline it.

- Find and underline each **topic sentence** (the statement of the paragraph's main point). If the paragraph has no topic sentence, compose one of your own in the margin.

- Draft a summary by paraphrasing the thesis in writing and then paraphrasing the topic sentence of each paragraph, adding whatever connecting material is necessary for coherence.

- Paraphrase the summary you have written, as an added measure against plagiarism.

- Check the summary against the original passage to ensure that your summary does not too closely match the original but that it accurately and objectively conveys the original's ideas.

- Make it clear to your reader throughout your summary that these are someone else's ideas, not yours.

Exercise 1-3

Read the following excerpt from Aristotle's *The Poetics* and the summaries that follow. Which summary of Aristotle's essay most completely fulfills the preceding guidelines for summarizing? Explain your choice and your rejection of the other summaries.

[To produce the tragic effect] it is clear: first, that decent people must not be shown passing from good fortune to misfortune (for that is not fearful or pitiful but disgusting); again, vicious people must not be shown passing from misfortune to good fortune (for that is the most untragic situation possible—it has none of the requisites, it is neither humane, nor pitiful, nor fearful); nor again should an utterly evil man fall from good fortune into misfortune (for though a plot of that kind would be humane, it would not induce pity or fear—pity is induced by undeserved misfortune, and fear by the misfortunes of normal people, so that this situation will be neither pitiful nor fearful). So we are left with the man between these extremes: that is to say, the kind of man who neither is distinguished for excellence and virtue, nor comes to grief on account of baseness and vice, but on account of some error; a man of great reputation and prosperity, like Oedipus and Thyestes and conspicuous people of such families as theirs.[3]

Summary #1: To achieve the tragic effect, according to Aristotle, the playwright should show a person who is neither particularly righteous nor particularly wicked falling on hard times because he or she has made some mistake in judgment.

Summary #2: Aristotle says that the only way to achieve the tragic effect is to show rich and famous people falling from high places because of bad luck and a character flaw.

Summary #3: The tragic effects of pity and fear can be achieved by showing conspicuous people like Oedipus and Thyestes and people of such families as theirs falling from grace not because of baseness and vice but because of some error.

Exercise 1-4

Summarize the following passage from Arthur Miller's essay, "Tragedy and the Common Man."

As a general rule, to which there may be exceptions unknown to me, I think the tragic feeling is evoked in us when we are in the presence of a character who is ready to lay down his life, if need be, to secure one thing—his sense of personal dignity. From Orestes to Hamlet, Medea to Macbeth, the underlying struggle is that of the individual attempting to gain his "rightful" position in his society.

Sometimes he is one who has been displaced from it, sometimes one who seeks to attain it for the first time, but the fateful wound from which the inevitable events spiral is the wound of indignity, and its dominant force is indignation. Tragedy, then, is the consequence of a man's total compulsion to evaluate himself justly.

In the sense of having been initiated by the hero himself, the tale always reveals what has been called his "tragic flaw," a failing that is not peculiar to grand or elevated characters. Nor is it necessarily a weakness. The flaw, or crack in the character, is really nothing—and need be nothing—but his inherent unwillingness to remain passive in the face of what he conceives to be a challenge to his dignity, his image of his rightful status. Only the passive, only those who accept their lot without active retaliation, are "flawless." Most of us are in that category.[4]

1-2: "Married to the law." Mrs. Hale and Mrs. Peters suppress a smile in the University of Wisconsin's 2001 production of *Trifles*, directed by Richard Kalinoski. Photographer: Mick Alderson.

A One-Act Play: *Trifles*

Before we move from objective responses to subjective ones, we will stop to read a play. Because many of the examples in this and subsequent chapters are based upon *Trifles*, the play is reprinted here in its entirety.

Susan Glaspell's classic one-act drama, *Trifles*, first performed in 1916 by the famous experimental theatre group, the Provincetown Players, is widely praised as one of the most powerful murder mysteries ever written. This absorbing tale lends itself well to analysis, since it can be read from many viewpoints, as well as to argument, since its moral imperative is questionable.

Trifles

Characters

George Henderson, *County Attorney*   Mrs. Peters
Henry Peters, *Sheriff*   Mrs. Hale
Lewis Hale, *a Neighboring Farmer*

Scene

The kitchen in the now abandoned farmhouse of John Wright, a gloomy kitchen, and left without having been put in order—unwashed pans under the sink, a loaf of bread outside the breadbox, a dish towel on the table— other signs of incompleted work. At the rear the outer door opens and the Sheriff *comes in followed by the* County Attorney *and* Hale. *The* Sheriff *and* Hale *are men in middle life, the* County Attorney *is a young man; all are much bundled up and go at once to the stove. They are followed by two women—the* Sheriff's wife *first; she is a slight wiry woman, a thin nervous face.* Mrs. Hale *is larger and would ordinarily be called more comfortable looking, but she is disturbed now and looks fearfully about as she enters. The women have come in slowly, and stand close together near the door.*

County Attorney. [*Rubbing his hands.*] This feels good. Come up to the fire, ladies.

Mrs. Peters. [*After taking a step forward.*] I'm not—cold.

Sheriff. [*Unbuttoning his overcoat and stepping away from the stove as if to mark the beginning of official business.*] Now, Mr. Hale, before we move things about, you explain to Mr. Henderson just what you saw when you came here yesterday morning.

County Attorney. By the way, has anything been moved? Are things just as you left them yesterday?

Sheriff. [*Looking about.*] It's just the same. When it dropped below zero last night I thought I'd better send Frank out this morning to make a fire for us—no use getting pneumonia with a big case on, but I told him not to touch anything except the stove—and you know Frank.

County Attorney. Somebody should have been left here yesterday.

Sheriff. Oh—yesterday. When I had to send Frank to Morris Center for that man who went crazy—I want you to know I had my hands full yesterday. I knew you could get back from Omaha by today and as long as I went over everything here myself—

County Attorney. Well, Mr. Hale, tell just what happened when you came here yesterday morning.

Hale. Harry and I had started to town with a load of potatoes. We came
along the road from my place and as I got here I said, "I'm going to see
if I can't get John Wright to go in with me on a party telephone." I spoke
to Wright about it once before and he put me off, saying folks talked too
much anyway, and all he asked was peace and quiet—I guess you know
about how much he talked himself; but I thought maybe if I went to the
house and talked about it before his wife, though I said to Harry that I
didn't know as what his wife wanted made much difference to John—

County Attorney. Let's talk about that later, Mr. Hale. I do want to talk
about that, but tell now just what happened when you got to the house.

Hale. I didn't hear or see anything; I knocked at the door, and still it was all
quiet inside. I knew they must be up, it was past eight o'clock. So I
knocked again, and I thought I heard somebody say, "Come in." I wasn't
sure, I'm not sure yet, but I opened the door—this door [*indicating the
door by which the two women are still standing*] and there in that
rocker—[*pointing to it*] sat Mrs. Wright.
[*They all look at the rocker.*]

County Attorney. What—was she doing?

Hale. She was rockin' back and forth. She had her apron in her hand and
was kind of—pleating it.

County Attorney. And how did she—look?

Hale. Well, she looked queer.

County Attorney. How do you mean—queer?

Hale. Well, as if she didn't know what she was going to do next. And kind
of done up.

County Attorney. How did she seem to feel about your coming?

Hale. Why, I don't think she minded—one way or other. She didn't pay
much attention. I said, "How do, Mrs. Wright, it's cold, ain't it?" And
she said, "Is it?"—and went on kind of pleating at her apron. Well, I was
surprised; she didn't ask me to come up to the stove, or to set down, but
just sat there, not even looking at me, so I said, "I want to see John." And
then she—laughed. I guess you would call it a laugh. I thought of Harry
and the team outside, so I said a little sharp: "Can't I see John?" "No,"
she says, kind o' dull like. "Ain't he home?" says I. "Yes," says she,
"he's home." "Then why can't I see him?" I asked her, out of patience.
"'Cause he's dead," says she. "*Dead?*" says I. She just nodded her head,
not getting a bit excited, but rockin' back and forth. "Why—where is
he?" says I, not knowing what to say. She just pointed upstairs—like that
[*himself pointing to the room above*]. I got up, with the idea of going up
there. I walked from there to here—then I says, "Why, what did he die
of?" "He died of a rope round his neck," says she, and just went on
pleatin' at her apron. Well, I went out and called Harry. I thought I
might—need help. We went upstairs and there he was lyin'—

County Attorney. I think I'd rather have you go into that upstairs, where you can point it all out. Just go on now with the rest of the story.

Hale. Well, my first thought was to get that rope off. It looked . . . [*stops, his face twitches*]. . . but Harry, he went up to him, and he said, "No, he's dead all right, and we'd better not touch anything." So we went back down stairs. She was still sitting that same way. "Has anybody been notified?" I asked. "No," says she, unconcerned. "Who did this, Mrs. Wright?" said Harry. He said it businesslike—and she stopped pleatin' of her apron. "I don't know," she says. "You don't *know*?" says Harry. "No," says she. "Weren't you sleepin' in the bed with him?" says Harry. "Yes," says she, "but I was on the inside." "Somebody slipped a rope round his neck and strangled him and you didn't wake up?" says Harry. "I didn't wake up," she said after him. We must 'a looked as if we didn't see how that could be, for after a minute she said, "I sleep sound." Harry was going to ask her more questions but I said maybe we ought to let her tell her story first to the coroner, or the sheriff. So Harry went fast as he could to Rivers' place, where there's a telephone.

County Attorney. And what did Mrs. Wright do when she knew that you had gone for the coroner?

Hale. She moved from that chair to this one over here [*pointing to a small chair in the corner*] and just sat there with her hands held together and looking down. I got a feeling that I ought to make some conversation, so I said I had come in to see if John wanted to put in a telephone, and at that she started to laugh, and then she stopped and looked at me—scared. [*The* County Attorney, *who has had his notebook out, makes a note.*] I dunno, maybe it wasn't scared. I wouldn't like to say it was. Soon Harry got back, and then Dr. Lloyd came, and you, Mr. Peters, and so I guess that's all I know that you don't.

County Attorney. [*Looking around.*] I guess we'll go upstairs first—and then out to the barn and around there. [*To the* Sheriff.] You're convinced that there was nothing important here—nothing that would point to any motive.

Sheriff. Nothing here but kitchen things.

[*The* County Attorney, *after again looking around the kitchen, opens the door of a cupboard closet. He gets up on a chair and looks on a shelf. Pulls his hand away, sticky.*]

County Attorney. Here's a nice mess.

[*The women draw nearer.*]

Mrs. Peters. [*To the other woman.*] Oh, her fruit; it did freeze. [*To the* County Attorney.] She worried about that when it turned so cold. She said the fire'd go out and her jars would break.

Sheriff. Well, can you beat the women! Held for murder and worryin' about her preserves.

County Attorney. I guess before we're through she may have something
   more serious than preserves to worry about.

Hale. Well, women are used to worrying over trifles.

   [*The two women move a little closer together.*]

County Attorney. [*With the gallantry of a young politician.*] And yet, for all
   their worries, what would we do without the ladies? [*The women do not
   unbend. He goes to the sink, takes a dipperful of water from the pail and,
   pouring it into a basin, washes his hands. Starts to wipe them on the
   roller towel, turns it for a cleaner place.*] Dirty towels! [*Kicks his foot
   against the pans under the sink.*] Not much of a housekeeper, would you
   say, ladies?

Mrs. Hale. [*Stiffly.*] There's a great deal of work to be done on a farm.

County Attorney. To be sure. And yet [*with a little bow to her*] I know there
   are some Dickson County farmhouses which do not have such roller
   towels.

   [*He gives it a pull to expose its full length again.*]

Mrs. Hale. Those towels get dirty awful quick. Men's hands aren't always
   as clean as they might be.

County Attorney. Ah, loyal to your sex, I see. But you and Mrs. Wright
   were neighbors. I suppose you were friends, too.

Mrs. Hale. [*Shaking her head.*] I've not seen much of her of late years. I've
   not been in this house—it's more than a year.

County Attorney. And why was that? You didn't like her?

Mrs. Hale. I liked her all well enough. Farmers' wives have their hands full,
   Mr. Henderson. And then—

County Attorney. Yes—?

Mrs. Hale. [*Looking about.*] It never seemed a very cheerful place.

County Attorney. No—it's not cheerful. I shouldn't say she had the
   homemaking instinct.

Mrs. Hale. Well, I don't know as Wright had, either.

County Attorney. You mean that they didn't get on very well?

Mrs. Hale. No, I don't mean anything. But I don't think a place'd be any
   cheerfuller for John Wright's being in it.

County Attorney. I'd like to talk more of that a little later. I want to get the
   lay of things upstairs now.

   [*He goes to the left, where three steps lead to a stair door.*]

Sheriff. I suppose anything Mrs. Peters does'll be all right. She was to take
   in some clothes for her, you know, and a few little things. We left in such
   a hurry yesterday.

County Attorney. Yes, but I would like to see what you take, Mrs. Peters,
   and keep an eye out for anything that might be of use to us.

Mrs. Peters. Yes, Mr. Henderson.

   [*The women listen to the men's steps on the stairs, then look about the
   kitchen.*]

Mrs. Hale. I'd hate to have men coming into my kitchen, snooping around and criticizing.
[*She arranges the pans under sink which the* **County Attorney** *had shoved out of place.*]
Mrs. Peters. Of course it's no more than their duty.
Mrs. Hale. Duty's all right, but I guess that deputy sheriff that came out to make the fire might have got a little of this on. [*Gives the roller towel a pull.*] Wish I'd thought of that sooner. Seems mean to talk about her for not having things slicked up when she had to come away in such a hurry.
Mrs. Peters. [*Who has gone to a small table in the left rear corner of the room, and lifted one end of a towel that covers a pan.*] She had bread set. [*Stands still.*]
Mrs. Hale. [*Eyes fixed on a loaf of bread beside the breadbox, which is on a low shelf at the other side of the room. Moves slowly toward it.*] She was going to put this in there. [*Picks up loaf, then abruptly drops it. In a manner of returning to familiar things.*] It's a shame about her fruit. I wonder if it's all gone. [*Gets up on the chair and looks.*] I think there's some here that's all right, Mrs. Peters. Yes—here; [*holding it toward the window*] this is cherries, too. [*Looking again.*] I declare I believe that's the only one. [*Gets down, bottle in her hand. Goes to the sink and wipes it off on the outside.*] She'll feel awful bad after all her hard work in the hot weather. I remember the afternoon I put up my cherries last summer. [*She puts the bottle on the big kitchen table, center of the room. With a sigh, is about to sit down in the rocking-chair. Before she is seated realizes what chair it is; with a slow look at it, steps back. The chair, which she has touched, rocks back and forth.*]
Mrs. Peters. Well, I must get those things from the front room closet. [*She goes to the door at the right, but after looking into the other room, steps back.*] You coming with me, Mrs. Hale? You could help me carry them. [*They go in the other room; reappear,* **Mrs. Peters** *carrying a dress and skirt,* **Mrs. Hale** *following with a pair of shoes.*]
Mrs. Peters. My, it's cold in there.
[*She puts the clothes on the big table, and hurries to the stove.*]
Mrs. Hale. [*Examining her skirt.*] Wright was close. I think maybe that's why she kept so much to herself. She didn't even belong to the Ladies Aid. I suppose she felt she couldn't do her part, and then you don't enjoy things when you feel shabby. She used to wear pretty clothes and be lively, when she was Minnie Foster, one of the town girls singing in the choir. But that—oh, that was thirty years ago. This all you was to take in?
Mrs. Peters. She said she wanted an apron. Funny thing to want, for there isn't much to get you dirty in jail, goodness knows. But I suppose just to make her feel more natural. She said they was in the top drawer in this

cupboard. Yes, here. And then her little shawl that always hung behind
the door. [*Opens stair door and looks.*] Yes, here it is.
[*Quickly shuts door leading upstairs.*]

Mrs. Hale. [*Abruptly moving toward her.*] Mrs. Peters?

Mrs. Peters. Yes, Mrs. Hale?

Mrs. Hale. Do you think she did it?

Mrs. Peters. [*In a frightened voice.*] Oh, I don't know.

Mrs. Hale. Well, I don't think she did. Asking for an apron and her little
shawl. Worrying about her fruit.

Mrs. Peters. [*Starts to speak, glances up, where footsteps are heard in the
room above. In a low voice.*] Mr. Peters says it looks bad for her. Mr.
Henderson is awful sarcastic in a speech and he'll make fun of her sayin'
she didn't wake up.

Mrs. Hale. Well, I guess John Wright didn't wake when they was slipping
that rope under his neck.

Mrs. Peters. No, it's strange. It must have been done awful crafty and still.
They say it was such a—funny way to kill a man, rigging it all up like
that.

Mrs. Hale. That's just what Mr. Hale said. There was a gun in the house. He
says that's what he can't understand.

Mrs. Peters. Mr. Henderson said coming out that what was needed for the
case was a motive; something to show anger, or—sudden feeling.

Mrs. Hale. [*Who is standing by the table.*] Well, I don't see any signs of
anger around here. [*She puts her hand on the dish towel which lies on the
table, stands looking down at table, one half of which is clean, the other
half messy.*] It's wiped to here. [*Makes a move as if to finish work, then
turns and looks at loaf of bread outside the breadbox. Drops towel. In
that voice of coming back to familiar things.*] Wonder how they are
finding things upstairs. I hope she had it a little more red-up up there.
You know, it seems kind of sneaking. Locking her up in town and then
coming out here and trying to get her own house to turn against her!

Mrs. Peters. But Mrs. Hale, the law is the law.

Mrs. Hale. I s'pose 'tis. [*Unbuttoning her coat.*] Better loosen up your
things, Mrs. Peters. You won't feel them when you go out.
[**Mrs. Peters** *takes off her fur tippet, goes to hang it on hook at back of
room, stands looking at the under part of the small corner table.*]

Mrs. Peters. She was piecing a quilt.
[*She brings the large sewing basket and they look at the bright pieces.*]

Mrs. Hale. It's log cabin pattern. Pretty, isn't it? I wonder if she was goin' to
quilt it or just knot it?
[*Footsteps have been heard coming down the stairs. The* **Sheriff** *enters
followed by* **Hale** *and the* **County Attorney.**]

Sheriff. They wonder if she was going to quilt it or just knot it!
[*The men laugh; the women look abashed.*]

County Attorney. [*Rubbing his hands over the stove.*] Frank's fire didn't do much up there, did it? Well, let's go out to the barn and get that cleared up.
[*The men go outside.*]

Mrs. Hale. [*Resentfully.*] I don't know as there's anything so strange, our takin' up our time with little things while we're waiting for them to get the evidence. [*She sits down at the big table smoothing out a block with decision.*] I don't see as it's anything to laugh about.

Mrs. Peters. [*Apologetically.*] Of course they've got awful important things on their minds.
[*Pulls up a chair and joins Mrs. Hale at the table.*]

Mrs. Hale. [*Examining another block.*] Mrs. Peters, look at this one. Here, this is the one she was working on, and look at the sewing! All the rest of it has been so nice and even. And look at this! It's all over the place! Why, it looks as if she didn't know what she was about!
[*After she has said this they look at each other, then start to glance back at the door. After an instant Mrs. Hale has pulled at a knot and ripped the sewing.*]

Mrs. Peters. Oh, what are you doing, Mrs. Hale?

Mrs. Hale. [*Mildly.*] Just pulling out a stitch or two that's not sewed very good. [*Threading a needle.*] Bad sewing always made me fidgety.

Mrs. Peters. [*Nervously.*] I don't think we ought to touch things.

Mrs. Hale. I'll just finish up this end. [*Suddenly stopping and leaning forward.*] Mrs. Peters?

Mrs. Peters. Yes, Mrs. Hale?

Mrs. Hale. What do you suppose she was so nervous about?

Mrs. Peters. Oh—I don't know. I don't know as she was nervous. I sometimes sew awful queer when I'm just tired. [Mrs. Hale *starts to say something, looks at* Mrs. Peters, *then goes on sewing.*] Well, I must get these things wrapped up. They may be through sooner than we think. [*Putting apron and other things together.*] I wonder where I can find a piece of paper, and string.

Mrs. Hale. In that cupboard, maybe.

Mrs. Peters. [*Looking in cupboard.*] Why, here's a birdcage. [*Holds it up.*] Did she have a bird, Mrs. Hale?

Mrs. Hale. Why, I don't know whether she did or not—I've not been here for so long. There was a man around last year selling canaries cheap, but I don't know as she took one; maybe she did. She used to sing real pretty herself.

Mrs. Peters. [*Glancing around.*] Seems funny to think of a bird here. But she must have had one, or why would she have a cage? I wonder what happened to it.

Mrs. Hale. I s'pose maybe the cat got it.

Mrs. Peters. No, she didn't have a cat. She's got that feeling some people have about cats—being afraid of them. My cat got in her room and she was real upset and asked me to take it out.

Mrs. Hale. My sister Bessie was like that. Queer, ain't it?

Mrs. Peters. [*Examining the cage.*] Why, look at this door. It's broke. One hinge is pulled apart.

Mrs. Hale. [*Looking too.*] Looks as if someone must have been rough with it.

Mrs. Peters. Why, yes.

[*She brings the cage forward and puts it on the table.*]

Mrs. Hale. I wish if they're going to find any evidence they'd be about it. I don't like this place.

Mrs. Peters. But I'm awful glad you came with me, Mrs. Hale. It would be lonesome for me sitting here alone.

Mrs. Hale. It would, wouldn't it? [*Dropping her sewing.*] But I tell you what I do wish, Mrs. Peters. I wish I had come over sometimes when she was here. I—[*looking around the room*]—wish I had.

Mrs. Peters. But of course you were awful busy, Mrs. Hale—Your house and your children.

Mrs. Hale. I could've come. I stayed away because it weren't cheerful—and that's why I ought to have come. I—I've never liked this place. Maybe because it's down in a hollow and you don't see the road. I dunno what it is but it's a lonesome place and always was. I wish I had come over to see Minnie Foster sometimes. I can see now—

[*Shakes her head.*]

Mrs. Peters. Well, you mustn't reproach yourself, Mrs. Hale. Somehow we just don't see how it is with other folks until—something comes up.

Mrs. Hale. Not having children makes less work—but it makes a quiet house, and Wright out to work all day, and no company when he did come in. Did you know John Wright, Mrs. Peters?

Mrs. Peters. Not to know him; I've seen him in town. They say he was a good man.

Mrs. Hale. Yes—good; he didn't drink, and kept his word as well as most, I guess, and paid his debts. But he was a hard man, Mrs. Peters. Just to pass the time of day with him— [*Shivers.*] Like a raw wind that gets to the bone. [*Pauses, her eye falling on the cage.*] I should think she would 'a wanted a bird. But what do you suppose went with it?

Mrs. Peters. I don't know, unless it got sick and died.

[*She reaches over and swings the broken door, swings it again. Both women watch it.*]

Mrs. Hale. You weren't raised round here, were you? [Mrs. Peters *shakes her head.*] You didn't know—her?

Mrs. Peters. Not till they brought her yesterday.

Mrs. Hale. She—come to think of it, she was kind of like a bird herself—
real sweet and pretty, but kind of timid and—fluttery. How—she—did—
change. [*Silence; then as if struck by a happy thought and relieved to get
back to everyday things.*] Tell you what, Mrs. Peters, why don't you take
the quilt in with you? It might take up her mind.

Mrs. Peters. Why, I think that's a real nice idea, Mrs. Hale. There couldn't
possibly be any objection to it, could there? Now, just what would I
take? I wonder if her patches are in here—and her things.
[*They look in the sewing basket.*]

Mrs. Hale. Here's some red. I expect this has got sewing things in it. [*Brings
out a fancy box.*] What a pretty box. Looks like something somebody
would give you. Maybe her scissors are in here. [*Opens box. Suddenly
puts her hand to her nose.*] Why— [Mrs. Peters *bends nearer, then
turns her face away.*] There's something wrapped up in this piece of silk.

Mrs. Peters. Why, this isn't her scissors.

Mrs. Hale. [*Lifting the silk.*] Oh, Mrs. Peters—it's—
[Mrs. Peters *bends closer.*]

Mrs. Peters. It's the bird.

Mrs. Hale. [*Jumping up.*] But Mrs. Peters—look at it! Its neck! Look at its
neck! It's all—other side to.

Mrs. Peters. Somebody—wrung—its—neck.
[*Their eyes meet. A look of growing comprehension, of horror. Steps are
heard outside.* Mrs. Hale *slips the box under quilt pieces, and sinks into
her chair. Enter* Sheriff *and* County Attorney. Mrs. Peters *rises.*]

County Attorney. [*As one turning from serious things to little pleasantries.*]
Well, ladies, have you decided whether she was going to quilt it or knot
it?

Mrs. Peters. We think she was going to—knot it.

County Attorney. Well, that's interesting, I'm sure. [*Seeing the birdcage.*]
Has the bird flown?

Mrs. Hale. [*Putting more quilt pieces over the box.*] We think the—cat got
it.

County Attorney. [*Preoccupied.*] Is there a cat?
[Mrs. Hale *glances in a quick covert way at* Mrs. Peters.]

Mrs. Peters. Well, not now. They're superstitious, you know. They leave.

County Attorney. [*To* Sheriff Peters, *continuing an interrupted
conversation.*] No sign at all of anyone having come from the outside.
Their own rope. Now let's go up again and go over it piece by piece.
[*They start upstairs.*] It would have to have been someone who knew just
the—
[Mrs. Peters *sits down. The two women sit there not looking at one
another, but as if peering into something and at the same time holding
back. When they talk now it is in the manner of feeling their way over*

strange ground, as if afraid of what they are saying, but as if they can not help saying it.*]*

Mrs. Hale. She liked the bird. She was going to bury it in that pretty box.

Mrs. Peters. [*In a whisper.*] When I was a girl—my kitten—there was a boy took a hatchet, and before my eyes—and before I could get there— [*Covers her face an instant.*] If they hadn't held me back I would have— [*catches herself, looks upstairs where steps are heard, falters weakly*]— hurt him.

Mrs. Hale. [*With a slow look around her.*] I wonder how it would seem never to have had any children around. [*Pause.*] No, Wright wouldn't like the bird—a thing that sang. She used to sing. He killed that, too.

Mrs. Peters. [*Moving uneasily.*] We don't know who killed the bird.

Mrs. Hale. I knew John Wright.

Mrs. Peters. It was an awful thing was done in this house that night, Mrs. Hale. Killing a man while he slept, slipping a rope around his neck that choked the life out of him.

Mrs. Hale. His neck. Choked the life out of him.

[*Her hand goes out and rests on the birdcage.*]

Mrs. Peters. [*With rising voice.*] We don't know who killed him. We don't know.

Mrs. Hale. [*Her own feeling not interrupted.*] If there'd been years and years of nothing, then a bird to sing to you, it would be awful—still, after the bird was still.

Mrs. Peters. [*Something within her speaking.*] I know what stillness is. When we homesteaded in Dakota, and my first baby died—after he was two years old, and me with no other then—

Mrs. Hale. [*Moving.*] How soon do you suppose they'll be through, looking for the evidence?

Mrs. Peters. I know what stillness is. [*Pulling herself back.*] The law has got to punish crime, Mrs. Hale.

Mrs. Hale. [*Not as if answering that.*] I wish you'd seen Minnie Foster when she wore a white dress with blue ribbons and stood up there in the choir and sang. [*A look around the room.*] Oh, I wish I'd come over here once in a while! That was a crime! That was a crime! Who's going to punish that?

Mrs. Peters. [*Looking upstairs.*] We mustn't—take on.

Mrs. Hale. I might have known she needed help! I know how things can be—for women. I tell you, it's queer, Mrs. Peters. We live close together and we live far apart. We all go through the same things—it's all just a different kind of the same thing. [*Brushes her eyes; noticing the bottle of fruit, reaches out for it.*] If I was you I wouldn't tell her her fruit was gone. Tell her it ain't. Tell her it's all right. Take this in to prove it to her. She—she may never know whether it was broke or not.

1-3: Mrs. Peters and Mrs. Hale seal their agreement to conceal the evidence with a conspiratorial look. This performance of Susan Glaspell's *Trifles* took place in 2000 at New York University's famous Provincetown Playhouse, the very theatre where Glaspell's play was first performed in 1916. Director: Ann MacCormack. Photographer: Melanie St. James.

Mrs. Peters. [*Takes the bottle, looks about for something to wrap it in; takes petticoat from the clothes brought from the other room, very nervously begins winding this around the bottle. In a false voice.*] My, it's a good thing the men couldn't hear us. Wouldn't they just laugh! Getting all stirred up over a little thing like a—dead canary. As if that could have anything to do with—with—wouldn't they laugh!
[*The men are heard coming downstairs.*]
Mrs. Hale. [*Under her breath.*] Maybe they would—maybe they wouldn't.
County Attorney. No, Peters, it's all perfectly clear except a reason for doing it. But you know juries when it comes to women. If there was some definite thing. Something to show—something to make a story about—a thing that would connect up with this strange way of doing it—
[*The women's eyes meet for an instant. Enter* **Hale** *from outer door.*]
Hale. Well, I've got the team around. Pretty cold out there.
County Attorney. I'm going to stay here a while by myself. [*To the* **Sheriff.**] You can send Frank out for me, can't you? I want to go over everything. I'm not satisfied that we can't do better.

Sheriff. Do you want to see what Mrs. Peters is going to take in?

[*The* County Attorney *goes to the table, picks up the apron, laughs.*]

County Attorney. Oh, I guess they're not very dangerous things the ladies have picked out. [*Moves a few things about, disturbing the quilt pieces which cover the box. Steps back.*] No, Mrs. Peters doesn't need supervising. For that matter, a sheriff's wife is married to the law. Ever think of it that way, Mrs. Peters?

Mrs. Peters. Not—just that way.

Sheriff. [*Chuckling.*] Married to the law. [*Moves toward the other room.*] I just want you to come in here a minute, George. We ought to take a look at these windows.

County Attorney. [*Scoffingly.*] Oh, windows!

Sheriff: We'll be right out, Mr. Hale.

[Hale *goes outside. The* Sheriff *follows the* County Attorney *into the other room. Then* Mrs. Hale *rises, hands tight together, looking intensely at* Mrs. Peters, *whose eyes make a slow turn, finally meeting* Mrs. Hale's. *A moment* Mrs. Hale *holds her, then her own eyes point the way to where the box is concealed. Suddenly,* Mrs. Peters *throws back quilt pieces and tries to put the box in the bag she is wearing. It is too big. She opens box, starts to take bird out, cannot touch it, goes to pieces, stands there helpless. Sound of a knob turning in the other room.* Mrs. Hale *snatches the box and puts it in the pocket of her big coat. Enter* County Attorney and Sheriff.]

County Attorney. [*Facetiously.*] Well, Henry, at least we found out that she was not going to quilt it. She was going to—what is it you call it, ladies?

Mrs. Hale. [*Her hand against her pocket.*] We call it—knot it, Mr. Henderson.

Curtain

Responding Subjectively

When we attend the theatre or read dramatic literature, we respond both intellectually and emotionally. We may sob, guffaw, gasp, or shake our heads in anger. Following are some readers' reactions after their first reading of Susan Glaspell's *Trifles*:

```
"I'm shocked that the women concealed the evidence at the
end. Two wrongs don't make a right."

"I can relate with Mrs. Wright. If someone had killed my
pet, I would have been tempted to kill him in revenge. I
```

might have done it, too, if I had already suffered years of abuse from him."

"I think Minnie would definitely have been convicted. Her alibi, that she was sleeping, is ridiculous. I envision the struggle that must have taken place: big John Wright in his nightshirt, being hoisted from his bed by a rope around his neck, and tiny Minnie Wright straining at the other end of the rope rigged up with pulleys."

"The men's attitude toward the women makes me angry. They think the women don't know anything but quilting and housework and that the women are too stupid to be able to help with the investigation. Things are not much different today."

All reactions are valid initially, but to engage more deeply with the work, we must invest some time and effort in assessing our reactions. In other words, we must ask not only *how* the work makes us feel but also *why* it makes us feel the way it does if our opinions are to transcend mere reaction.

Following are some questions that may help you to define and assess your responses to theatre and drama. Unwritten responses are fleeting; you are not likely to remember them or be able to use them to launch further inquiry. Therefore, it is important that you write your responses; doing so will lead you to ever deeper ones.

Questions to Guide Your Responses to Theatre and Drama

1. What is the overall subject matter?
2. What are the larger components (such as setting and plot)?
3. What are the smaller details (such as props and word choices)?
4. What is the predominant mood?
5. What details contribute to the predominant mood? What details contradict it?
6. Do any details strike you as symbolic?
7. What does the title of the work tell you?
8. What is the style of the work? For example, is it realistic? expressionistic? Why would the artist have chosen this style?

9.   What is the historical setting of the work—its place, time, and political influences?

10.   What critical theories could you apply to the work? (Refer to chapter 3).

11.   What do you believe the artist meant for you to feel?

12.   Do your feelings coincide with what you perceive the artist intended you to feel?

13.   Does the work confirm or challenge your experiences? your values? your beliefs? your assumptions? Explain.

14.   How is the work like or unlike comparable works? What accounts for the works' similarities and differences?

15.   Has your response to the work changed from your initial reaction, now that you have examined the work in more detail?

16.   What questions do you have about the work?

Inferring

To **infer** is to draw a conclusion that is not readily apparent, but is based, if the inference is valid, on evidence.

Exercise 1-5

Write a short response paper on one of the following topics. Support your answer with details and examples from the text. In *Trifles* . . .
- Who killed John Wright?
- Why did the killer kill John Wright?
- Why do the women hide the dead canary from the men?
- What is the men's attitude toward the women in the play?
- Why do the women say Minnie was probably going to knot the quilt?

Comparing or Contrasting

To **compare** means to note similarities; to **contrast** means to note differences. Whether we are comparing or contrasting, the effort sharpens our observations.

Exercise 1-6

Write a short response paper on one of the following topics. Support your answer with details and examples from the text. In *Trifles*, compare or contrast . . .

- Mrs. Peters to Mrs. Hale
- Mrs. Peters at the beginning of the play to Mrs. Peters at the end
- Minnie Wright to a bird
- Mrs. Hale and Mrs. Wright to Antigone (heroine of the play by Sophocles)
- Mrs. Hale and Mrs. Peters to Rosa Parks or Harriet Tubman, or any historically famous lawbreaker

Interpreting

To **interpret** is to make the meaning clear. Interpretation can be merely a matter of translation, as when we say that *deus ex machina* is a Latin phrase meaning "a god out of a machine." With regard to literature, however, to interpret is to convey a work's **subtextual**, or implied, meaning. We often find the key to a work's subtext by interpreting the symbolic significance of its elements.

Exercise 1-7

Write a short response paper on one of the following topics. Support your answer with details and examples from the text. In *Trifles* . . .

- What does the canary symbolize?
- What does the quilt, especially the log cabin pattern, symbolize?
- What does the jar of preserves symbolize?
- How does the setting of the play reinforce the theme of respect for women's work?
- What is the significance of the title of the play?

Evaluating

When we **evaluate**, we estimate the worth, or value, of a thing.

Exercise 1-8

Write a short response paper on one of the following topics. Support your answer with details and examples from the text.
- Do Mrs. Hale and Mrs. Peters have worthy reasons for hiding the canary?
- What is the worth of women's work in *Trifles*?
- Is *Trifles*, first published in 1916, still worth being read and performed?

Arguing

To **argue** in an academic setting is to take a position on an issue that can be debated by reasonable, informed people. An argument presupposes a skeptical audience, one that is inclined to disagree.

Exercise 1-9

Write a short response paper supporting one of the following propositions. In *Trifles* . . .
- The women are right to conceal the evidence.
- The women are wrong to conceal the evidence.

Writing Informally

There are many purposes for writing informally. For one, we learn, when we write, what we are thinking and feeling. Also, writing works as an aid to reading: we read texts more closely and more thoughtfully when we plan to write about them. Another reason to write informally is to begin the process of organizing a formal essay: our observations, opinions, and reasons for our opinions tend to take shape naturally when we allow ourselves to write uninhibitedly.

Still, an invitation to write informally is not an invitation to sloppiness. Take the time to decide on the focus of your response paper. Organize your thoughts. Write in complete sentences. Choose your words carefully and spell them correctly. A response paper that will be useful later is not hastily conceived or written. It offers evidence of close, thoughtful reading.

The following short response to *Trifles*, written by student Benjamin Fisher, addresses one of the propositions in Exercise 1-9.

A Story of Moral Issues

by Benjamin Fisher

In her famous one-act play, Trifles, Susan Glaspell details the story of a woman accused of murdering her husband. The story starts with the sheriff, the county attorney, a neighbor, and two women, Mrs. Hale and Mrs. Peters, going to the Wrights' house and searching for evidence in the murder of Mr. Wright. While waiting for the men to find the evidence, Mrs. Peters and Mrs. Hale uncover a dead bird hidden in Mrs. Wright's sewing basket, and this is where the story becomes interesting. These women must make the choice either to show the bird to their husbands or hide the evidence that links Mrs. Wright to the murder of her husband.

The story brings up several moral questions. Throughout the story, we are informed more and more of the life that Mrs. Wright has been living. She spends most of her time locked up in her house by herself, doing chores. She has no children to raise and doesn't talk much with anyone from the area. She relates to her caged bird that was killed by her husband. Just like her, the bird is locked up all the time, has no little birds to raise, and doesn't have anyone else to talk/relate to. This connection between the bird and Mrs. Wright has caused her to become attached to the bird. When her husband chokes her bird to death, he metaphorically kills a part of her as well.

So we ask the question, does the death of her bird justify Mrs. Wright's murder of her husband? If Mrs. Wright lives in danger of Mr. Wright's violence, is it wrong for her to protect herself by killing him? If her husband is as abusive as he seems, does he not deserve punishment? These are some of the moral questions a reader faces when reading this play.

My opinion is that the women should not have concealed the evidence. Anyone who has killed another human being should face the consequences. Mrs. Wright may have been justified, if she had been abused, in killing Mr. Wright, or she may have been insane at the time. The court is in a better position to decide than Mrs. Peters and Mrs. Hale.

On one hand, Benjamin's essay reveals a close reading and an understanding of some of the play's subtextual elements—that Mrs. Wright identified with her pet bird and that Mr. Wright had metaphorically murdered his wife—as well as the moral questions that the play raises. Benjamin then proceeds to venture an opinion about the ethical dilemma at the center of the play and to offer some reasons for his opinion. This short response paper bears many of the marks of careful, thoughtful reading and writing.

On the other hand, Benjamin's essay bears some marks of informality. For instance, his comment "this is where the story becomes interesting" would not appear in a formal essay. Also, the essay is not directed toward the support of a single, focused thesis statement; it is more loosely constructed. Benjamin's reasons for his thesis have not yet been tested. For example, his last reason (that the courts are better suited than the women to make a decision about Mrs. Wright's guilt) does not take into account that the all-male jury Mrs. Wright would be facing might not understand her frame of mind after the emotional abuse she suffered. This is not to say that Benjamin's opinion is faulty, only that in formal writing he will have to recognize and address this crucial issue.

These marks of informality are not flaws in a response paper. On the contrary. In formal writing, we test ideas more deliberately, organize more carefully, and polish our phrases. The important thing at this juncture is to *start writing*, and the short, informal response is often the first step.

Notes

[1] Brooks Atkinson, *"Death of a Salesman*, A New Drama by Arthur Miller, Has Premiere at the Morosco," *New York Times* 11 Feb. 1949: 27.

[2] Frederick Morgan, "Notes on the Theatre," *Hudson Review* 2 (1949): 272-73.

[3] Barnet, Sylvan, Morton Berman, and William Burto, eds., *Types of Drama,* 2nd ed. (Boston: Little, 1972) 303-04.

[4] Arthur Miller, "Tragedy and the Common Man," *Types of Drama*, ed. Sylvan Barnet, Morton Berman, and William Burto, 2nd ed. (Boston: Little, 1972) 306.

2

Principles of Effective Writing

Doctor Faustus is caught between two angels. One whispers in his left ear to stop his pursuit of knowledge; the other whispers in his right ear to press on. Which is the good angel and which is the bad? Faustus has no way of knowing. Every writer knows the feeling. The creator in our heads gives us a

2-1: A dangerously curious Doctor Faustus asks Mephistophilis, "How comes it then that thou art out of hell?" Mephistophilis's chilling reply is "Why this is hell, nor am I out of it." This 1997 production of *Doctor Faustus* at Grand Canyon University was directed by Claude Pensis. Photographer: Claude Pensis.

sentence, and we write it down. Then the critic in our heads says, "No, that's no good," and we delete it. And so it goes. The night wears on, our deadline approaches, and we lurch forward and backward as the creator and the critic engage in battle. What we need is a dependable process for writing that allows the creator and the critic to work together amicably. This chapter offers such a process, and you won't have to sell your soul to the devil to obtain it.

Types of Essays

As a student, you will be called upon to write, primarily, essays and research papers. An **essay** is a prose, nonfiction literary composition. The invention of the essay is attributed to Michel de Montaigne, a sixteenth-century French writer. Montaigne considered his own experiences and opinions worthy of study in his search of the truth, believing that to study himself was to study humankind. "Every man bears the whole stamp of the human condition," he wrote.[1] The word *essay* is from the French *essayer*, which means "to try"—an appropriate term, since it recognizes the difficulty of expressing one's thoughts.

An essay consists of more than one paragraph, and it is shorter than a book, but within those wide parameters, an essay may be any length. An essay may make use of sources, but not to the extent that a research paper does. An essay may be objective or subjective. An **objective essay** offers information without commentary, opinion, or interpretation. A **subjective essay**, on the other hand, does offer an opinion. For example, a newspaper article that informs the reader that the University Theatre Department will produce August Wilson's *Fences* during the spring semester is objective. An article that evaluates that production is subjective.

A **critical essay** is subjective. The purpose of the critical essay is not, as the term may imply, to criticize, but rather to critique. To *criticize* is to denounce or find fault; to *critique* is to exercise careful judgment or to offer scholarly interpretation. Critical essays are either analytical or argumentative.

To *analyze* means, literally, to take a thing apart to discover how the pieces work together to create a whole. An **analytical essay** examines various pieces of a whole in order to evaluate, interpret, or speculate about causes and effects. Analytical writing differs from objective writing in that inference is at its core. An *inference* is a conclusion derived from facts, but it is not itself a fact. It is a guess or a theory, albeit an educated one. Take, for example, Hamlet's comment in act 2, scene 2: "What a piece of work is man! How noble in reason, how infinite in faculty, in form and moving how express and admirable, in action how like an angel, in apprehension how like a god—the beauty of the world, the paragon of animals!" Do you infer that Hamlet is being sincere or sarcastic? What evidence can you offer for your inference? To answer the question, you will have to take the play apart and examine the pieces.

An **argument essay** assumes a contrary audience, one that is predisposed to disagree with the writer, but also one that is both rational and educated. When you write an argument essay, your task is not only to defend your position, but also to refute your opponent's position.

Remember that the word *argument* is often used broadly to mean "main point" or "thesis." Your instructors may speak of your "central argument" with regard to the thesis or main point of your paper, even if the paper is purely analytical and does not engage in refutation at all. Be sure that you understand the meaning of the word *argument* as it pertains to your assignment.

Planning Your Essay

The process for writing essays and research papers about theatre and drama is the same as the process for writing about any topic: plan, draft, revise, and edit. First, we will look at the steps in planning: prewriting, narrowing your topic, posing a research question, doing research, formulating a thesis, identifying the counterarguments, asking the proof question, designing points of proof, organizing the evidence, and outlining your essay.

The process is seldom absolutely linear. You may find yourself skipping a step or backing up a step or two before moving forward. For example, you may have formulated a workable thesis without researching the topic. Or you may need to do additional research after you have identified the counterarguments. Still, it helps to have a planning process.

Prewriting

You can use any of several prewriting strategies to begin planning your essay. You might begin by **brainstorming**. Many people use a **mind map**, a diagram of connecting words to free-associate ideas and begin the process of seeing the relationships among them.

Another brainstorming device is **freewriting**. Set a timer for a certain number of minutes, say ten, and write for that length of time without stopping, without lifting pen from paper, and without correcting grammar or spelling errors. Your words will be garbled and incoherent; you will repeat yourself. These are not problems. The objective is to allow your thoughts to flow freely and reveal your interests and ideas. Now that you can see them, you can begin to shape them.

Choosing and Narrowing Your Topic

Your **topic** is the broad subject matter of your paper. It can be stated in a few words, such as "Ibsen's realism" or "Arthur Miller's critique of society." You will need to narrow your focus, however, to some particular aspect, such as "the influence of heritage in Ibsen's *Hedda Gabler*" or "the perversion of moral values in capitalist societies in Miller's *Death of a Salesman.*"

Many students make the mistake of thinking that the goal of an essay is to cover as much territory as possible—to show how much they know. The result is a paper that can be described as shallow and wide; it touches upon many topics but pursues none in depth. In fact, most instructors prefer papers that are narrow and deep; that is, they explore one idea thoroughly.

Posing a Research Question or a Proposition

An analytical paper answers a **research question,** whereas an argument paper debates a **proposition**. Posing a proper research question is a crucial step in the design of your analytical essay because some research questions will lead you to an objective essay, and some will lead you to an analytical one.

For example, the question "In *Death of a Salesman,* what happened between Willy and Biff in Boston to cause so much tension between them?" will lead to an objective paper. To answer the question, you need only summarize a part of the plot.

However, the question "How does the impressionistic setting of *Death of a Salesman* contribute to the theme of the failed American dream?" will probably lead to an analytical paper because no definite answer to that question exists.

Be sure to ask only one research question. Asking more than one will lead to a disunified paper. Also, remember that a research question is not a thesis. You will try to prove the truth of your thesis; you cannot prove the truth of a question. Chapter 3 offers many examples of research questions that will lead to analytical papers.

If your essay is argumentative, you will need to state a proposition—a statement that the paper will either defend or refute. "Willy Loman is a tragic hero" is an example of a proposition. Chapter 4 offers many examples of such statements.

Researching Your Topic and Taking Notes

Not all academic essays about theatre and drama require **sources**—books and articles that relate to the topic—other than the play itself. But if your essay will use sources, now is the time to begin collecting and reading them. Chapter 6, "Writing the Research Paper," offers detailed information on finding sources through your campus library or the World Wide Web.

After you have collected your sources, read them with your pen and highlighter. Highlight the pertinent passages and write your reactions and thoughts in the margins as you read. If you are using borrowed books, use sticky notes to mark the interesting passages. Take notes on index cards, one note per card. On each card, write a fact or a quotation that you may want to include in your paper. Be sure to note on each card the source from which you obtained the information, including the page number. Later, you will find that the index cards are easily shuffled and reorganized as your paper takes shape.

Formulating Your Thesis

In an analytical paper, your **thesis** answers your research question. In an argument essay, your thesis states your position in the debate. In both kinds of essay, the thesis articulates your main point and is, therefore, the most important sentence in the essay. Chapters 3 and 4 offer specific criteria for a workable thesis.

Your thesis statement is also important because it determines your essay's **mode of discourse**: *narration, description, analysis,* or *argument*. A narrative thesis will lead to a narrative essay, a descriptive thesis will lead to a descriptive essay, and so forth. Narration and description are objective modes; in other words, the writer need offer no insights or evidence of critical thinking. Analysis and argument are subjective modes; the writer must offer his or her own ideas and support them. Obviously, it is more challenging to write in the analytical and argument modes. Compare the following examples:

2-2: "God, timberland! Me and my boys in those grand outdoors!"
Willy Loman dreams of another life in *Death of a Salesman*, produced
by the University of Wyoming in 1998 and directed by William Missouri
Downs. Photographer: Ted C. Brummond.

Narrative Thesis: Biff is shocked to learn that his father has been unfaithful to Linda. [What follows will merely recount the episode in Willy's hotel room in Boston.]

Descriptive Thesis: Willy imparts a skewed value system to his sons. [What follows will illustrate a thesis that needs no proving because it is readily apparent to anyone who has read or seen the play.]

Analytical Thesis: *Death of a Salesman* indicts the false values of the American dream. [Most readers would need to see support for this statement before they would accept it as true.]

Argumentative Thesis: Willy is a tragic hero. [A rational, educated person might disagree with this statement.]

Identifying the Counterarguments

If your essay is argumentative, you must articulate your opponents' arguments, which are your **counterarguments**. Like your own argument, they consist of a thesis and points of proof, which you will regard as the **counterthesis** and **counterpoints**. Your paper will **refute** the counterarguments. Identify what you believe to be the strongest, not the weakest, arguments against your opinion, if you want your paper to be convincing.

Asking the Proof Question

After you have found a thesis, you must support, or *prove*, it. What constitutes support? One way to ascertain what sort of information will support your thesis is to ask a **proof question**, or simply convert the thesis statement into a question, beginning usually with *how* or *why*. For example, if your thesis is "*Death of a Salesman* indicts the false values of the American dream," the proof question arises naturally in response to that claim: "*How* does *Death of a Salesman* indict the false values of the American dream?" Answers to this question will support, or prove, your thesis. Although the proof question rarely appears in the final version of an essay, it is a critical step in planning the essay because it tests the workableness of your thesis. If you cannot answer the proof question, you need to rethink your thesis. Chapter 3 further explains this step in planning the analytical paper.

In an argument paper, there are often two proof questions. The first asks why you disagree with the counterarguments. The second asks why you believe your own thesis to be true. Chapter 4 expounds upon this concept in more detail.

Designing Your Points of Proof

Your **points of proof** answer your proof question. They are the reasons why you think your thesis is true. Each point of proof must be general enough to require one, two, or more paragraphs' worth of supporting facts, details, and examples, depending on the length of the essay you are writing.

Each point of proof should directly answer the proof question, but it will not, by itself, provide the complete answer. For example, if the proof question is "How does *Death of a Salesman* indict the false values of the American dream?" one point of proof could be that "The character of Willy Loman embodies the American emphasis on success rather than honesty." This is not a complete answer to the proof question, but a partial one. Collectively, your points of proof will fully support your thesis.

Be sure that each point of proof answers the proof question and supports the thesis and not some other idea. Sentences such as "First, this essay will examine the character of Willy Loman" and "Secondly, this essay will examine the heartlessness of American enterprise" are not points of proof. Rather than answer the proof question, they delay the task. Chapter 3 further discusses these concepts with regard to the analytical essay.

If your essay is argumentative, your points of proof may be subdivided into two categories: refutations and constructive arguments. **Refutations** tell why you disagree with the counterarguments. **Constructive arguments** give additional reasons why you believe your thesis to be true, in the absence of counterarguments. Chapter 4 explains these concepts in more detail.

Organizing the Evidence

Before you begin writing the body paragraphs, gather the index cards on which you took notes from your sources. Write your points of proof on separate index cards and lay them out side by side. Place each note card beneath the point of proof that it supports. Continue to compile the evidence until you have enough to support each point of proof adequately. You may find, if you are like most writers, that some of your notes are not usable and that you need to find others that better illustrate and support your points of proof. Having to go back to your sources and look for new evidence is typically part of the writing process.

2-3: The balance of power shifts in *Oleanna*, a play that has been causing arguments since its premier in 1992. David Mamet's controversial drama was performed at Central Washington University in 1994, directed by Wesley Van Tassel. Photographer: Leslee Caul.

Outlining Your Essay

Before they begin drafting their essays, most writers save time and avoid frustration by organizing their ideas in the form of an outline like the ones that follow. Whether it is analytical or argumentative, an essay has three main parts: introduction, body, and conclusion. The following section, "Drafting Your Essay," discusses the contents of these sections in detail. The number of points of proof and supporting facts and examples will, of course, vary according to each essay's needs.

Sample Outline for Analytical Essay

I.   Introduction
- A. Occasion
  - 1. Background information
  - 2. Statement of the issue
- B. Thesis
- C. Points of proof
  - 1. Point 1
  - 2. Point 2
  - 3. Point 3
  - 4. Point 4

II.   Body (develop each point of proof in turn)
- A. Point of proof 1
  - 1. Supporting fact
  - 2. Supporting example
- B. Point of proof 2
  - 1. Supporting fact
  - 2. Supporting fact
  - 3. Supporting example
- C. Point of proof 3
  - 1. Supporting example
- D. Point of proof 4
  - 1. Supporting fact
  - 2. Supporting example

III. Conclusion

Sample Outline for Argument Essay

I.   Introduction
   A. Occasion
      1. Background information
      2. Statement of the issue
      3. Counterarguments
        a. Counterthesis
        b. Counterpoints
          (1) Counterpoint 1
          (2) Counterpoint 2
   B. Thesis
   C. Points of proof
      1. Refutations
        a. Refutation of counterpoint 1
        b. Refutation of counterpoint 2
      2. Constructive arguments
        a. Constructive argument 1
        b. Constructive argument 2

II.   Body
   A. Refutation of counterpoint 1
      1. Supporting fact
      2. Supporting example
   B. Refutation of counterpoint 2
      1. Supporting fact
      2. Supporting fact
      3. Supporting example
   C. Constructive argument 1
      1. Supporting example
   D. Constructive argument 2
      1. Supporting fact
      2. Supporting example

III. Conclusion

Drafting Your Essay

Now that you have planned your essay, the next step is to begin writing. Remember that you will probably need to revise your essay several times before you arrive at a final version.

Drafting the Introduction

There are many forms for introductory paragraphs for critical essays, most of which will lead to interesting and organized essays. This text recommends an introductory paragraph with three parts: occasion, thesis, and points of proof. Such an introductory paragraph bears the advantages of getting to the point quickly, which most readers appreciate, and exhibiting mastery of the subject matter: it is obvious that the writer knows not only what the main point of the essay is, but also precisely how it will be supported.

   1.   **Occasion** is a term for the sentences that precede the thesis. These sentences express the writer's reason, or *occasion,* for writing. They offer necessary background information, such as the title of the play and the name of the playwright, and a statement of the issue that the paper will address. It might offer a brief plot summary. In the excerpt from Zachary M. Bush's essay on the next page, the issue is whether Willy Loman qualifies as a tragic hero.

   Occasions are difficult to write because they must strike just the right balance. They must orient the reader and not simply say what the reader already knows. Occasions must begin somewhat generally, but not too generally. Occasions must engage the topic directly, but not abruptly. It helps some writers to remember the journalistic formula: *who, what, when,* and *where.* (The *why* will come later.) Stick to the facts. Do not begin with a platitude or an overly general expression, such as "Throughout history . . ." or "Humankind has always . . . ."

   If the essay is an argument, the introductory remarks should also contain the counterthesis and, if necessary, the counterpoints. In the first paragraph of Zachary's essay on the next page, the opinion of Fred Ribkoff and Robert Brustein that Willy does not qualify as a tragic hero is offered as a counterthesis. No counterpoints (reasons for their opinion) are given.

   In short, the occasion should provide the reader with whatever information he or she needs to be able to understand the thesis, which comes next. Do not labor too long over the occasion. If you are struggling with the first few sentences or are stalled altogether, proceed directly to the composition of your thesis and return to the introductory remarks later.

2.   Your *thesis statement* is the most important sentence in the entire essay, so you must construct it carefully. As a rule, let your thesis be the first general statement that you make. If the thesis is preceded by several generalizations, it is difficult for the reader to recognize it as the thesis. Be sure that the thesis is written in the appropriate mode of discourse to let your reader know whether you plan to narrate, describe, analyze, or argue.

3.   Some introductory paragraphs end with the thesis statement; others go on to list *points of proof.* If you list your points of proof after your thesis, use transitional expressions, such as *first, second,* and *finally,* to help your reader understand that these claims are subordinate to the thesis and coordinate with each other.

End the introductory paragraph with the final point of proof. Whereas in body paragraphs, concluding sentences are often desirable, in introductory paragraphs, concluding sentences tend to compete with the thesis statement and confuse the essay's plan.

Following is an example of an introductory paragraph for an argument paper, containing an occasion, a thesis, and points of proof.

2-4: "Bernard is not well liked, is he?" The Loman boys taunt their studious next door neighbor in this 1998 production of *Death of a Salesman* at the University of Wyoming, directed by William Missouri Downs. Photographer: Ted C. Brummond.

Willy Loman's Moment of Recognition

by Zachary M. Bush

Much of the criticism that Arthur Miller's Death of a Salesman has received is rooted in the written records of Aristotle's lectures on dramatic tragedy. One of the central criteria that Aristotle asserts for the composition of a tragedy is the point of anagnorisis, in which the hero is enlightened to the nature of the tragedy that his actions have occasioned. Critics such as Fred Ribkoff and Robert Brustein contend that Willy Loman fails to fulfill this aspect of the tragic hero. However, if the audience allows itself to be drawn into the action of the drama and the realm of Willy's fabricated reality, it becomes evident in the climactic final scene that Willy does recognize his errors and as a result becomes a tragic hero. When Biff and Happy desert their father in the restaurant, Willy's overwhelming humiliation triggers the full memory sequence of his affair, and his remorse for what he has done surfaces in his self-directed rambling in the garden at the end of Act 2. In addition, the vulnerability that Biff demonstrates when he cries in his father's arms awakens Willy to the genuine love of his son; love embraces forgiveness, which in turn acknowledges mistakes. As a result, the motivation behind Willy's contemplation of suicide changes from a self-absorbed attempt to escape the dismal reality of his life to a sincere attempt to better the lives of his loved ones.

Exercise 2-1

In the preceding paragraph, identify: (1) the occasion and the counterthesis contained within it, (2) the thesis, (3) and the first, second, and third points of proof.

Drafting the Body Paragraphs

Well-written body paragraphs usually have four qualities: unity, adequate development, organization, and coherence.

Unity in paragraphs is the quality of having only one main idea. Unity is best achieved by the use of a **topic sentence** that makes a general claim, which will be supported by evidence presented in the remainder of the paragraph. The topic sentence is often the first sentence of the paragraph.

The following paragraph, written by Ronald Hingley, in his introduction to *Anton Chekhov: Five Plays,* demonstrates the concept of paragraph unity. Hingley begins with a topic sentence and then dedicates the remainder of the paragraph to supporting, or proving, the truth of that sentence.

> From Chekhov's own early plays and from the bulk of pre-Chekhov drama in general, the mature works differ . . . in the relatively slight emphasis placed on action. True, the occasional happening is to be observed, and there are even deeds of violence. Tuzenbakh of *Three Sisters* is killed in a duel; Uncle Vanya twice fires a revolver at his ludicrous brother-in-law. Yet we note that the former calamity takes place off stage, and that the briefly murderous Vanya predictably misses his target. Even *The Cherry Orchard*, last and most pacific of the plays, features a revolver: that carried by Yepikhodov in case he should feel the urge to commit suicide. But it is never fired, and if during the play's exquisite last scene the aged manservant, Firs, may be thought a victim of homicide, it is homicide by culpable negligence, not by direct action. With all this may be contrasted Chekhov's earliest play, *Platonov*, with its two attempted suicides, one attempted murder, one successful murder, and one lynching.[2]

Another type of paragraph, called the **topic-restriction-illustration (TRI)** paragraph, begins with a topic sentence that is too broad for development in a single paragraph. It may be intended to govern several succeeding paragraphs. Next comes a statement that restricts the topic to a manageable size. Then come the facts and examples that illustrate the restriction sentence. The following two paragraphs, from Oscar Brockett and Robert J. Ball's *The Essential Theatre*, demonstrate:

> Scene designers need a variety of skills, many of them pertinent to other arts, especially architecture, painting, interior design, and acting. Like architects, scene designers conceive and build structures for human beings to use. Although scene designers do not design entire buildings, as architects do, they sculpt space and, like architects, must be concerned with its function, size, organization, construction, and visual appearance. Also, like architects, they must be able to communicate their ideas through sketches, scale models, and construction

drawings that indicate how each element is built and how it will look when completed.

Scene designers, in some aspects of their work, use skills similar to painters'. For example, one of the designer's primary ways of communicating with the director and other designers is through sketches and drawings. During preliminary discussions of a production, designers usually make numerous sketches to demonstrate possible solutions to design problems; before these designs are given final approval, they usually are rendered in perspective and in color. In addition to making sketches showing entire settings, designers also make painters' elevations—scale drawings of each piece of scenery showing how it is to be painted and the painting techniques to be used. Designers sometimes must paint (or supervise others who paint) the scenery they have designed.[3]

In some cases, writers find the topic sentence best placed at the *end* of the paragraph, as in the following example from Richard Hornby's 1989 review of the Royal Shakespeare Company's production of *The Merchant of Venice*:

> The set, for instance, had a prettified design with Italian Renaissance arches and columns that was all wrong. Shakespeare's Venice is no honeymoon dream world, like the actual Venice of today, but a harsh commercial town of deals, ventures, debts, and scarcity. We never hear of gondolas, canals, or St. Mark's Square (as we do, for example, in Ben Jonson's *Volpone*, written soon after), but only of the Rialto, the commercial center. We see only men there (except for Jessica, who escapes), who are typically spiteful or troubled. Portia's world of Belmont ("beautiful mountain"), by contrast, has only women living in it (her father is dead); it is exotic, romantic, and unbelievably wealthy. When Portia hears of Antonio's debt to Shylock, she offers to pay it twelve times over, and then ups it to twenty times! Chris Dyer's set designs, however, made no contrast between the two worlds whatsoever, so that audience members unfamiliar with the play had trouble even figuring out where scenes were taking place, much less feeling the proper emotional response to them.[4]

Sometimes a **concluding sentence** for the paragraph is in order. This sentence might restate the assertion made in the topic sentence, or it might speak of the broader implications of the evidence offered in the paragraph and its connection to the thesis. See, for example, the following paragraph from Martin Esslin's biography of Bertolt Brecht, which explains an aspect of Brecht's "epic theatre":

> It must at all times be made apparent to the spectators that they are not witnessing real events happening before their very eyes at *this very moment*, but that they are sitting in a theatre, listening to an account (however vividly presented) of things that have happened in the *past* at a certain time in a certain place. They are to sit back, relax, and reflect on the lessons to be learned from

those events of long ago, like the audience of the bards who sang of the deeds of heroes in the houses of Greek kings or Saxon earls, while the guests ate and drank. Hence the term *epic* theatre. While the theatre of illusion is trying to re-create a spurious present by pretending that the events of the play are actually taking place at the time of each performance, the "epic" theatre is strictly *historical*; it constantly reminds the audience that they are merely getting a report of past events.[5]

The second quality of well-written paragraphs, **adequate development**, is achieved by providing sufficient evidence for the assertion in the topic sentence. **Evidence** consists of specific details, facts, and examples. Assume that your audience is not going to believe a word you say unless you present specific supporting evidence. The following paragraph, from Robert Brustein's review of Ingmar Bergman and the Royal Dramatic Theatre of Sweden's 1988 production of *Hamlet*, exemplifies the concept of adequate development; compare the number of sentences that make general assertions to the number of sentences that offer specific supporting information.

Ophelia is witness to [Hamlet's murder of Polonius], as she witnesses almost every brutal event in this brutalized court. But this is no consumptive, sensitive suffering plant. As played by Permilla Östergren (the promiscuous maid of *Fanny and Alexander*), she is a somewhat chunky lass, feisty and argumentative, and, until her father's death, possessed of a strong will. Gertrude gussies her up for Hamlet by rouging her lips and fitting her out with red high heels, pulling down the strap of her slip as an afterthought. Östergren plays her mad scene—in Bergman's hands a powerful study of degenerative female psychosis—in a heavy brocaded gown and marching boots, carrying the bloody handkerchief Polonius used to stanch the wound to his eye. She also carries a dangerous pair of shears, with which she cuts off large tufts of hair, and, instead of offering flowers to Gertrude and Claudius, she hands out iron nails. A central character throughout, she even appears at the rainy funeral that follows her own death. The chorus of courtiers, now wearing black mourning coats and black beribboned top hats, makes a dancing exit carrying black umbrellas. Instead of the usual chiaroscuro, a harsh light illuminates the entire stage area including water pipes and exit signs. And Ophelia materializes at the back, in bare feet, blue slip, and flowered crown—now a ghost haunting her own burial service.[6]

The third quality of well-written paragraphs, **organization,** is achieved simply by giving the details in a logical order. If, for example you are recounting the plot of a story, the logical order of details is *chronological*. If you are describing a physical entity, such as a set design, you might begin at the top and progress downward, or begin on the left and progress to the right. In other words, the organization of your paragraph would be *spatial*.

Another useful organizational pattern is the *question-answer* pattern, demonstrated in the following excerpt from Frank Rich's 1991 review of *Marvin's Room*:

> Is there any chance you will believe me when I tell you that *Marvin's Room*, which was written by Scott McPherson and opened at Playwrights Horizons last night, is one of the funniest plays of this year as well as one of the wisest and most moving? Maybe not. And that's how it should be. When the American theater gains a new voice this original, this unexpected, you really must hear it for yourself.[7]

Because comparison is a valuable tool in the study of art, it is particularly important to be able to organize a **comparison paragraph**. You can proceed in one of two ways, using either the **point-by-point pattern** or the **block pattern**. In the point-by-point pattern, you make a point about the first item and then a corresponding point about the second item. Then you make a second point about the first item and a corresponding point about the second item, and so forth. The block pattern, on the other hand, divides the paragraph roughly into halves, or blocks, and discusses the first item thoroughly before going on to the second item. The paragraph that follows, borrowed from *Tragedy and Comedy*, a treatise by drama critic Walter Kerr, uses the block pattern to compare the two dramatic forms. The first half of the paragraph discusses tragedy; the second half discusses comedy. The concluding statement generalizes about the difference.

> The tragic statement is the original and fundamental statement, the mother statement, because it coincides exactly with the intention of drama as a whole. If drama's impulse is to display an action, tragedy is the form that sets man free enough to act, to act extensively, even to act absolutely. When the tragic hero says "I *will*," he is doing drama's work without reserve. Comedy, which we feel in our bones to be the lesser form, is indeed the lesser form because it comes into existence as a comment upon tragedy, and in fact upon drama. It is a species of criticism and, hence, parasitical. It does not initiate action; its desires are all passive. Rather it derides action for the inhibited and otherwise oppressed thing it is. "Oh, no, you won't," it says, pointing to the stone wall just ahead. Comedy could not create drama of its own power; its feet are too sore, its burdens too heavy, for it to cross the circle unaided. Comedy will cross the circle when it is kicked across or chased across or carried across; left to its own devices it will simply run in circles forever, or until it is tired enough to lie down. Comedy is dependent. It requires tragedy to budge it into its characteristic posture of dragging its feet while thumbing its nose. Tragedy is the thought of drama, and comedy the afterthought.[8]

The following comparison paragraph, from Virginia Woolf's essay "If Shakespeare Had Had a Sister," illustrates the point-by-point pattern of comparison. Here, Woolf expounds upon the conspicuous presence of women in Elizabethan drama and their conspicuous absence from historical records in England during the seventeenth century.

> A very queer, composite being thus emerges. Imaginatively she is of the highest importance; practically she is completely insignificant. She pervades poetry from cover to cover; she is all but absent from history. She dominates the lives of kings and conquerors in fiction; in fact she was the slave of any boy whose parents forced a ring upon her finger. Some of the most inspired words, some of the most profound thoughts in literature fall from her lips, in real life she could hardly read, could scarcely spell, and was the property of her husband.[9]

The fourth quality of the well-written paragraph, **coherence**, is the smooth progression from one idea to the next. One way that coherence is achieved is by the use of **transitional expressions** such as *for example*, *nevertheless*, and *however*. These expressions keep the reader from getting lost in the maze of evidence you are presenting. Some useful transitional expressions are listed here.

Additional idea: *and, also, in addition, too, indeed*

Alternative idea: *more importantly, furthermore, moreover, or*

Comparison: *similarly, likewise*

Contrast: *but, yet, however, on the other hand, conversely, rather*

Numbered ideas: *first, second, third, finally*

Result: *so, hence, therefore, consequently, thus, then*

Exemplification: *for example, for instance, in fact*

Summary: *in short, on the whole, to sum up, in other words*

In the preceding extract from *Tragedy and Comedy*, note how Kerr uses the transitional expressions, *indeed, in fact, hence,* and *rather*.

Repetition is another tool for bringing coherence to a paragraph. Kerr's paragraph, for example, repeats the word *too*: "too sore," "too heavy." And it repeats the word *across* as well as the structure of phrases: "when it is kicked across or chased across or carried across." Such parallel structure aids the reader in comparing the ideas.

Your readers have a difficult task, processing all of the information that you are delivering. You can assist them by providing coherent paragraphs.

Exercise 2-2

Explain how the following body paragraph, from an early draft of an essay about Chekhov's *The Seagull*, fails to exhibit the principles of *unity, adequate development, organization,* and/or *coherence*. What suggestions would you have for revising the paragraph? You might begin by identifying all the sentences that could serve as topic sentences. How many are there? How does having more than one topic sentence affect paragraph unity? (It is not necessary to be familiar with the play in order to analyze the paragraph.)

Treplev is an honest and introspective character. He is very in tune with his emotions and has no shame in divulging their sources. Treplev recognizes his own pathetic nature at the threat of losing either Nina or his mother, and this in turn aggravates him to death. Upon realizing that Nina no longer cares for him, Treplev immediately returns to the arms of his mother and says to her, "I've nothing left. She [Nina] doesn't love me and I can't write any more. My hopes have all come to nothing" (97). He seeks his mother's pity. This quiet desperation displays Treplev's feelings of futility. He believes that his hopes have become nothing, as a result of a woman and before his life has reached its maturation. He continues to say, "I've no one left but you now" (97) to his mother. Treplev has no problem verbalizing the emptiness of his existence. Later in act four after Nina leaves, and directly before he kills himself, Treplev rips all his writing to shreds. Nina has left, and as we have already learned earlier in the play, Arkadin has never read any of his work. This fact adds to his feeling of inadequacy, because his mother dotes on Trigorin, an author he finds completely untalented, while she refuses to even read any of his published work. Treplev believes his work has no meaning without Nina and lacks justification without his mother's acknowledgement. Because of these reactions, he feels he has accomplished nothing.

2-5: Arkadina, the actress, believes she "could play a girl of fifteen." Chekhov's *The Seagull* was performed in 1996 at DePaul University. Director: Bella Itkin, with associate direction by Phyllis E. Griffin. Photographer: John Bridges.

Drafting the Conclusion

The conclusion is your last chance to evoke a nod of approval from your reader as you reinforce your main idea. Do not waste the opportunity by merely repeating your thesis and points of proof. The reader has already read and been convinced of these points. However, the conclusion must not raise a new issue.

How do writers, under these restrictions, reiterate their main ideas without repeating themselves, while sustaining the attention of their readers to the last word? Good conclusions usually develop a **controlling idea**. Following are some ideas you might develop in your conclusion.

- Return to an illustration or anecdote written in the introductory remarks.
- Discuss a quotation.
- Develop an analogy or a comparison.
- Predict the future of the situation or issue.
- Describe the current status of the issue.

- Discuss the broader implications of the topic.
- Call your readers to action.

The following paragraph concludes an essay titled "Eugene O'Neill's Claim to Greatness" by Joseph Wood Krutch. In the essay, Krutch argues with O'Neill's critics who claim that O'Neill's writing was "not only strained and turgid, but awkward, inarticulate, banal."[10]

> Somerset Maugham once declared that all the great novelists—Balzac, Dickens and Dostoevsky, for example, "wrote badly." He did not say that the novels were great because they were badly written or that no writer is both a great stylist and great in other ways besides. But he did suggest that, as novelists, his favorites were superior to the Flauberts and the Jameses whom another school admires so much more. He felt that they were superior because Balzac and Dickens and Dostoevsky had virtues more important than those they lacked and because, instead of torturing themselves in the vain attempt to "get a style," they wrote what they had it in them to write. An O'Neill who wrote better would have been a better O'Neill. But he will last longer and mean more than many who can, in the ordinary sense, write rings around him.[11]

The controlling idea of the above conclusion is to develop a comparison of O'Neill and novelists who were also said to "write badly."

After you have written your conclusion, look at your introductory remarks again. Do you perceive a shift in tone, attitude, emphasis, or even topic? If so, you will need to revise, perhaps extensively. The whole paper should work as a unit.

Citing Your Sources

If you have used sources in your essay in a way that obligates you to credit them, you must document the necessary passages and create a list of **works cited** or a **bibliography**, depending upon which documentation style your instructor requires. Chapter 6 gives detailed information on this step in the process.

Inventing a Title

Some writers create a title for their essay early in the process, saying it helps them narrow their topic and focus on their main idea. Others wait until they have finished the essay to compose a title. These suggestions may help you invent your title:

- It might indicate the form of the essay, as the title of Denise Bush's essay in chapter 3, "Bianca and Othello: An Honest Whore and a Murderous Hero" indicates a comparison/contrast paper.

- It might offer a pun, like Joe Darden's "Absurd, Absurder, Absurdist," also in chapter 3.

- It might state your central argument, as does Rebecca Penkoff's "Torvald Isn't Such a Bad Guy" in chapter 4.

- It might offer a particularly apt turn of phrase from the body of the essay.

- Or it might ask a question.

Do give your essay its own title, not the title of the work it discusses. For example, "A Doll's House" will not do as a title for an essay about Ibsen's *A Doll's House*, although you might include the name of the play in the title, such as "Name-calling and Terms of Endearment in *A Doll's House*."

The essay title is not punctuated with quotation marks, nor is it italicized, boldfaced, underlined, or otherwise adorned. Capitalize the first letter of the first and last words and all other words in between except for articles, prepositions, and coordinating conjunctions. Titles of books, plays, operas, record albums or compact discs, and artworks included in the title of the essay are underlined or italicized; titles of poems, songs, short stories and essays are set in quotation marks. Look carefully at the titles of the essays presented in this book for further guidance.

Revising and Editing Your Essay

Good writing usually entails extensive **revision**. Ernest Hemingway once told an interviewer that he rewrote the ending of *A Farewell to Arms* thirty-nine times. When the interviewer asked him what the problem was, he replied, "Getting the words right."[12] Hemingway's answer may seem obvious, but most of us have difficulty knowing when we have reached the point where our words are "right."

Most of us benefit greatly from having others read our writing and comment upon it. Usually the person who reviews your writing will be a friend, roommate, or classmate—in other words a peer. At times, **peer review** can be helpful; other times not. Generally, peer review goes more smoothly and is more beneficial for not only the author but also the reader (whose own writing and critical thinking skills will improve as a result of the process) if you have guidelines. The following "Guidelines for Peer Review," much of which summarizes the advice of Peter Elbow, author of *Writing Without Teachers* and *Sharing and Responding*, will provide you with a procedure for productive peer review and for revision that results from it.

There are two kinds of feedback: **reader-based feedback** and **criterion-based feedback**. The first type, all readers are qualified to do. The second type is only for those who can judge your writing based upon the same criteria that your instructor will use to grade your essay, usually your classmates.

Guidelines for Peer Review

Author Whose Paper Is Being Reviewed:

- If you have more than one peer reviewer at a time, give assignments: pointing, summarizing, and telling, as explained below. It is your responsibility to decide what kind of feedback you want and from whom.

- Have a peer read your essay aloud, one section at a time. Hearing your words will give you an auditory sense of the work. You will hear the rough spots.

- Be quiet and listen. Do not, by gesture or facial expression, express disagreement with your peers' comments, or your peers will stop commenting.

- Do not decide yet which comments you will take seriously and which ones you will reject. For now, accept all comments. Later, you may realize that a comment that seemed "off" during your peer review actually indicated a problem or a chance for improvement.

- Do not ask your peers to fix your essay.

- Know that ultimately you are responsible for your essay. It is up to you to decide what to do with the feedback you receive.

Readers Giving Reader-Based Feedback:

- Know that you do not have to be an English teacher to give valuable feedback to your peer. You have been reading most of your life and are perfectly qualified, as a reader, to respond to writing.

- Remember throughout the process that you do not have to justify any of your reactions. It is the author's task to solve the essay's problems, not yours.

- Never quarrel with someone else's reaction.

- Be specific. If you say, "This paper keeps saying the same thing over and over," the writer may simply feel judged. If you say, "Paragraph five makes the same point as paragraph three," the writer will have a clearer sense of direction.

- With your finger or a pen, **point** at the places in the text that you believe are well written. Point to the places that are not as well written.

- **Summarize** the main point of the section you have just read and describe its dominant mood.

- **Tell** what happened to you during the reading. Mark the places where you smiled, where your brow wrinkled, where you thought, "Huh?" How did you feel at the end? Concentrate on your feelings about the writing.

- Do not discuss grammar, punctuation, spelling, or mechanics.

- Do not fix the essay.

Readers Giving Criterion-Based Feedback:

- Find the thesis, or what you believe to be the intended thesis. Could other statements be mistaken for the thesis? Is the thesis written in the proper mode of discourse? Does it fulfill the criteria for a workable thesis?

- What question does the thesis provoke? In other words, what is the proof question?

- Where are the points of proof? Do they follow the thesis directly? If not, is there a good reason? Are they explicit in the body of the essay?

- Do the points of proof fulfill the criteria for workable points of proof?

- Does the occasion contain specific, rather than general, information?

- Does the occasion lead directly to the thesis? Or does there seem to be some lack of continuity from occasion to thesis?

- Do the body paragraphs exhibit the qualities of unity, adequate development, organization, and coherence?

- Is the evidence presented in the body convincing?

- Does the conclusion reiterate the main point without simply repeating the thesis and points of proof? Does the conclusion develop a controlling idea?

- What suggestions for improvement do you have for the author?

After peer review, the author must decide which comments and suggestions to act upon. Remember that the author alone, not his or her peers, is responsible for the essay.

If review by your peers is not an option, put yourself in the place of a reader who is reading the essay for the first time and answer the questions for reader-based and criterion-based feedback.

Guidelines for Editing and Proofreading

William Strunk, coauthor of the renowned *The Elements of Style*, writes, "Vigorous writing is concise. A sentence should contain no unnecessary words, a paragraph no unnecessary sentences, for the same reason that a drawing should have no unnecessary lines and a machine no unnecessary parts."[13] Such economy is rarely achieved without extensive editing.

Like the procedures for planning, drafting, and revising, the procedures for editing are rarely linear. A word change in one place in the essay may create a need to reconstruct a sentence or reorganize a paragraph elsewhere. Still it makes sense to start with the larger issues in editing, and work toward the smaller ones.

- Examine your sentences individually. Each one should be solidly constructed. **Run-ons** and **fragments** are very serious errors. Try reading your sentences in reverse order, the last sentence first. This way, you are reading each sentence out of context and can concentrate on its structure rather than its content.

- Consider sentence punctuation, especially of quoted material.

- Look at your words individually. Is each word chosen carefully in terms of meaning and tone?

- Is each word spelled correctly? Your computer's grammar and spell check functions are useful, but they will not catch every error, particularly the homonymic ones. If, for example, you have written *medal* where you should have written *mettle* or *where as* instead of *whereas*, your computer, being only a machine, is of no help. Use a dictionary!

- Have you used upper- and lower-case correctly and consistently? Have you used italics and underlining correctly? Are numbers correct and presented consistently?

- Review your source citations and works cited page or bibliography. Are they presented correctly and in the style preferred by your instructor?

Consult the Handbook at the end of the textbook for advice in all the aforementioned matters.

Formatting Your Essay

See the sample essays in this book for a generally accepted, MLA-recommended format for college papers. You probably do not need a title page because they are generally for book-length papers with multiple chapters. If you need one, of if your professor prefers one, center the information on the page, as follows:

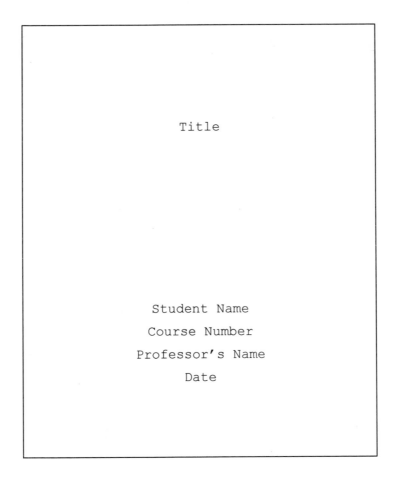

```
                          Title




                      Student Name
                     Course Number
                   Professor's Name
                          Date
```

Finally, check with your instructor for any special requests in the formatting and packaging of your paper.

2-6: A love triangle in *Hedda Gabler*, produced at Wake Forest University in 1999, directed by J.E.R. Friedenberg. Photographer: Bill Ray III.

Notes

[1] Michel de Montaigne, "Of the Art of Discussion" *The Complete Essays of Montaigne*, trans. Donald M. Frame (Stanford: Stanford UP, 1958) 704.

[2] Ronald Hingley, Introduction, *Anton Chekhov: Five* Plays, trans. Ronald Hingley (Oxford: Oxford UP, 1977) xxiii-iv.

[3] Oscar Brockett and Robert J. Ball, *The Essential Theatre*, 8th ed. (Belmont, CA: Wadsworth/Thomson Learning, 2004) 364-65.

[4] Richard Hornby, *Mad about Theatre* (New York: Applause, 1996) 109.

[5] Martin Esslin, *Brecht: The Man and His Work* (Garden City, NY: Doubleday, 1961) 125.

[6] Robert Brustein, "Twenty-first Century Hamlet," *Dumbocracy in America* (Chicago: Dee, 1994) 84-85.

[7] Frank Rich, "*Marvin's Room*," *Hot Seat* (New York: Random, 1998) 839.

[8] Walter Kerr, *Tragedy and Comedy* (New York: Simon, 1967) 266.

[9] Virginia Woolf, "If Shakespeare Had Had a Sister," *The Rinehart Reader,* ed. Jean Wyrick and Beverly J. Slaughter, 3rd ed. (Fort Worth: Harcourt, 1999) 216.

[10] Joseph Wood Krutch, "Eugene O'Neill's Claim to Greatness," *Essays in the Modern Drama*, ed. Morris Freedman (Boston: Heath, 1964) 91.

[11] Krutch 95.

[12] Ernest Hemingway, *Good Advice on Writing*, eds. William Safire and Leonard Safir (New York: Simon, 1992) 210.

[13] William Strunk and E. B. White, *The Elements of Style* (Boston: Allyn, 1979) 23.

Writing the Analytical Essay

Susy Hendrix is blind and someone is trying to kill her. Her life depends upon figuring out who, and why. Clues emerge in the course of Frederick Knott's thriller, *Wait Until Dark*. Susy pieces them together to create a theory—a story that would explain the bizarre recent events of her life. The evidence points to Mike, a man she believes to be her protector. Should Susy

trust her instincts or her reasoning skills? How would you fare in Susy's
position? How reliable is your judgment in a life-or-death situation? This
chapter is intended to help you hone your analytical skills, to give you
confidence in your ability to posit a theory, test the support for it, and act on
it. Or not. There is a reason they call it "critical" thinking.

3-1: Susy Hendrix's critical thinking skills are tested in
Wait Until Dark, produced by Castleton State College in
1999. Director: Harry McEnerny. Photographer: Ennis
Duling.

The Nature of Analysis

When you write an analytical essay, you attempt to convey your own perspective. The analytical essay might focus on some particular symbol or image and discuss its implications. For example, you might discuss Shakespeare's use of the moon in *A Midsummer Night's Dream*. Sometimes it is a "silver bow"; other times it is "cold" or "wat'ry." Sometimes it "gracious, golden, glittering gleams"; other times it is the "governess of floods, / Pale in her anger." What moods, what themes, what messages are implied by this ever-changing object? The analytical essay might employ a fresh critical approach. For example, you might apply Marxist criticism (explained later in this chapter) to *Antigone* by discussing the influence of money on Creon's personality. Your analytical essay might explain the theory of deconstruction, using as an extended example Vladimir's round song in the second act of *Waiting for Godot*. There is no end to the possible ways in which drama can be analyzed.

Drawing Inferences

At the heart of the analytical essay is an **inference**. In other words, the writer examines a fact, or perhaps a collection of facts, and from them draws a conclusion or an inference. Take, for a brief example, Lucky's speech in act 1 of *Waiting for Godot*. At first, it reads like nonsense:

> Given the existence as uttered forth in the public works of Puncher and Wattmann of a personal God quaquaquaqua with white beard quaquaquaqua outside time without extension who from the heights of divine apathia divine athambia divine aphasia loves us dearly with some exceptions for reasons unknown but time will tell. . . .

However, a close reading of the entire speech and a genuine desire to make some sense out of it may lead to a new dimension of understanding of the play.

Approaches to Analysis

There are three primary approaches to analysis: **interpretation, speculation about causes or effects**, and **evaluation**. In all three approaches, you will be drawing inferences.

In the following paragraph, Susan Sontag *interprets* Ionesco's peculiar language, particularly his use of the cliché and of what Sontag calls "language-as-thing":

> Ionesco's discovery of the cliché meant that he declined to see language as an instrument of communication or self-expression, but rather as an exotic substance secreted—in a sort of trance—by interchangeable persons. His next discovery, also long familiar in modern poetry, was that he could treat language as a palpable thing. (Thus, the teacher kills the student in *The Lesson* with the word "knife.") The key device for making language into a thing is repetition. This verbal repetition is dramatized further by another persistent motif of Ionesco's plays: the cancerous, irrational multiplication of material things. (Thus: the egg in *The Future Is in Eggs*; the chairs in *The Chairs*; the furniture in *The New Tenant*; the boxes in *The Killer*; the cups in *Victims of Duty*; the noses and fingers of Roberta II in *Jack*; the corpse in *Amédée, or How to Get Rid of It*.) These repeating words, these demonically proliferating things, can only be exorcised as in a dream, by being obliterated.[1]

In the following paragraph, Sigmund Freud *speculates about the cause* of Hamlet's famous hesitation to wreak revenge upon his father's murderer:

> What is it then, that inhibits [Hamlet] in fulfilling the task set him by his father's ghost? The answer, once again, is that it is the peculiar nature of the task. Hamlet is able to do anything—except take vengeance on the man who did away with his father and took that father's place with his mother, the man who shows him the repressed wishes of his own childhood realized. Thus the loathing which should drive him on to revenge is replaced in him by self-reproaches, by scruples of conscience, which remind him that he himself is literally no better than the sinner whom he is to punish.[2]

In the following paragraph, drama critic Frank Rich *evaluates* Tony Kushner's *Angels in America*. The 1992 review was written upon the play's premiere:

> Such is the high-voltage theatricality achieved by both play and production that the English audience at *Angels in America* is totally gripped even as it must consult a program glossary to identify phenomena like Ethel Rosenberg (who materializes to call an ambulance for the stricken [Roy] Cohn), Ed Meese, Shirley Booth, and the Yiddish expression "Feh!" Even a graphic simulation of rough anonymous sex—brilliantly accomplished by two fully dressed actors miming their actions at opposite sides of the stage—becomes a funny and affecting metaphor for Mr. Kushner's larger, painful canvas of a country splintering at every public and private level. There are scenes of *Angels in America* that run on too long and thoughts that are not clear (though they may become so in part two). But the excitement never flags. Mr. Kushner has created

an original theatrical world of his own, poetic and churning, that, once entered by an open-minded viewer of any political or sexual persuasion, simply cannot be escaped.[3]

Critical Theories

Certain philosophical discourses often inform our analyses of theatre and drama. They give us a lens through which to view the literature as well as the performance of plays. Chances are that you are already applying certain philosophies to your reading and writing. If you are interested in politics, you read literature with an eye toward some political message. If you are interested in psychology, you read with an eye toward the psychological motivation of the author or the characters. These discourses, or critical theories, simply validate what you are already doing and broaden your range of ideas for generating your own analyses of dramatic literature.

Following is a brief summary of several of the more widely recognized critical approaches to drama. These philosophies can be extremely complex and obscure, and this overview in no way pretends to capture any of them in their entirety, but it can provide a starting point for the generation of ideas.

New Criticism

This philosophy is not new anymore, really. It has been a prevalent approach to literature since the 1950s. The theory assumes that every part of the work contributes to a unifying theme. The theme is an idea about the real world, outside the text. Each element represents figuratively that central idea. For example, the quilt in Susan Glaspell's *Trifles* represents, among other things, the idea that women should stand together against a male-dominated legal system. How does the quilt do that? An essay on the topic would explain the connection.

New Criticism is probably the most fundamental approach to literary analysis. To use it, first articulate the theme, or at least one of the themes of the play, and then ask why the author has chosen some particular detail, speech, or action and how it contributes to the theme. You might explain how the moon in *A Midsummer Night's Dream* contributes to the idea that love is an irrational state. You might explain how the unicorn in *The Glass Menagerie* represents the idea that life brutalizes sensitive people.

Structuralism

If you love art for art's sake and not for its message, you may be a structuralist at heart. This interpretive approach focuses on the text as an independent, aesthetic object, detached from real world ideas. Its primary interest is in how the parts interrelate and what laws govern their interactions.

Examining **binary oppositions** is one way to approach a text. Some binary oppositions are night/day, awake/asleep, straight/crooked. You could explore the masculine and feminine as binary opposites in *Trifles*. You could write about the town and the country as binary opposites in *A Midsummer Night's Dream*. How about success versus failure in *Death of a Salesman*? Or reality versus fantasy in *The Glass Menagerie*? Bianca and Othello are presented as binary opposites in the essay titled "Bianca and Othello: An Honest Whore and a Murderous Hero" later in this chapter.

Another structuralist approach is to examine the text as **metonym** or **metaphor**. Though the two are not always clearly separable, you might think of metonymic fiction as realistic and metaphoric fiction as surrealistic. Key concepts are "selection" and "substitution."

3-2: A bewildered Yank on 5th Avenue, from the 2004 production of *The Hairy Ape* at the State University of New York at New Paltz. Director: John Wade. Photographer: David Cavallaro.

In metonymic fiction, some selected detail represents a character or some other larger element of the text. For example, ballet shoes might represent the dancer herself; a swastika might represent a Nazi; a combat helmet might represent a dead soldier. In *The Glass Menagerie*, you might see the unicorn as representing Laura. In *Trifles*, Minnie Wright, who never appears on stage, is defined metonymically through selected details: her pots and pans, unbaked bread, rocking chair, jar of preserves, quilt, and apron. Since these details represent her, when she is away from her kitchen, she loses her identity. That is why she asks the women to bring her apron to her in jail—so that she can feel more "natural"—more like herself.

A metaphoric text is not realistic. It substitutes one element for another element from a completely different context. Eugene O'Neill's *The Hairy Ape* is a classic example. The workers on a steamship cannot really be Neanderthals, but they certainly look subhuman with their stooped, knuckle-dragging postures; their living space is not really a cage, but it is presented as such. Everything that happens in the play is predicated upon these metaphors—images substituted for the real thing.

Our Town could be read either metonymically or metaphorically. The details—Mrs. Webb's string beans, Mrs. Gibbs's chickens, Emily's school books—are realistic details, but they are imaginary, which gives the play a surreal quality. You might be able to write an essay that shows how the details of the play you are analyzing work metonymically or metaphorically or both to determine the play's action.

Post-Structuralism

Like structuralism, post-structuralism is not interested in external reality or in some moral or theme that the literature points to. However, it differs from structuralism in that it does not insist upon consistency or meaning within the text. The world, so the philosophy goes, is essentially unknowable, and language is particularly unreliable.

Semiotics is a post-structuralist idea about language as a combination of signifiers and the things they signify. A semiotic reading of a play would show that what the signifier signifies is not reliable. In *Trifles*, for example, the word *quilt* is a signifier. To the men, it signifies domesticity, women's work, nothing very dangerous. The women read the word differently; in it they see crime, madness, injustice, and a call to sisterhood.

Deconstruction is another post-structuralist theory; it is one of the most difficult to grasp and use because its central idea is that the text's meaning is indeterminate. Language, so goes the philosophy, can never entirely capture the thought. Something is always lost in the translation. Therefore, what is unsaid is as important as what is said. Any meaning you assign to the literature, therefore, is suspect. The thing to do is argue for indeterminacy.

In *Trifles*, it can be argued that the meaning of Mrs. Peters's statement, "the law is the law," is indeterminate. You could assume the phrase means that the rules and regulations of society are what one must obey. That seems to be what Mrs. Peters means. The text, however, dismantles that idea when the women disobey the law. At some level, as well, Mrs. Peters probably does not believe this cliché herself, even when she says it. **Clichés** are phrases that have been overworked to the point that they have lost their ability to convey meaning. "The law is the law" is meaningless also because it is a circular definition. Saying it is like saying, "A kangaroo is a kangaroo." The phrase's meaninglessness undercuts attempts to assign it meaning. Later, Mrs. Peters, who uttered the cliché, is deemed trustworthy by the County Attorney because she is "married to the law." Mrs. Peters seems to realize an irony when the County Attorney makes this remark: the law is not the law after all, and she is no more obliged to observe the laws of marriage (love, honor, and, in those days *obedience*) than she is any other law.

This whole exercise may seem like nothing more than a stunt, but remember the idea behind deconstruction is that language is the product of a supple mind. Deconstruction is useful as a tool for uncovering layers of meaning in language that the characters utter unconsciously. Why *did* Mrs. Peters utter such an empty phrase as "the law is the law"?

You might take what Edmund says in *King Lear*, "Now, gods, stand up for bastards," and explore it from the possibility that this "prayer," which implies belief in a higher power, is equally an expression of disbelief in gods as well as the concept of bastardy. The prayer may be both sincere and ironic. At the end of Eugene Ionesco's *The Chairs*, a character writes a meaningless word, "ANGELFOOD." Or *is* the word meaningless? Perhaps, in its meaninglessness, it conveys meaning.

Deconstruction is an obscure concept, and the examples above are simplistic in the extreme, but if you can grasp and clarify the idea, you might enjoy the exercise. Read the works of the French philosophers Jacques Derrida and Michel Foucault and American philosopher Paul de Man, who are deconstruction's most famous proponents, if you want to learn more about this critical approach.

Psychological Criticism

The assumption of **psychological criticism** is that the play is a reflection of the playwright's or the characters' psyche and can be interpreted as such. The theories of Sigmund Freud, Jacques Lacan, and Carl Jung most often influence psychological literary criticism.

Freud offers the following famous explanation for the appeal of Sophocles's *Oedipus Rex*:

> [Oedipus's] destiny moves us only because it might have been ours— because the oracle laid the same curse upon us before our birth as upon him. It is the fate of all of us, perhaps, to direct our first sexual impulse toward our mother and our first hatred and our first murderous wish against our father. Our dreams convince us that that is so. King Oedipus, who slew father Laius and married his mother Jocasta, merely shows us the fulfillment of our own childhood wishes. But, more fortunate than he, we have meanwhile succeeded, in so far as we have not become psychoneurotics, in detaching our sexual impulses from our mothers and in forgetting our jealousy of our fathers. Here is one in whom these primeval wishes of our childhood have been fulfilled, and we shrink back from him with the whole force of the repression by which those wishes have since that time been held down within us.
>
> . . . There is an unmistakable indication in the text of Sophocles' tragedy itself that the legend of Oedipus sprang from some primeval dream material which had as its content the distressing disturbance of a child's relation to his parents owing to the first stirrings of sexuality. At a point when Oedipus, though he is not yet enlightened, has begun to feel troubled by his recollection of the oracle, Jocasta consoles him by referring to a dream which many people dream, though, as she thinks, it has no meaning:
>
>> Many a man ere now in dreams hath lain
>> With her who bare him. He hath least annoy
>> Who with such omens troubleth not his mind.
>
> Today, just as then, many men dream of having sexual relations with their mothers and speak of the fact with indignation and astonishment. It is clearly the key to the tragedy and the complement to the dream of the dreamer's father being dead. The story of Oedipus is the reaction of the imagination to these two typical dreams.[4]

Note that Freud offers evidence from the text of Sophocles's play to support his theory.

A popular interpretation of *Hamlet* is that his fury at his mother's hasty remarriage is motivated by an Oedipus complex. Such psychological readings sometimes inform the directing of plays. In more than one production, Hamlet has thrown his mother on the bed and made overtly sexual advances toward her, even though Shakespeare wrote no such stage direction, as far as we know.

In another example, if you read *Coriolanus* and the *Diagnostic and Statistical Manual of Mental Disorders*, published by the American

Psychiatric Association, you may come to believe that Coriolanus is driven by narcissism resulting from the way in which he was breast-fed. The psychological approach can lead to intriguing research questions. What psychological force drives Frankie, in *The Member of the Wedding*, to fall in love with a wedding? Why can't Brick have an honest and deep relationship with Maggie in *Cat on a Hot Tin Roof*? Why does Martha so cherish the illusion that she has a son in *Who's Afraid of Virginia Woolf*? Why does Hedda Gabler kill herself with her father's pistol in front of his portrait?

Reader-Response Criticism

At the heart of most **reader-response theories** is the idea that a text's meaning is incomplete until a reader reads it. One theory says that you interpret according to the dictates of your own identity. If you distrust legal authority, for example, you are likely to read *Trifles* as an endorsement of the subversion of legal authority, and you will see the various details of the text as supportive of that main idea. If, on the other hand, you are not inherently suspicious of authority, you might see the values and customs of the era in which *Trifles* is set as the problem, and you will see the details corroborating that theme. This is different from New Criticism in the assumption that the reader produces the meaning; the text does not dictate its own interpretation.

Another reader-response approach is to show how the text creates expectations in the reader and then satisfies them (or fails to). For example, in the opening scene of Harold Pinter's *The Homecoming*, a conversation takes place between Max and his son Lenny. Max's speech contains several pauses that seem to imply unspoken ideas or emotions. Readers tend to try, whether they are aware of it or not, to fill in the gaps and "read" the pauses. As a reader, you might analyze how these subtle moments create expectations or contribute to the tension of the play. Or consider, in another example, how *Waiting for Godot* creates the expectation that Godot will appear and the reader's emotional reaction to his non-appearance.

You might, on the other hand, reverse the process by noticing your reaction and then analyzing how the text elicited that response from you. For example, many people are moved to tears by a small moment in Thornton Wilder's *Our Town*—Rebecca's description of the address on the envelope of a letter. The passage is not at all sentimental; it does not seem intended to make a person cry, yet it does. Why? If you can get a handle on how the passage works to create a response, you are using the reader-response approach.

3-3: Emily Webb joins the dead in a 2003 production of *Our Town* at Louisiana State University, directed by Jane Drake Brody. Photographer: Chipper Hatter.

Marxist Criticism

Just as Karl Marx was interested in the struggle for power among social and economic classes, the Marxist critic is interested in what dramatic literature has to say about the struggle. **Marxist criticism** focuses upon the treatment of members of the underclass by those in power as well as by the playwright. *Trifles* could be examined in terms of its turning the hierarchy of power upside down, especially as a result of economic disparity between the women and the men.

Many powerful dramatists, such as Clifford Odets, have been influenced by Marxist thinking, and Marxist criticism is often the logical approach to a critical essay on such authors' plays. For example, you might examine the speeches of the cab drivers in *Waiting for Lefty* to come to a conclusion about Odets's feeling about the working class. One of the cab drivers, Sid, in reference to the owners of the cab company, says, "They know if they give in just an inch, all the dogs like us will be down on them together—an ocean knocking them to hell and back and each singing cuckoo with stars coming from their nose and ears." Sid's speech is a curious mixture of images, both the language of a common working man and a poet. Thus, Odets conveys his message that working class people are worthy of respect.

Nora Helmer's defiant abandonment of her husband and children in Ibsen's *A Doll's House* has been studied from a Marxist perspective as a reaction against capitalistic oppression. Oscar Wilde's comedy *The Importance of Being Earnest* is often read as a critique of upper class morality and values. Wherever in literature there is an underclass, there is the potential for Marxist criticism.

Feminist Criticism

Feminist criticism, like Marxist criticism, is based upon a political philosophy: women deserve rights and opportunities equal to those of men. Sometimes the goal of feminist criticism is to articulate the implied message of drama produced by feminist thinking, such as Glaspell's *Trifles*. Other times the goal is to discover how the literature promotes or disparages feminist principles, consciously or not. For example, Henry Higgins in Shaw's *Pygmalion* is a likable fellow, but his sexism is troublesome. Should we read the play as an exposé of sexism, since Higgins is clearly a sexist, or as a subtle endorsement of it, since Higgins is so likable?

Not all works by women have a clearly feminist intent. While the characters are women in Marsha Norman's *'night, Mother*, the play is not primarily about women's issues. Many works by men, on the other hand, do engage in the examination of women's issues. Ibsen's *A Doll's House* is an example. Some plays do not have any female characters, like David Mamet's *American Buffalo*, but can still be examined from a feminist perspective *because* women are absent—their very absence gives us something to think about—and because the male characters talk about women. Mamet's *Oleanna* is another case in point. Is Mamet discrediting women's complaints about sexual harassment? Is he claiming that there is a tendency toward excess in the women's movement? In *The Taming of the Shrew*, does Shakespeare endorse or object to women's subjection to their husbands? What does Caryl Churchill's *Cloud Nine* say about female sexuality?

Queer Theory

Queer theory examines the treatment of homosexuals in drama. Queer theory, like feminist criticism, is based upon the belief that everyone deserves equal treatment and respect, and plays are examined with that idea in mind. In *Cat on a Hot Tin Roof*, is Brick a homosexual or not? Why doesn't Tennessee Williams just tell us? What does Brick mean by "pure" love? What are we to make of the two schoolteachers' relationship in *The Children's Hour*? What does the play say about Lillian Hellman's attitude toward lesbianism? Is Tony Kushner's *Angels in America* really as good as the critics say? Or is it simply capitalizing upon what Robert Brustein calls the "theatre of guilt"—the attitude that criticism of plays that protest against the mistreatment of women and minorities, including gays, is socially *verboten*? These are the kinds of questions that queer theory asks.

Queer theory also explores the ways in which society constructs and rewards certain sexual behaviors and punishes others. In Shakespeare's *Antony and Cleopatra*, for example, Marc Antony is a Roman soldier who would rather make love than war. Antony's comrades in arms believe he has become womanish, which, in their opinion, is a revolting development. What can we deduce about Shakespeare's attitude toward sexual identity and its social constructions from the play? In Shakespeare's day, men and boys played all the female roles in the theatre. Meanwhile, the Puritans eschewed theatre because they believed that cross dressing was immoral. What might Shakespeare have been saying about such disputes when he has Cleopatra predict that someday some "squeaking Cleopatra" would "boy" her greatness?

Multiculturalism

Used interchangeably with **post-colonial criticism, multiculturalism** examines the treatment of those who are underprivileged as the result of belonging to a cultural (racial, ethnic, social, economic, etc.) minority. Some readers have seen *Othello* as proof positive of Shakespeare's abhorrence of racism; some have seen *The Merchant of Venice* as proof positive of his anti-Semitism. Could Shakespeare have been of both opinions—both sympathetic to blacks and antithetic to Jews? It seems unlikely, but many critics have enjoyed trying to discern Shakespeare's attitude.

Lorraine Hansberry's enduring *A Raisin in the Sun* is often analyzed in terms of multiculturalism: how, a multiculturalist might ask, does racial discrimination affect Walter Lee's view of manhood? Why is Beneatha so much less affected by prejudice than Walter Lee? Plays by August Wilson, Suzan-Lori Parks, Luis Valdez, Wole Soyinka, and countless others lend themselves to multicultural analysis, not just because their authors are minorities, but because they deal with multicultural issues.

New Historicism

New historicists view the text as both a product of and an influence upon the time in which it was written. *Trifles*, for example, can be read as a treatise on legal structures in America at the turn of the 20th century. Many critics thought that the enormous appeal of *Oklahoma!* in 1943 was that it offered audiences an escape from the reality of World War II, to a simpler time. In the play, however, Judd is a dark, malignant presence. Curly kills him, and the community exonerates its protector. Seen in this light, the play may have appealed to Americans' need for reassurance that the war was morally justifiable.

How a text treats "the other" in society is of major concern to the new historicist, and since "the other" is a prevalent trope in literature, there is no shortage of plays to be studied through this lens—*Antigone*, for example, and Arthur Miller's *The Crucible*.

Critical theories often cohabit. You may find the New Criticism and the psychological approach to be compatible. Marxist and feminist criticisms often work well together since their philosophies overlap. Both are concerned with equal rights for the disenfranchised. The main thing to understand is that these philosophies and theories can help you get a handle on the literature you are examining. When teamed up with your own notes, responses, and ideas, philosophies and theories can help you figure out what approach you will take in your analysis.

Following is a list of some useful books in the field of critical theory:

Recommended Reading: An Introduction to Critical Approaches to Literature

Carlson, Marvin A. *Theories of the Theatre: A Historical and Critical Survey from the Greeks to the Present.* Ithaca, NY: Cornell UP, 1993.

Case, Sue-Ellen. *Feminism and Theatre.* New York: Methuen, 1988.

Eagleton, Mary, ed. *Feminist Literary Theory: A Reader.* 2nd ed. Oxford: Blackwell, 1995.

Eagleton, Terry. *Literary Theory: An Introduction.* 2nd ed. Minneapolis: U of Minnesota P, 1996.

Fortier, Mark. *Theory/Theatre: An Introduction.* New York: Routledge, 1997.

Jefferson, Ann. *Literary Theory, A Comparative Introduction.* 2nd ed. New York: Rowman, 1987.

Reinelt, Janelle G., and Joseph R. Roach, eds. *Critical Theory and Performance.* Ann Arbor: U of Michigan P, 1992.

Richter, David H. *Critical Tradition: Classic Texts and Contemporary Trends.* 2nd ed. Boston: St. Martin's, 1998.

Showalter, Elaine, ed. *The New Feminist Criticism*. New York: Pantheon, 1985.

Williams, Raymond. *Marxism and Literature*. 2nd ed. Oxford: Oxford UP, 1985.

Wright, Elizabeth. *Psychoanalytic Criticism: A Reappraisal*. 2nd ed. New York: Routledge, 1998.

Young, Robert, ed. *Untying the Text*. Boston: Routledge, 1981.

Planning and Drafting Your Analytical Essay

Before you draft your analytical essay, spend some time getting to know your reader and planning. A process for planning essays is described generally in chapter 2. The following section further describes the process as it applies to the analytical essay.

Understanding Your Purpose

Analytical essays, as distinguished from performance reviews, which are discussed in chapter 5, are usually written by academics (like yourself) for the purpose of helping readers understand drama as a work of literature. Such essays discuss how the drama works on a subtextual level. The essay is about the play as read, not as performed.

Libraries are brimming with such essays, collected both in books and periodicals such as *Modern Drama* and the *Journal of Dramatic Theory and Criticism*.

Recognizing Your Audience

Wise writers try to create a profile of their readers by asking questions: What do my readers already know? What do they need to know? What do they believe? How are they likely to react to my opinions? The more you know about your readers, the more successful you will be in aiming your writing toward them and in persuading them.

In a college course you have certain ready-made readers: yourself, your instructor, and your peers. These are worthy readers, to be sure, but who else reads analytical essays about theatre and drama? Certainly it is a long list, from the highly motivated—playwrights and theatre practitioners (actors, directors, costume designers, etc.)—to the barely motivated—the casual theatergoer and students pressed into service for the sake of a grade—all of whose experiences and reading needs vary widely.

It will be difficult if not impossible to tailor your essay to suit the needs of every member of such a diverse group, so your best course of action is to aim somewhere in the middle—at the reader who has read the play and who is familiar with its themes as well as basic theatrical terms and concepts. This reader, therefore, does *not* need you to recount the plot in its entirety, but does need reminders about the particulars, as they pertain to the point you are making.

Think of your reader as skeptical, not easily persuaded. You will have to prove to your reader that your analysis is valid by presenting carefully laid out evidence. While in actuality your instructor may be your only reader, try to envision someone other than your instructor reading your essay, and write for that person. Students writing solely for their instructors tend to omit and gloss over evidence that they know their instructor already knows. This is a mistake because your instructor, when reading your essay, adopts the mindset of a less informed reader, one who needs a carefully structured and supported analysis in order to be persuaded.

Think of your reader as somewhat reluctant. This person wants to know more about your subject but does not want to waste time reading a rehash of shopworn observations. Your reader is hoping you will provide a fresh perspective—not, necessarily, a startling, never-before-conceived theory, but an approach that sheds new light on a familiar subject.

Assume your reader is not willing to work very hard to understand your analysis. He or she is certainly capable of filling in the gaps in the evidence, and of seeing connections between ideas, but does not want to go to the trouble, and justifiably so. After all, it is not your reader's responsibility to make sense of your writing; it is your responsibility to write clearly.

Choosing and Narrowing Your Topic

Isolate one remarkable element of the work that intrigues you. Consider the length of the essay, and narrow your topic accordingly. A two- or three-page essay cannot discuss classical drama in depth. Nor would that amount of space allow for a deep discussion of Sophocles's work, or even of one play, such as *Antigone*. But a three- to five-page essay might discuss in some depth the implications of the fact that Antigone's tomb is also her bridal chamber.

Posing a Research Question

Your task, in writing the analytical essay, is to answer a research question; therefore, a properly posed research question is essential to the process of composition. It is almost always a wise decision to ask your question about some small element of the work, such as a set piece in a play, and discuss its broader implications, rather than to ask a question about the broader elements, such as theme or plot, and plan to discuss it in its entirety. Following are six generally stated research questions, each of which stands a good chance of leading to an analytical essay:

1. What does some element of the work mean?
2. What is the appeal of the work?
3. How does one work, character, or element compare to another?
4. How do certain elements of the work contribute to a larger concept?
5. Why does the playwright make certain choices?
6. What is the cause or effect of some element of the work (or the work as a whole)?

In the following section, these same six general questions are used as the basis of research questions about specific plays. These narrowed questions could provide you with a topic for your own analytical essay, or they may spark ideas for other topics. Or you may use them simply as models of the sort of question you should devise for your own project.

Remember that in analysis, no definitive answer to your research question is available. You are expected to support an inference, not a fact. If an answer to your research question is readily available, you will be writing an objective, not an analytical, essay.

Sample Research Questions

1. What does some element of the work mean?

- What does the tree in Beckett's *Waiting for Godot* mean? the boots? the rope?
- What does Lucky's speech in *Waiting for Godot* mean?
- What does the word "ANGELFOOD" in Ionesco's *The Chairs* mean?
- What does the fact that the oracle was right in *Oedipus Rex* mean?

- What does Nora mean when she tells Torvald in *A Doll's House* that millions of women have sacrificed their honor for the men they loved?
- What did Chekhov mean when he called *The Seagull* a comedy?
- What did David Mamet mean when he said, in defense of *Oleanna*, "I'm an artist. I write plays, not political propaganda. If you want easy solutions, turn on the boob tube"?[5]
- What does it mean that Mrs. Warren, the prostitute in Shaw's *Mrs. Warren's Profession*, is a sympathetic character?
- What does the existence of the six characters in Pirandello's *Six Characters in Search of an Author* mean?
- What does it mean that the coin lands on heads more than ninety times consecutively in Stoppard's *Rosencrantz and Guildenstern Are Dead*?

2. **What is the appeal of the work or artist?**

- What is the appeal of Shakespeare's character Richard III?
- What is the appeal of Iago in *Othello*?
- What is the appeal of *Antigone* to modern audiences who have no experience with the burial rites at issue in the play?
- What is the appeal of the "collective character"—the shift away from the focus upon an individual and toward the focus upon a group—in Gorki's *The Lower Depths*?
- What is the appeal of Rebecca's description of the address on the envelope in *Our Town*?
- What is the appeal of Sid's use of language in Odets's *Waiting for Lefty*?
- What is the appeal of Federico Garcia Lorca's frequent use of verse in *Blood Wedding*?
- What is the appeal of the music in Brecht's *Mother Courage and Her Children*?
- What is the appeal of "epic theatre"?
- What is the appeal of the theatre of cruelty?
- What is the appeal of the sparseness of the scenery in *Our Town*?
- What is the appeal of Lady Macbeth's character?
- What is the appeal of *The Taming of the Shrew* in an age of women's liberation?

- What is the appeal of the dialogue in Sheridan's *The School for Scandal*?

3. **How does one work, character, or element compare to another?**

- How does Ros and Guil's attitude toward death in *Rosencrantz and Guildenstern Are Dead* compare to that of Vladimir and Estragon in *Waiting for Godot*?

- How do Sophocles's and Aeschylus's versions of the myth of Electra differ?

- How does Mrs. Peters's attitude toward the law at the beginning of *Trifles* compare to her attitude at the end?

- How does Larry's attitude toward death at the beginning of *The Iceman Cometh* compare to his attitude at the end?

- How does the issue of sexism in Shaw's *Pygmalion* compare with the issue of sexism in the classical tale?

- How does Regina's dream of Chicago compare to Birdie's dream of Lionet in *The Little Foxes*?

- How do ideas about courage and cowardice compare in *Hedda Gabler*?

- How does Mary in Lillian Hellman's *The Children's Hour* compare to Iago in *Othello*?

- How does the character of Birdie in *The Little Foxes* compare to the character of Amanda in *The Glass Menagerie*?

- How does the role of Tom in *The Glass Menagerie* compare to that of the chorus in Greek tragedy?

- How does Vladimir and Estragon's relationship compare to Pozzo and Lucky's in *Waiting for Godot*?

- How does *Waiting for Godot* compare to a medieval morality play?

- How does the structure of Valdez's *I Don't Have to Show You No Stinking Badges* compare to the structure of Pirandello's *Six Characters in Search of an Author*? How does it compare to the structure of *Hamlet*?

- How does Mrs. Hale and Mrs. Peters's conversational style in *Trifles* compare to the conversational style typical of women according to Deborah Tannen in her book *You Just Don't Understand: Women and Men in Conversation*?

- How does the character of Antigone in Sophocles's play compare to the character in Jean Anouilh's play?

- How does Nora's evolution in Ibsen's *A Doll's House* compare to the mythical hero's journey?

4. **How do certain elements of the work contribute to larger concepts?**

- How does the black and white imagery of *Othello* contribute to the idea of racism?

- How does the setting of *Trifles* contribute to the theme of respect for women's work?

- How does the complexity of Hedda Gabler's character contribute to the concept of "realism" in drama?

- How does the discovery of Yorick's skull contribute to Hamlet's dilemma?

- How does Blanche's frequent bathing in *A Streetcar Named Desire* contribute to our understanding of her character?

- How does the subplot of Gloucester's family contribute to the main plot in *King Lear*?

- How does the lack of action in *The Cherry Orchard* contribute to the idea of naturalism in drama?

- How do the double identities in *The Importance of Being Earnest* contribute to the play's subversiveness?

- How does the rhinoceros in Ionesco's *Rhinoceros* contribute to the concept of the theatre of the absurd?

- How do the cousins Shen Te and Shui Ta in Brecht's *The Good Woman of Setzuan* contribute to the idea of relative morality?

- How does Joseph Kesselring's *Arsenic and Old Lace* contribute to the theatrical tradition of the farce?

- How does the chorus in *Antigone* contribute to our understanding of the play's action?

- How does the fire escape in *The Glass Menagerie* contribute to our perception of the characters?

- How does the lantern-slide technique in *The Glass Menagerie* contribute to the mood of the play?

- How does the setting of *Dutchman* contribute to our understanding of the theme?

- How do the concealed facts and identities contribute to the tone of Sheridan's *The School for Scandal*?

- How does mixing the commonplace with the tragic in Synge's *Riders to the Sea* contribute to our understanding of the play's theme?

- Using *Miss Julie* as a case in point, how does August Strindberg's philosophy contribute to his art?

- How does Doctor Faustus's bargain with the devil contribute to the Biblical theme of forbidden knowledge?

5.   Why does the playwright make certain choices?

- Why does Shaw not have Professor Higgins marry Eliza at the end of *Pygmalion*?

- Why does Molière give *Tartuffe* its *deus-ex-machina* ending?

- Why does Synge have his characters in *The Playboy of the Western World* use coarse language when he knew it would offend audiences?

- Why does Tom Stoppard have characters from different eras appear on the stage together in act 3 of *Arcadia*?

- Why does Marsha Norman set *'night, Mother* in real time?

- Why does Bertolt Brecht choose to alienate his audiences?

- Why does Harold Pinter tell the story backwards in *Betrayal*?

- Why does Martin McDonagh use such grotesque imagery (such as a dead, half-headless cat with bits of its brain plopping out) in *The Lieutenant of Inishmore*?

6.   What is the cause or effect of some element of the work (or the work as a whole)?

- Why does King Lear take off his clothes in the storm?

- What causes King Lear and the Fool's role reversal?

- What is the cause of Eben's inability to resist Abbie's seduction in *Desire under the Elms*?

- What is the cause of Willy Loman's suicide?

- What causes Frankie to fall in love with a wedding in *The Member of the Wedding*?

- What causes the workers in *The Hairy Ape* to stoop?

- What causes Mrs. Peters to conceal the evidence in *Trifles*?

- What causes Hamlet to hesitate?

- What causes critics to designate Ibsen's *An Enemy of the People* a "well-made play"?
- What causes the inadequacy of Gayev's and Lyubov's reactions to disaster in *The Cherry Orchard*?
- What causes Lopakhin to destroy the cherry orchard?
- What causes Brick's coldness to Maggie in *Cat on a Hot Tin Roof*?
- What causes Martha to pretend she has a son in *Who's Afraid of Virginia Woolf*?
- What causes Leonardo to be the only character with a name in Federico Garcia Lorca's *Blood Wedding*?
- What caused the demise of the theatre of cruelty?
- What caused the demise of the theatre of the absurd?
- What is causing the popularity of musicals on Broadway?

3-4 "Turn, hell-hound, turn," snarls Macduff in his final confrontation with Macbeth. This 1997 production of *Macbeth* at the University of Wyoming was directed by Lou Anne Wright. Photographer: Ted C. Brummond.

Stating Your Thesis

Your *thesis* is a declarative statement of your main point. It is the statement that the whole essay will prove. A workable analytical thesis usually possesses the following qualities:

- answers the research question
- is one complete, precise, unified statement about the work or the artist
- is narrow enough to limit the material
- is general enough to need support
- is defensible
- is not too obvious

These guidelines for a workable thesis are malleable to some degree. For the beginning writer, though, it is advisable to adhere to them strictly.

Exercise 3-1: Faulty Analytical Theses

Imagine you have been assigned to write a three- to five-page essay on Susan Glaspell's *Trifles* that answers the following research question: "How does the quilt in *Trifles* contribute to the theme of the play?" Use the guidelines for formulating a thesis to determine the problem(s) with the following theses. After you have determined the problems, compare your answers to those in the next box.

1. The quilt is an important symbol.
2. The quilt is an important symbol for three reasons.
3. This paper will analyze the importance of Minnie Wright's quilt.
4. The importance of the quilt is how it contributes to the theme of the play.
5. The importance of the quilt is how it contributes to the theme of justice for women.
6. Quilts are symbols of the value of women's work.
7. The quilt symbolizes the concerns of women.
8. The quilt is sewn in the log cabin pattern.
9. The importance of the quilt cannot be overstated.
10. The quilt is evidence that Minnie Wright was angry at her husband.

Answers to Exercise 3-1:
Faulty Analytical Theses

1. The thesis does not answer the research question, is imprecise, and is too obvious. That the quilt is an important symbol is readily apparent. The thesis should state what the importance of the quilt *is*.
2. Eliminate "for three reasons," which is extraneous in any thesis, and you have the same thesis as in number one above, with the same problems. In addition, "for three reasons" renders the thesis indefensible. It is simply not true that the quilt is an important symbol for *exactly three* reasons. Surely there are more reasons than that, but no one knows how many reasons there are.
3. The thesis fails to make a precise statement about the theme and fails to answer the research question. It promises an analysis rather than delivers one. What does the writer conclude is the importance of Minnie Wright's quilt's contribution to the theme? The answer to that question would be the thesis.
4. The thesis does not answer the research question. Also, it fails to make a precise statement about the theme or tell how the quilt contributes to that theme.
5. The thesis does not answer the research question; also it fails to make a precise statement about the theme.
6. The thesis does not make a statement about the play. Support for this thesis need never mention *Trifles*.
7. The thesis is not precise enough to limit the material. Women have far too many concerns for a three- to five-page paper to discuss in depth.
8. The thesis is too narrow; it needs no support, for it is a fact.
9. The thesis is indefensible. The importance of the quilt most certainly can be overstated. It is also imprecise and does not answer the research question.
10. The thesis is too obvious.

Asking the Proof Question

Suppose your thesis is "The quilt in *Trifles* symbolizes the need for women to defy the law in order to get justice." Your readers will naturally ask the question "*How* does the quilt in *Trifles* symbolize the need for women to defy the law in order to get justice?" That question is your *proof question*. It is your readers' natural reaction to the assertion your thesis makes: it is your thesis with a *how* or a *why* in front of it.

Designing Your Points of Proof

If you can offer at least two answers to the proof question, you can support your thesis. These answers to the proof question are your *points of proof.* The points of proof are mini-theses: they need to be illustrated, using details and examples from the text if you are analyzing a play, facts from history if you are analyzing theatre history. Ideally, points of proof

- answer the proof question
- exhibit a clear connection to the thesis
- are stated in precise, complete sentences
- are general enough to need support
- are narrow enough to be supportable in one, two, or several paragraphs each (depending on the desired length of the essay)
- state reasons for the thesis rather than examples that illustrate it

Think of the points of proof as topic sentences for your body paragraphs, as that is how they will ultimately serve you.

Exercise 3-2: Faulty Points of Proof

Imagine that your task is to support the following thesis: "In *Trifles*, Minnie Wright's quilt symbolizes the need for women to defy the law to get justice." The proof question, then, is "How does Minnie Wright's quilt symbolize the need for women to defy the law to get justice?" The points of proof should answer that question. Use the guidelines for formulating points of proof to determine the problems with the following points of proof. After you have determined the problems, compare your answers to those on the next page.

1. The women's words and actions prove that they must defy the law in order to get justice.
2. The quilt shows that Minnie Wright was angry at her husband.
3. The quilt is sewn in the log cabin pattern.
4. Isn't the quilt a symbol of rage against male domination?
5. This essay will examine the effects of isolation upon abused women.

Answers to Exercise 3-2:
Faulty Points of Proof

1. The sentence contains two points of proof, ostensibly: "words" and "actions." However, neither is developed into a point. What point will the writer make about the women's words? What point will the writer make about the women's actions? And what do either of them have to do with the quilt? The writer who cannot answer these questions has not yet given the essay enough thought.

2. The statement is true enough, but its connection to the thesis is not clear. If all the writer does is prove the truth of this statement, the thesis will remain unsupported. How does the fact that the quilt shows that Minnie was angry at her husband prove that the quilt shows that women have to defy the law to get justice?

3. The statement, like #2, is true, but its connection to the thesis is not clear. Besides, the statement needs no support. It is a fact that the quilt is sewn in the log cabin pattern. What are the implications of that pattern?

4. The sentence is a question rather than a statement. The point of proof must be supported, or proved. You cannot prove the truth of a question.

5. The statement does not answer the proof question. It only promises that an answer will come. Once the writer has examined the effects of isolation upon abused women, what conclusion will she or he draw about the quilt as a symbol of the need for women to defy the law to get justice?

As you can see from the previous exercises, devising an analytical thesis and points of proof is a difficult task. So many things can go wrong. The following thesis and points of proof, however, would probably yield a suitable essay:

Thesis: In *Trifles*, the quilt symbolizes the need for women to defy the law in order to get justice.

Proof Question: How does the quilt in *Trifles* symbolize the need for women to defy the law in order to get justice?

Points of Proof:

1. First, the quilt shows that the legal system has no respect for women's work, and by extension for women themselves, and is therefore inadequate in protecting women like Minnie Wright from abuse.

2. Second, the quilt shows that women like Minnie, who retaliate against injustice, cannot expect mercy from the male-dominated legal system, entrenched in either/or thinking and therefore incapable of grasping the subtleties of Minnie's situation.

3. Finally, the quilt facilitates and therefore endorses the women's defiance of the law.

Each of the points of proof above needs the support of details and examples from the text. Yet each point is supportable, and each will in its turn support the thesis.

3-5: "Look at this one. Why, it looks as if she didn't know what she was about!" Mrs. Hale and Mrs. Peters begin to piece together the clues to the mystery in this 2003 production of *Trifles* at Messiah College, directed by Kasi L. Krenzer Marshall. Photographer: Melissa Engle.

A few notes about variations in points of proof are in order:

Some instructors and students do not like to see a list of points of proof accompanying the thesis. Many essays end the introductory paragraph with the thesis statement. Such a form is, of course, perfectly acceptable, and sometimes more graceful than the one that includes the points of proof. Other instructors believe that including the points of proof in the thesis paragraph results in superior essays.

This author and teacher encourages students, whether they plan to include points of proof in their thesis paragraphs or not, to use the strategy explained here for devising points of proof while planning their essays. Then, once the points have served their purpose, they can delete them when printing the final version of the essay.

- Another way in which your essay may deviate from the form prescribed in this book is to offer the points of proof before instead of after the thesis.

- Usually the points of proof should be stated in separate, complete sentences; sometimes, however, they can be offered as items in a series without loss of clarity.

Organizing Your Essay

Now that you have chosen and narrowed your topic, organize your evidence, using your note cards as described in chapter 2. Then use one of the following templates to assist you in outlining your essay. Tailor the template to suit the needs of each essay, as the number of points of proof and supporting details is variable.

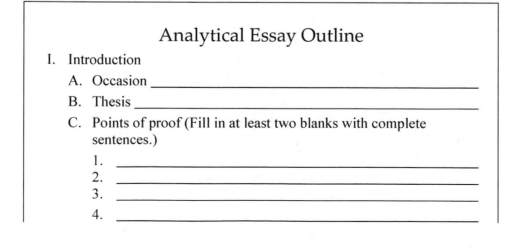

Analytical Essay Outline

I. Introduction

    A. Occasion _____

    B. Thesis _____

    C. Points of proof (Fill in at least two blanks with complete sentences.)

        1. _____

        2. _____

        3. _____

        4. _____

II. Body (Develop each point of proof. Copy your points of proof from C
     above; there should be at least two. Assemble your notes and fill in
     details that will illustrate or support each point. The number of details
     will vary from point to point. You must tailor the template to suit your
     own needs.)

   A. Point of proof 1 _____

       1. Detail _____

       2. Detail _____

       3. Detail _____

   B. Point of proof 2 _____

       1. Detail _____

       2. Detail _____

       3. Detail _____

   C. Point of proof 3 _____

       1. Detail _____

       2. Detail _____

   D. Point of proof 4 _____

       1. Detail _____

       2. Detail _____

III. Conclusion _____

Organizing the Comparison-Contrast Essay

As noted in chapter 2, comparison-contrast can be a useful organizational
pattern when analyzing a dramatic work. However, some special
considerations are necessary when you are planning a comparison-contrast
essay. First, be specific about the elements you are comparing. For example,
the question "How does *Othello* compare to *Macbeth*?" is too open-ended.
Everything there is to say about both plays could appear in an essay that asks
such a broad, vague question. One purpose of the research question is to help
you narrow your focus and eliminate material. "How do Iago's motives
compare to Lady Macbeth's?" is a more specific question and will lead to a
more focused essay.

For a comparison-contrast essay to be successful, you must point out the
differences in things that appear similar, or the similarities in things that

appear different. For example, if you write an essay showing that the premises of both *Waiting for Godot* and *Six Characters in Search of an Author* are absurd, you have wasted your time. Your reader already knows the two plays are similar in that way. If you write an essay showing that Brecht's and Ibsen's theatrical styles are different, you have made the obverse mistake. Again, your reader can see that without your help.

The comparison-contrast essay must offer a reason for the comparison or contrast. You are showing that these two things are alike (or different) in order to prove what?

Comparison-contrast essays usually fall into one of two organizational patterns: the block pattern or the point-by-point pattern. The **block pattern** discusses one of the two items being compared, and then the other. The **point-by-point pattern** discusses one point of comparison as it applies to each item, then the next point of comparison, and so forth. Following are examples of two organizational patterns, using, for demonstration purposes, the subject matter of Denise Bush's essay, "Bianca and Othello: An Honest Whore and a Murderous Hero."

Standard Block Pattern	**Standard Point-by-Point Pattern**
I. Introduction	I. Introduction
A. Occasion	A. Occasion
B. Thesis	B. Thesis
C. Points of proof	C. Points of proof
1. Bianca	1. Self-assessment
a. Self-assessment	a. Bianca
b. Treatment of lover	b. Othello
c. Dealing with jealousy	2. Treatment of lover
2. Othello	a. Bianca
a. Self-assessment	b. Othello
b. Treatment of lover	3. Dealing with jealousy
c. Dealing with jealousy	a. Bianca
	b. Othello
II. Body	II. Body
A. Bianca	A. Self-assessment
1. Self-assessment	1. Bianca
2. Treatment of lover	2. Othello
3. Dealing with jealousy	B. Treatment of lover
B. Othello	1. Bianca
1. Self-assessment	2. Othello
2. Treatment of lover	C. Dealing with jealousy
3. Dealing with jealousy	1. Bianca
	2. Othello
III. Conclusion	III. Conclusion

If your essay will be a comparison-contrast, block pattern, use the following template to outline your essay, remembering that the number of points and examples will vary, depending upon your material. Tailor the outline to suit your own needs.

Comparison-Contrast Essay Outline: Block Pattern

I. Introduction

    A. Occasion _____

    B. Thesis _____

    C. Points of proof

        1. Item 1 _____

            a. Point 1 _____

            b. Point 2 _____

            c. Point 3 _____

        2. Item 2 _____

            a. Point 1 _____

            b. Point 2 _____

            c. Point 3 _____

II. Body

    A. Item 1

        1. Point 1 _____

            a. Example _____

            b. Example _____

        2. Point 2 _____

            a. Example _____

        3. Point 3 _____

            a. Example _____

            b. Example _____

    B. Item 2

        1. Point 1 _____

            a. Example _____

        2. Point 2 _____

            a. Example _____

        3. Point 3 _____

            a. Example _____

III. Conclusion _____

If your comparison-contrast essay will use the point-by-point pattern, outline your essay with the following template, remembering that the number of points and examples will vary, depending upon your material. Tailor the outline to suit your needs.

Comparison-Contrast Essay Outline: Point-by-Point Pattern

I. Introduction

   A. Occasion _____

   B. Thesis _____

   C. Points of proof

      1. Point 1 _____

         a. Item 1 _____

         b. Item 2 _____

      2. Point 2 _____

         a. Item 1 _____

         b. Item 2 _____

      3. Point 3 _____

         a. Item 1 _____

         b. Item 2 _____

II. Body

   A. Point 1 _____

      1. Item 1 _____

         a. Example _____

         b. Example _____

      2. Item 2 _____

         a. Example _____

         b. Example _____

   B. Point 2 _____

      1. Item 1 _____

         a. Example _____

         b. Example _____

      2. Item 2 _____

         a. Example _____

                b. Example _____

      C. Point 3 _____

          1. Item 1 _____

               a. Example _____

               b. Example _____

          2. Item 2 _____

               a. Example _____

               b. Example _____

III.   Conclusion _____

Student Essays

Following are two essays written by college students. Both exemplify an analytical mode of discourse as well as the organizational patterns recommended throughout this book.

Denise Bush, the author of the first essay, has observed that the prostitute of the play *Othello* is named "Bianca," which means "white," in contrast to the "noble" Othello, who is black. Denise explains Bianca's importance to the play by illuminating these binary opposites.

Exercise 3-3

Determine which comparison-contrast pattern—the block or the point-by-point—Denise Bush uses in the following essay.

3-6: "Oh my dear Cassio, my sweet Cassio," says Bianca, the much-maligned courtesan, in *Othello*, performed here at the University of Kansas in 2002 by the University Theatre, directed by Paul Meier. Photographer: Luke Jordan.

Denise Bush

Professor Joan Lord Hall

Tragic Drama

22 Mar. 2000

Bianca and Othello: An Honest Whore

and a Murderous Hero

Why does Shakespeare bestow the name "Bianca" (white) upon the "courtesan" figure of his play, <u>Othello</u>, a drama that is dark with deception and twisted lies? If the reader compares

Bianca to Othello, the noble warrior and central

> Occasion

character of the story, the contrast first favors Othello, as their reputations precede them both--Othello's brave deeds exalt him far above his fellow soldiers, while Bianca's occupation of ill-repute drags her far below the other women. Othello is honored, Bianca mocked. However, as the play

proceeds, the white of Bianca, being her candor and

> Thesis

frankness, becomes a welcomed contrast to the black Othello, who is manipulated by Iago's deception and becomes increasingly less candid. Bianca's honesty in her self-

assessment (which is not clouded by other people's

> Points
> of
> Proof

perception of her), in her generous relationship with her lover, and in the way she deals with jealousy makes her image shine bright and pure, while Othello's heart darkens through his delusion.

    Bianca, negatively labeled a "huswife," "strumpet" and

"customer" by those around her (including her

> Point 1,
> Item 1:
> Bianca's
> self-
> assessment

lover, Cassio), does not allow her reputation to taint her self-perception or her actions. "I am no strumpet, but of life as honest as you that thus abuse me," she retorts to Emilia's accusations (5.1.22). Her loyalty to Cassio--she is never seen with any other man in the play--supports her own evaluation of herself as "honest" (which can also mean <u>chaste</u> in Shakespeare's English) and

belies the allegations of others. When Iago accuses her of
treacherous involvement in Cassio's attack, she refutes
the charge and stands on her integrity, as one of the only
characters not intimidated by Iago's lies. To this charge of
"whoring" and possible violence against her lover, she firmly
replies, "He [Cassio] supped at my house; but I therefore shake
not" (5.1.119).

    Othello, embracing his fame and lineage, readily defines
himself by the reputation that surrounds him as a
"valiant" warrior and "worthy general" (4.1.218);
it serves as a comfortable refuge that protects
him from self-scrutiny and from recognizing his
own weaknesses. The narration of his heroic

Point 1, Item 2: Othello's self-assessment

history wins the love of Desdemona--"She loved me for the
dangers I passed" (1.3.166)--and he continues to make use of
it, both in his defense before the senate when he's accused of
stealing Desdemona's heart by devious means, and to encourage
himself with reminders of his past "feats of broils and
battles" (1.3.86). Since he is noble, level-headed, and wise in
war (Iago recalls how cool Othello remains under cannon-fire
while his troops, including his own brother, are blown away
(3.4.136), Othello assumes these qualities are present in all
areas of his life. Because of this narrow assessment of himself
as the noble stoic, he does not recognize his rage and extreme
jealousy as flaws, so that these become easy prey to Iago's
lies. Responding to Iago's lie that Cassio lay with Desdemona,
Othello declares, "I tremble" (4.1.40). When Lodovico, a
statesman and cousin of Desdemona, witnesses Othello striking
Desdemona and assaulting her with insults, he questions his
earlier admiration for Othello's virtue, wondering, "Is this
the nature whom passion could not shake?" (4.1.265). Unlike

Bianca, who can stand unshaken before the onslaught of Iago's lies, Othello loses his composure.

When she first appears, Bianca hails her lover with "Save you, friend Cassio" (3.4.167). It is a frank public disclosure of their sexual relationship, for in early modern English the title "friend" also means lover or sweetheart. She repeats this bold reference to their relationship when complaining how tedious are "lovers' absent hours" (3.4.173). Clearly Bianca is smitten by Cassio. "I think, i' faith she loves me," admits Cassio (4.1.113), and her focus is on him. When Cassio cries out in pain after being wounded by Roderigo, she comes to his aid without thought of danger, exclaiming, "Oh my dear Cassio, my sweet Cassio" (5.1.76). We deduce that the lack of encouragement she receives from Cassio in public doesn't diminish her hope of gaining his love, for she seems to accept his weakness of putting his reputation first, as when he claims it's best for him not to appear to be "womaned" (3.4.193). She understands the awkward situation her reputation as a courtesan puts him in--she actually takes the brunt of the ridicule--and persists in trying to gain his love regardless of how he responds to her in public. This does not mean she is happy with their situation, and she does not hide her frustration over his flimsy, noncommittal defense of his neglect. She responds to his tentative "Not that I love you not" with an angry "Not that you do not love me!" (3.4.195-96). Bianca's persistence in the relationship--"I pray you bring me on the way" (3.4.196)--and her later referring to him as "sweet" demonstrate her understanding and perception--she knows her lover--and she exercises patience, saying, "I must be circumstanced [accept things as they are]" (3.4.200).

> Point 2, Item 1: Bianca's generosity

What a contrast we have in the prestigious relationship of Othello and Desdemona! Othello's marriage to the beautiful Desdemona, daughter of the important "magnifico" (1.2.10) furthers his prestige among his fellow soldiers and the

> Point 2,
> Item 2:
> Othello's
> lack of
> generosity

senate. Othello loved her, he says, because she "pitied" him for the hardships he suffered in youth, suggesting he is more enamored with her adoration and her favorable image of him than with Desdemona herself. Since it is her response to his monologue that fires their "love," we learn little about her life. Othello wants Desdemona to be perfect (her perfection will adorn his nobility), so he prefers to focus on her exterior "alabaster" beauty. Her discourse is welcomed only when it esteems Othello; in front of the senate, he asks that she have the opportunity to speak (in his defense) in order to put an end to her father's accusation that Othello has bewitched her. How unfair, then, Othello is when he denies Desdemona the opportunity to speak on her own behalf when she is accused of having a love affair with Cassio! Because he does not really know or understand her, he is quick to believe Iago's evil assessment of Desdemona. Unlike Bianca, Othello would rather forgo his love than be made a fool of in public. The idea of being a "cuckold" haunts him (3.3.165), and his fear drives his rage towards Desdemona and prevents him from confronting her.

Interestingly, both Bianca and Othello are presented with the same damning handkerchief as proof against their lovers' faithfulness. When Cassio offers this handkerchief that has mysteriously appeared in his room as a gift to Bianca, her suspicions

> Point 3,
> Item 1:
> How Bianca
> handles
> jealousy

are aroused--so this is why Cassio has been absent: another woman, the owner of the embroidered handkerchief, has kept him occupied. Her immediate question, "O Cassio, whence came

this?" (3.4.179), reveals her jealousy, but for the moment she
has to accept his reply: "I found it in my chamber" (3.4.187).
However, time and brooding increase Bianca's consternation, and
when she next encounters Cassio, her fury lets loose. "There!"
she spits out as she throws down the handkerchief and rids
herself of the object that represents the possibility of
another woman in her lover's life: "Give it to your hobbyhorse"
(3.4.155).

What can be said to defend Bianca's misconstrued jealousy
and anger? How is it different from the jealous rage of
Othello? Bianca wastes no time in confronting Cassio with her
jealous suspicions and giving him the opportunity to defend
himself. She has good reason to doubt Cassio, and his public
belittling of her gives her little reassurance. Yet she has no
desire to cling to a piece of evidence that would prove the
falsehood of her lover. In spite of her anger, she never
defames Cassio's name, and, most telling of her generosity, she
gives him the opportunity to redeem himself: "If you'll come to
supper tonight, you may" (4.1.159).

In comparison, Othello accentuates the significance of the
handkerchief, allowing it to grow to mammoth proportions to
conceal from his eyes the innocence of

> Point 3, Item
> 2: How Othello
> handles
> jealousy

Desdemona. Initially, the embroidered
handkerchief is a token of Othello's love
for Desdemona, for, following his mother's
instruction, he has saved it for the woman he marries. But in
the third act, when Desdemona attempts to bind Othello's head
with it to ease his pain, he impatiently pushes it aside while
rejecting Desdemona's comfort. Iago's first onslaught of lies
against Othello's wife has already taken effect. When Iago
offers the false report that he overheard Cassio making
passionate references to Desdemona in a dream as "proof" of an
illicit affair between the two, Othello casts away any

reasonable defense for his wife. Since her guilt has already
been decided, Othello needs only some bit of tangible evidence
to justify his rage. Thus Othello magnifies the significance of
the handkerchief, this "napkin" that is "too little" (3.3.287)
for Desdemona to comfort him with, to enormous proportions in
order to condemn innocent Desdemona. He vows never to love her
again: "Even so my bloody thoughts, with violent pace, / shall
nev'r look back, nev'r ebb to humble love" (3.3.455).

This downward spiral of Othello's emotions from lofty
feelings of love towards his wife to embittered hatred takes
place without her being given a chance to counter Iago's
accusations and lies. Unlike Bianca with Cassio, he never
confronts her directly with his jealous assumptions and causes
her only to wonder at his anger. Desdemona's previous actions
and character should give Othello reason to doubt Iago, since
she has left the comforts of familiar Venice and endured the
ire of her father to marry Othello. Yet he assaults her with
abusive words, calling her "devil" and "strumpet," and he
humiliates her before others without explaining the cause of
his anger. Unlike Bianca, he gives no opportunity for his loved
one to redeem herself. Knowing she has the power to change his
heart, he tells Iago, "I will not expostulate with her, lest
her body and beauty unprovide my mind again" (4.1.206). This
very night he must kill her or else time might give him reason
to reassess his suspicions.

When comparing Bianca's simple manner of dealing with her
lover to Othello's twisted one, we can see how well her name
befits her, as her purity stands out sharply against the
darkness of Othello. It isn't until the end of the third act,
after the audience has begun the ordeal of watching the
seemingly ideal marriage crumble, that Bianca makes an
appearance. Shakespeare chooses this unlikely, minor character,

Bush 7

the supposed whore, to display the traits that are so lacking
in Othello. Bianca, refreshingly unencumbered by a "good name,"
pursues the man she loves with honest bluntness. Othello, beset
with delusions, murders the woman he loves with a blind
vengeance. We, the audience, yearn to see someone who does not
succumb to the devious workings of Iago. The brave warrior,
Othello, disappoints us, but Bianca, the "poor caitiff," the
 "strumpet" who is scorned by all, shows us how to defy evil
with honesty and generous love.

Bush 8

Work Cited

Shakespeare, William. *The Tragedy of Othello*. New York:
    Penguin, 1998.

3-7: "Precious villain!" The Moor
of Venice attacks the evil Iago in
the University of Illinois 2002
production of *Othello*. Director:
Henson Keys. Photographer: R.
Eric Stone.

The following essay by student Joe Darden offers an interpretation of Samuel Beckett's *Waiting for Godot*, particularly in terms of the protagonists' suffering. Notice the topic sentences of each body paragraph and the smooth presentation of evidence from the text for each point of proof.

3-8. "With Estragon my friend, at this place, until the fall of night, I waited for Godot," says Vladimir, resigned to wait just one more day. The 2003 production of *Waiting for Godot* at DePaul University was directed by John Jenkins. Photographer: John Bridges.

Joe Darden

Professor Suzanne Hudson

Writing about Theatre and Drama

10 Dec. 2003

Absurd, Absurder, Absurdist

Samuel Beckett's <u>Waiting for Godot</u> was written in 1948 during the aftermath of World War II. The play was one of several written during the post-war years to be later characterized by critics and academics as "theatre of the absurd." <u>Waiting for Godot</u> focuses on the seemingly meaningless activities of two men, Vladimir and Estragon, as they wait for a man named Godot, who never appears. In the meantime, the shabbily dressed men pass the time and suffer in a barren landscape. Only a small mound and a desiccated tree occupy the stage. The suffering of Vladimir and Estragon reinforces <u>Waiting for Godot</u>'s central theme: human existence is simply absurd. First, Vladimir and Estragon represent all of humanity; the problems they face, Beckett is saying, are faced by all of us. Second, Godot represents God and the deliverance from suffering that comes with God's coming. Third, the cyclical structure of <u>Waiting for Godot</u> makes it clear both that Godot will never appear and that Vladimir and Estragon will continue to wait indefinitely. Finally, Vladimir and Estragon's suffering raises their existence to the level of absurdity.

Vladimir and Estragon represent all of humanity. They say so explicitly near the end of the play: "[All] mankind is us, whether we like it or not" (90). Though this is not absolute proof, it is also not the only evidence.

Many of the concerns that Vladimir and Estragon face are basic to the point of being symbolic. Like all of humanity they seek food, clothing, and shelter. Like much of humanity, they lack these necessities. Their general state of want is

Darden 2

established early in the play with several lines and stage directions. When Estragon asks Vladimir for the meager meal of a single carrot, he discovers not only that there is just one carrot left, but that "the more [he eats] the worse it gets" (17).

Likewise, Estragon's struggle with his boots and Vladimir's dissatisfaction with his hat demonstrate their lack of adequate clothing. Estragon has been wearing his too-tight boots for so long that they have fused to his feet. Only with a "supreme effort" (4) does he succeed in removing a single boot. He later notes that his foot is "swelling visibly" (6) due to the poor condition of his boots.

Shelter is perhaps the basic need that Vladimir and Estragon most lack. In the play's first lines, Estragon reveals that he has spent the night "in a ditch" (2). He spends the night between acts 1 and 2 in a similar location. From Vladimir's shabby dress and his conversation with Estragon in the beginning of act 2 (where the two compare notes on their night apart), one can infer that he is also homeless. With such broad, symbolic struggles, Vladimir and Estragon should be viewed more broadly than as two literal men.

That Godot represents God is a fairly quick but necessary point to make. First, the word God is featured none too subtly in the word Godot. Second, when asked by Vladimir in the second act to describe the color of Godot's beard, the boy responds, "I think it's white, Sir" (106). A man with a white beard is the stereotypical depiction of God. Indeed, Vladimir seems to ask the question in order to determine the nature of Godot. Having feared that the boy's response would reveal Godot to be God, Vladimir utters the despairing and ironic oath, "Christ have mercy on us!" (106) after the boy's revelation. That Godot represents God is confirmed in a simple manner on the last page of the play. In response to Estragon's question, "And if [Godot] comes?" Vladimir muses, "We'll be saved" (109).

In order to understand <u>Waiting for Godot</u>'s theme, one must understand both that Godot is never coming (one could argue that Godot doesn't even exist, but in a practical sense for Vladimir and Estragon, there is no difference between Godot not coming and Godot not existing at all) and that Vladimir and Estragon will continue to wait. The play is divided into two acts that mirror each other. The implication of this structure is that nothing fundamental ever changes. There <u>are</u> minor changes such as the appearance of new boots for Estragon, leaves on the tree, and Pozzo's deteriorated state. Rather than diluting the mirrored shape of the two acts, these minor aesthetic changes accentuate it. Much like the real world, window dressing changes, but fundamental concepts remain the same.

Both acts begin with Vladimir and Estragon meeting in the same spot. In both acts, Vladimir and Estragon focus on passing the time while waiting for Godot, with varying amounts of success. In both acts they face the same struggles--Estragon with his boots, Vladimir with his hat and bladder, both lacking adequate food and shelter. Pozzo and Lucky appear twice: in the middle of each act. The boy appears twice: at the end of each act. In both acts, Vladimir and Estragon contemplate suicide and decide against it. And, of course, Godot fails to appear in both acts. Vladimir himself acknowledges the cyclical nature of existence at the end of the play when he says:

> Tomorrow when I wake, or think I do, what shall I say of
> today? That with Estragon my friend, at this place,
> until the fall of night I waited for Godot? That Pozzo
> passed with his carrier, and that he spoke to us?
> Probably. But in all that what truth will there be?

> He'll know nothing. He'll tell me about the blows he
>
> received and I'll give him a carrot. (104)

Vladimir almost reaches his breaking point with this
realization, but in the end continues his endless wait along
with Estragon.

All of the preceding makes for an existence that is odd,
perhaps silly, but it is Vladimir and Estragon's suffering that
raises that existence (and symbolically all of humanity's
existence) to the level of absurdity. Waiting is one thing if
those waiting enjoy, or are at least indifferent to, the
process. Vladimir and Estragon suffer constantly throughout the
play. In addition to the symbolic concerns that identify the
pair as representatives of all humanity, Vladimir and Estragon
face seemingly endless extra suffering. Estragon is beaten
nightly by ten men. It happens so regularly that he simply
expects it. "Beat me? Certainly they beat me," (2) he says at
the beginning of act 1. Vladimir suffers from a pain in his
abdomen that causes him to suffer doubly because it steals the
humor from his existence. "One daren't even laugh any more,"
(5) he notes after experiencing terrible pain during a hearty
laugh. Estragon is haunted by unspeakably terrible nightmares,
which are alluded to in act 1 when Vladimir screams, "DON'T
TELL ME!" (10) as Estragon tries to relate his dream. In act 2,
Estragon has a nightmare on stage and is again silenced by
Vladimir when he tries to describe the dream.

In the middle of act 2, Vladimir is finally moved to
exclaim that "this [waiting for Godot] is awful!" (70). He
casts about for a solution, but in the end he and Estragon can
only continue waiting. Why? That's simply what they've always
done. The end of the play is broadcast from its beginning with
Vladimir's remark, "What's the good of losing heart now, that's
what I say. We should have thought of it [suicide] a million
years ago" (3). The situation is hopeless, but Vladimir and

Darden 5

Estragon have simply invested too much time in waiting to stop
now, regardless of how awful their situation is. They wait
indefinitely in a state of perpetual suffering for a God who
either doesn't exist or who doesn't care enough to visit
because that is what they've always done. They (we) are
completely, utterly, simply absurd.

Darden 6

Work Cited

Beckett, Samuel. Waiting for Godot. New York: Grove, 1982.

Exercise 3-4

Study Joe Darden's essay by performing the following tasks:
In the first paragraph
1. Underline Joe's thesis.
2. Place brackets around each point of proof stated in the first paragraph.
3. Draw a box around the occasion.
In the body of the paper
1. Draw a line across the page where each of the four points of proof begins development.
2. Underline the sentence that reiterates the corresponding point of proof listed in the first paragraph.
3. Draw a squiggly line under the topic sentence of each body paragraph.
4. Place brackets around each piece of evidence presented for each topic sentence. (These "pieces of evidence" will often consist of more than one sentence.)
For the conclusion
1. State what you think is the controlling idea.

Revising and Editing Your Essay

Use the following checklist to be certain that your essay is ready for submission. Consult the Handbook at the end of this book for guidance in word choice, sentence structure, and punctuation.

Revision and Editing Checklist

☐   Thesis statement is clear and present. It makes an inference about the work. It is narrow and specific enough to be adequately supported in the space of the paper but general enough to need support.

☐   Points of proof are clear and present. Each answers the proof question. Each is narrow and specific enough to be supported adequately in one to three paragraphs and general enough to need support.

☐   Introduction contains specific details. It leads the reader to the thesis; it does not mislead the reader about the subject of the paper.

☐   Essay adheres to the essay plan set out in the list of points of proof.

☐   Body paragraphs are unified, adequately developed, organized, and coherent.

☐   Conclusion solidifies the essay's main point without resorting to mere repetition of thesis and points of proof. Conclusion is unified and developed. Conclusion does not bring up any new issues.

☐   Sentences are well constructed. There are no run-ons or fragments. Sentences are correctly punctuated.

☐   Words are correct and well chosen.

☐   All quotations use acknowledgment phrases.

☐   Sources are correctly cited in text.

☐   Title is appropriate.

☐   Paper is properly formatted.

Notes

[1] Susan Sontag, *Against Interpretation* (New York: Farrar, 1966) 119.

[2] Lee A. Jacobus, ed., *The Bedford Introduction to Drama*, 4th ed. (Boston: Bedford/St. Martin's, 2001) 384.

[3] Frank Rich, "*Angels in America*: Millennium Approaches," *Hot Seat* (New York: Random, 1998) 861.

[4] Lee A Jacobus, ed., *The Bedford Introduction to Drama*, 4th ed. (Boston: Bedford/St. Martin's, 2001) 101-02.

[5] Arthur Holmberg, "The Language of Misunderstanding," *American Theatre* (Oct. 1992): 94-95.

Writing the Argument Essay

Let's say you are able to go back in time to the 1940s and make a decision about whether to pursue nuclear technology. You know for a fact that the technology will be used to create a nuclear weapon that could destroy millions of innocent people with the flick of a switch. Would you be in favor of free scientific inquiry or the suppression of the research? This is not an easy decision. Even those of us most dedicated to resisting government control might be tempted just this once to suppress the research. A good playwright recognizes that some decisions are not easy, but that ultimately one must take a stand. In Bertolt Brecht's *The Life of Galileo*, the Inquisition presents a surprisingly convincing case against free inquiry, as it does in George Bernard Shaw's *St. Joan*. These plays succeed because the playwright has captured a true ethical dilemma and dealt with it, rather than simply have a villain elucidate the "wrong" point of view and have a hero demolish it easily—a strategy that would be most *un*dramatic and would only bore the audience. By the same token, an essay that argues against a weak opponent, or one that contrives to make the opposition *appear* weak, will bore the reader. This chapter is intended to help you structure and strategize arguments that address the difficult issues presented in drama and to support a considered, informed opinion, even in the face of strong opposition.

The Nature of Argument

The word *argument* is used in so many contexts and toward so many purposes that there is no single comprehensive definition of it. Some rhetoricians distinguish between *argument* and *persuasion*, claiming that argument intends to lead audiences to a certain belief or conviction, and that persuasion intends to move audiences to action. This distinction becomes exceedingly fine, as the aims of arguments tend to blend and overlap.

Some rhetoricians make a distinction between Rogerian, Toulmin and Aristotelian arguments. The Rogerian argument, named after psychotherapist Carl Rogers, emphasizes approaching audiences in a nonthreatening manner, expressing understanding of the opposing position, finding common ground with those who hold it, and enlarging the common ground of agreement. The emphasis is upon achieving consensus rather than "defeating" the opposition. The Toulmin argument, named after British philosopher Stephen Toulmin, begins with a debatable claim and offers reasons to support it. The Aristotelian argument, named after the Greek philosopher Aristotle, is designed to silence opposition by citing authorities and presenting overwhelming evidence. These types of arguments are not mutually exclusive, and this textbook recommends a combination of the three.

The essential distinction that this textbook makes between the argument essay and the analytical essay is that the argument essay engages directly in **refutation**. The argument writer's job, therefore, is not only to defend a proposition but also to refute an opposing opinion. In so doing, it is essential to articulate the opposing viewpoint in fair and generous terms and to treat the opponent with respect.

Argument Appeals

Arguments succeed or fail often as a result of having made, or not made, the proper appeal to the proper audience. The terms *ethos*, *pathos*, and *logos* (Greek for *character*, *emotion*, and *reason*) are useful in classifying types of appeals.

Ethos is the appeal to the audience's sense of ethics—its sense of right and wrong. In *Antigone*, for example, Creon, king of Thebes, has forbidden the burial of Polyneices, a traitor; Antigone believes that to deny her brother Polyneices a proper burial is wrong according to a higher law than Creon's. She tells Creon:

> I never thought your edicts had such force
> They nullified the laws of heaven, which,
> Unwritten, not proclaimed, can boast
> A currency that everlastingly is valid;
> An origin beyond the birth of man.
> And I, whom no man's frown can frighten,
> Am far from risking Heaven's frown by flouting these.[1]

Pathos is the appeal to the audience's emotions. Emotional appeals often take on the appearance of a rant—an argument fueled by mean-spiritedness. However, appeals to the emotion can be useful in certain situations, such as the one in which George Bernard Shaw found himself after the 1905 New York premiere of *Mrs. Warren's Profession*, a play that views a prostitute sympathetically. The police commissioner closed the play for "offending public decency." A *Theatre Magazine* opinion piece that agreed with the censors called Shaw

> a pseudo-anarchist who believes in no family tie (except for himself, perhaps), who proclaims free love, who preaches the seduction of our daughters by wholesale, not by means of wine suppers and "delicate" attentions, but by a false philosophy of specious half-truths. . . .[2]

Shaw's scathing condemnation of the critics who caused the uproar is persuasive because it equals its opponents' indignation. When one's integrity has been questioned, sometimes it is best to react with passion.

The entire blame for the agitation against *Mrs. Warren's Profession* lies in the hands of the New York critics. Their stupidity, inhumanity and scurrilous and obscene language in dealing with the play drove the poor, wretched little Police Commissioner to steps he was reluctant to take. No words of mine are adequate to describe my feelings toward these critics. They should all be gathered in a dustpan and thrown into a dust heap. Had they any sense of decency, they would make a barefooted pilgrimage somewhere or shoot themselves, but I don't suppose they will.[3]

Logos is the appeal to the audience's logic, or sense of order. In *Tartuffe*, Molière, a playwright whose dramatic style characterizes the Age of Reason, has given us the character of Cléante, who uses analogy, a tool of logical persuasion, to argue that the appearance of goodness is not necessarily proof of its existence:

> There's a vast difference, so it seems to me,
> Between true piety and hypocrisy:
> How do you fail to see it, may I ask?
> Is not a face quite different from a mask?
> Cannot sincerity and cunning art,
> Reality and semblance, be told apart?
> Are scarecrows just like men, and do you hold
> That a false coin is just as good as gold?[4]

Here again, as in the critical theories described in chapter 3, there may be overlapping appeals. Shaw's argument, for example, appeals both to his readers' emotions and to their sense of ethics.

Types of Reasoning

Reasoning is sometimes classified as **inductive** or **deductive.** Inductive reasoning moves from specific facts to a general conclusion. That movement requires an inductive leap, a leap from certainty to uncertainty. Your conclusion is considered valid when there are enough facts in support of it to convince a skeptical audience. If you base your inference on scant evidence, as Othello does when he concludes that a missing handkerchief signifies that Desdemona has been unfaithful, your audience may accuse you of "jumping to conclusions."

Deductive reasoning moves from the general to the specific, as demonstrated by a **syllogism**. A syllogism begins with a major premise, or general rule, moves to a minor conclusion, or more specific fact, and finally arrives at a conclusion. For example:

Major Premise:	Neil Simon writes only comedies.
Minor Premise:	Neil Simon wrote *Barefoot in the Park.*
Conclusion:	Therefore, *Barefoot in the Park* is a comedy.

Such an argument is considered valid if the major premise would not be disputed by an intelligent, rational audience, and the minor premise is adequately supported.

Given these requirements, is the following syllogism valid?

Major Premise:	Neil Simon writes only comedies.
Minor Premise:	*Barefoot in the Park* is a comedy.
Conclusion:	Therefore, Neil Simon wrote *Barefoot in the Park.*

As you can see, some appeals to logic are faulty. In his absurd drama *Rhinoceros*, Eugene Ionesco satirizes the uncritical thinker's attraction to the framework of logic:

Logician:	Here is an example of a syllogism. The cat has four paws. Isidore and Fricot both have four paws. Therefore, Isidore and Fricot are cats.
Old Gentleman:	My dog has got four paws.
Logician:	Then it's a cat. . . .
Old Gentleman:	So then logically speaking, my dog must be a cat?
Logician:	Logically, yes. But the contrary is also true. . . .
Old Gentleman:	Logic is a very beautiful thing.
Logician:	As long as it is not abused.

Logical Fallacies

Fallacies are lapses in logic. They are the result of presenting faulty premises as valid ones, misusing evidence, or distorting counterarguments. These lapses are not always accidental; politicians, for example, use them frequently, especially when they consider their audiences to be gullible enough to be persuaded by them. Dramatic characters often commit logical fallacies. Following are some of the more common logical fallacies:

Ad hominem is a Latin term meaning "against the man." One attacks the person rather than the argument. In Yasmina Reza's play, *"Art,"* Marc and his friend Yvan disagree about the aesthetic value of an expensive painting purchased by their friend Serge. Marc says, "If Yvan tolerates the fact that Serge has spent two hundred grand on some piece of white shit, it's because he couldn't care less about Serge."

The *appeal to tradition* claims that something should be done in a certain way simply because it has always been done that way. This is the argument of Old Man Warner in Shirley Jackson's one-act play, *The Lottery*. "There's *always* been a lottery," he says, in defense of the barbaric practice of human sacrifice.

The *bandwagon fallacy* asserts if everyone believes something to be true, it is true. In Friedrich Dürrenmatt's *The Visit*, one sees the townspeople gradually moving from the position of defending their fellow citizen, Ill, to a position of reviling him. The people, one by one, hop on the bandwagon.

Begging the question is sidestepping the issue, thereby leaving the question unanswered. Suppose that the question "How did theatre begin?" is answered with "Cave dwellers acted out ancient stories around the campfire." The answer begs the question. It gives an early use of theatre but doesn't say how the cave dwellers' theatre began.

Circular reasoning mistakes a cause for an effect, and vice versa. "Scholars continue to write about Hamlet because he is a fascinating character" is a circular explanation of why so many words have been written about Hamlet, Shakespeare's "melancholy Dane." In essence, the sentence says that Hamlet is fascinating because he is fascinating. The explanation should instead answer the question, "What is so fascinating about Hamlet that scholars continue to write about him?"

Either/or reasoning, also called a *false dichotomy*, assumes that there are only two options, whereas there may be many more. Shakespeare's Richard III claims that he cannot be a lover, deformed as he is; therefore, he must be a villain.

False analogy assumes that because two things are alike in some ways, they must be alike in other ways. An example is "If we can put a man on the moon, surely we can find a way to fund a dramatic arts program in this college."

Hasty generalization, or *sweeping generalization*, is unlikely to be true because exceptions are easy to find, as in the claim that actresses are temperamental. Surely some actresses are even-tempered. "Everyone recognizes Shakespeare's greatness" is a hasty generalization. Surely there is someone on the planet who does not recognize Shakespeare's greatness.

Oversimplification leaves out relevant considerations about an issue, as in "More funding for the arts would result in better art."

Post hoc ergo propter hoc is Latin, meaning "After this therefore because of this." The fallacy assumes that because one event followed another, it was caused by the first one. For example, night follows day; therefore, day causes night. If an actor forgets to wear his lucky charm and gives a bad performance, it would be a logical fallacy to claim that the bad performance was the result of forgetting the charm.

Non sequitur is Latin, meaning "It does not follow." The fallacy draws a conclusion that doesn't follow from the previous premise. "Romeo is a Montague; therefore, his family would disapprove of his relationship with Juliet." The minor premise is missing. It would need to be supplied for the validity of the statement to be judged.

The *slippery slope* fallacy asserts that granting one concession will lead to total surrender. In *Antigone*, Creon argues that to allow one person to break the law will plunge Thebes back into anarchy.

A *straw man* is an artificial opponent that is easily knocked down. One attributes to his opponent a stupid argument, which is an inaccurate statement of his position, and then shows it to be stupid. Suppose your opponent has

4-1: Teireisus lays a curse on Creon in this 2002 production of *Antigone*, performed by the Department of Theatre and Dance at the University of South Carolina. Director: Jay Berkow. Photographer: Jason Ayer.

said, "Funding for a drama program is not a top priority for our college."
You would be setting up a straw man for an opponent if you claimed that
your opponent does not value the dramatic arts.

Exercise 4-1

Examine the following arguments and explain why they are illogical or
fallacious. Tell whether the appeal of each argument is to *ethos, pathos,
logos,* or some combination.

1. Orgon, Marianne's father in Molière's *Tartuffe*, wants his daughter to
    marry a man she loathes rather than the man she loves. When she
    protests, he says:

    > When crossed in their amours,
    > All lovesick girls have the same thoughts as yours.
    > Get up! The more you loathe the man, and dread him,
    > The more ennobling it will be to wed him.

2. In act 3, scene 1 of *Julius Caesar*, Brutus delivers the following speech:

    Brutus: If there be any in this assembly, any dear friend of Caesar's, to him I
    say that Brutus' love to Caesar was no less than his. If then that
    friend demand why Brutus rose against Caesar, this is my answer:
    not that I loved Caesar less, but that I loved Rome more. Had you
    rather Caesar were living, and die all slaves, than that Caesar were
    dead, to live all free men? As Caesar loved me, I weep for him. As
    he was fortunate, I rejoice at it. As he was valiant, I honour him. But
    as he was ambitious, I slew him. There is tears for his love, joy for
    his fortune, honour for his valour, and death for his ambition. Who is
    here so base that would be a bondman? If any, speak, for him have I
    offended. Who is here so rude that would not be a Roman? If any,
    speak, for him have I offended. Who is here so vile that will not love
    his country? If any, speak, for him have I offended. I pause for a
    reply.

    All the Plebeians: None, Brutus, none.

    Brutus: Then none have I offended.

3. In act 2, scene 1 of *Othello*, Iago says of beautiful women, "She never
    yet was foolish that was fair, / For even her folly helped her to an heir."

Planning and Drafting the Argument Essay

In chapter 2 you studied the steps toward writing the argument essay. This chapter discusses those and additional concepts related to argument in further depth.

Understanding Your Purpose

Often, we use the word *argument* to mean *quarrel*—that is, to engage in a discourse fueled by anger. This definition of *argument* reduces the act of arguing to a contest of wills or personalities. Or perhaps we think in terms of winning and losing arguments, which reduces a noble occupation to a competition. Argument, at its highest purpose, is an effort at arriving at the truth. Opposing points of view are presented and defended. Who wins is not important; what *is* important is that every salient point has been considered from every reasonable viewpoint. Only when this condition has been met can we draw the wisest conclusions.

Arguing about theatre and drama may seem on the surface a trivial pursuit. The characters are fictitious, after all, so why do their opinions and actions matter to us out here in the real world? To answer that question, we must understand that one of the basic functions of drama is to provide us with the opportunity to put ourselves into unfamiliar situations and ask, "What would I have done?" If you were Mrs. Peters or Mrs. Hale in *Trifles*, would you have hidden the incriminating evidence? If you were Nora in *A Doll's House*, would you have left your husband and children? If you were Antigone, would you have allowed your sister, Ismene, to share the blame for your crime? Too often in this life, we cannot know right from wrong. Drama allows us to understand the dilemma. Argument allows us to grow from experiences outside the limitations of our own.

Recognizing Your Audience

Readers of your argument essay may have mild distaste for your opinion or outright hostility. Or they may be impartial judges who will look at both sides of the argument before arriving at any conclusions. To be persuasive you are well advised to analyze your readers' needs, wants, and attitudes. Answering the following questions could aid your efforts:

- How much detail do your readers need? How much background information?
- What organizational structure will work best for these readers?
- To what degree will your readers be persuaded by appeals to their sense of ethics? logic? emotions?
- Are your readers likely to appreciate irony? informality? irreverence?
- Will your readers respect a tone of authority or one of modesty?

Student writers usually do well to envision their readers as people outside the classroom—not their instructor nor their classmates. The essay should make sense to the readers who have neither taught nor heard the class lectures. Assume instead that the readers are as familiar with the play as you are but need to see how you put the supporting evidence together to arrive at your opinion.

Choosing and Narrowing Your Topic

For your argument essay, choose a topic that is controversial. Your professor, textbook, and class discussions will alert you to some current debates in theatre and drama, but new issues are constantly arising. Be on the lookout for such topics as you read newspapers, magazines, and journals.

You must also find a rational, educated opinion against which to argue. Arguing against a weak opinion makes you look like the bully who is really a coward—afraid to pick on someone his own size. Your professor may suggest an opinion to refute, or you may need to find credible opponents on your own through library research. You might consult chapter 6 of this book, "Writing the Research Paper," for advice on finding essays and articles on theatre and drama. Perhaps one of the following topic suggestions for argument essays will be workable or spark more ideas for writing.

Topic Suggestions for Argument Essays

In debate, arguments are based upon **propositions**, statements that may be either defended or refuted. If you were to defend one of the following propositions, it would be your thesis. If you were to refute it, it would be your counterthesis.

- In Sophocles's *Antigone*, Creon, not Antigone, is the true tragic hero.

- In Sophocles's *Antigone*, Antigone was wrong to refuse to let her sister share the blame for her crime.

- In Anouilh's *Antigone*, Antigone dies for no reason.

- In Henrik Ibsen's *A Doll's House,* Nora is wrong to leave her family.

- Torvald Helmer, in *A Doll's House*, does not deserve his punishment.

- *A Doll's House* is too dated to be of interest to modern audiences.

- In Susan Glaspell's *Trifles,* the women are wrong to conceal the evidence that would have implicated Minnie Wright.

- Petruchio, in Shakespeare's *The Taming of the Shrew*, is a wife abuser.

- Marc's opinion of the painting Serge purchased in Yasmina Reza's *"Art"* is correct.

- *The Merchant of Venice* proves Shakespeare to be anti-Semitic.

- The ending of *Tartuffe* is an example of the *deus ex machina* flaw.

- Oedipus's fatal flaw is hubris.

- Tom Stoppard's *Rosencrantz and Guildenstern Are Dead* is, as Robert Brustein writes, "a theatrical parasite, feeding off *Hamlet, Waiting for Godot,* and *Six Characters in Search of an Author.*"[5]

- The title character of Brecht's *Mother Courage and Her Children* is a sympathetic character.

- Stanley, in *A Streetcar Named Desire*, though a rapist, is nonetheless a sympathetic character.

- Tennessee Williams betrayed the cause of respect for homosexuals in *Cat on a Hot Tin Roof.*

- Paula Vogel's *How I Learned to Drive* is more soap opera than art.

- Constantine Stanislavsky was right to direct Chekhov's *The Seagull* as a tragedy, not a comedy, against Chekhov's wishes.

- Lopakhin, in Chekhov's *The Cherry Orchard*, is a villain.

- *Waiting for Godot* ends on a positive note.

- The theatre of the absurd died because it had exhausted the idea that drove it.

- Margaret Edson's *Wit* is essentially a diatribe against teachers and doctors, both undeserving targets.

- David Rabe's *Streamers* is too violent for the stage.

- Willy Loman, of Arthur Miller's *Death of a Salesman*, is a tragic hero.

- *Children of a Lesser God* is highly praised because of its political correctness, not its artistic merit.

- Troy Maxson, of August Wilson's *Fences*, is a victim of centuries of racial oppression.

- The Asian community was right to object to the casting of Jonathan Pryce in *Miss Saigon*.

- George Gershwin's *Porgy and Bess*, according to August Wilson, "bastardizes" African-Americans' music and experience.[6]

Drafting the Occasion

Your occasion, in other words, the introductory remarks of your first paragraph, should probably identify the work(s) about which you are writing, the artist(s), and the issue in contention. You might also offer a short synopsis of the plot, like the following plot summary of Henrik Ibsen's *A Doll's House*, if you believe your reader would benefit by it.

> Nora, a seemingly happy Norwegian wife and mother, has forged a signature on a loan in order to afford her deathly ill husband, Torvald, time to recuperate in sunny southern Italy. Torvald does not know, nor would he approve of, either the loan or the forgery. Back home in Norway, now that Torvald has been restored to health, Nora must resort to deception in order to obtain the funds with which to repay the loan. Her web of deceit unravels, she and Torvald argue, and she understands for the first time the state of ignorance, poverty, and immorality in which she has been living. Rather than live one more day in such a state, she leaves her husband and children. The play ends with the resounding slam of the door behind her.

Stating the Counterarguments

Next, identify the **counterthesis** and **counterpoints**. Be as specific as possible about who said (or wrote) what, and when and where it appeared. Keep in mind that this may well be the view of a larger, like-minded group. Present the strongest counterarguments, and present them in terms that their proponents would consider fair. If you present only the weakest arguments, or if you make the strongest counterarguments seem weak or ridiculous, you only arouse suspicion about your own integrity and undermine your argument. In her essay printed at the end of this chapter, Rebecca Penkoff fully explains the counterargument in a tone of respect.

Stating Your Thesis

If the occasion and counterarguments constitute a full paragraph in their own right (six or seven sentences), you may want to begin a new paragraph for your thesis and points of proof. Use a transition to cue the reader that you are moving from counterpoint to thesis. Something as simple as the word *however* at the beginning of the thesis may suffice, as is the case in Rebecca Penkoff's essay at the end of this chapter. Other times, a whole sentence is in order.

The thesis must be in your own words; this is not the time to quote or paraphrase a source. You must be the person to make all the major assertions. Your sources will corroborate your assertions, but you must not let them speak for you. Like the thesis of the analytical essay, the thesis of the argumentative essay fulfills the following criteria:

4-2: Nora teases Dr. Rank with her bag of macaroons in this 2004 performance of *A Doll's House*, directed by Daniel Yurgaitis at Northern State University in Aberdeen, South Dakota. Photographer: Larry Wild.

- is one complete, unified statement about the issue in contention
- is narrow enough to limit the material
- is general enough to need support
- is defensible
- is not too obvious

To this list, add two more criteria specific to the argumentative thesis:

- answers the charge made in the counterthesis
- makes a statement with which a rational, educated person could disagree.

Exercise 4-1: Faulty Argumentative Theses

Following are ten faulty argumentative theses. The issue in contention is the manner in which Torvald Helmer, the antagonist of Henrik Ibsen's drama, *A Doll's House*, should be played. In this exercise, the thesis should contradict theatre critic Marvin Rosenberg's assertion that Torvald is a "true villain."[7] Use the preceding guidelines to determine the problems with the following argumentative theses. Then compare your answers to those in the next box.

1. Torvald's character is complicated.
2. Torvald's character is complicated for three reasons.
3. This paper will argue the merits of Torvald's character.
4. Torvald is a conscientious businessman.
5. But *is* Torvald a "true villain"?
6. *A Doll's House* is purely feminist propaganda.
7. If readers and theatregoers understood Torvald's character, they might change their minds about him.
8. Torvald's detractors are simply being narrow-minded.
9. Only radical feminists would agree with this criticism of Torvald.
10. Torvald reflects the social influences of the time in which he lived.

Answers to Exercise 4-1:
Faulty Argumentative Thesis

1. This thesis doesn't contradict the charge made in the counterthesis. Torvald could be both complicated and a villain.

2. This thesis has the same problem identified #1. Adding "for three reasons" does not solve the problem. This thesis is also indefensible, for there are an indeterminate number of reasons why Torvald's character is complicated. It is highly unlikely that there are exactly three.

3. This thesis is really a statement of purpose. It tells what the paper will do, but not what it will argue.

4. This thesis is a fact, not an arguable statement. Support for it will result in a descriptive paper.

5. This thesis is a question; it should be a statement. The essay must prove the truth of the thesis. One cannot prove the truth of a question.

6. This thesis has many problems. For one, it does not contradict the counterthesis. For another, it is an overstatement: the play may be partly feminist propaganda, but any thoughtful person would know that literature is never "purely" anything. Another problem with this thesis is its tone; it is more emotional than rational, especially in its use of the loaded word *propaganda*.

7. This thesis assumes that those with the opposite view are uninformed and that simply describing Torvald's character will persuade them. Thus, this thesis will lead to a descriptive paper. You must assume that your opponent possesses the same facts that you possess but interprets them differently.

8. This thesis resorts to name-calling and assumes that the opposing view is not rational. A strong argument takes on strong arguments.

9. This thesis does not answer the counterthesis. It is an example of an *ad hominem* attack: it attacks the opponent rather than the argument. This thesis is also indefensible: it is impossible that "only" radical feminists would believe it; logic dictates that there must be at least one person in the entire universe who is not a radical feminist but agrees with this criticism of Torvald.

10. This thesis is more analytical than argumentative. No rational, educated person would be predisposed to disagree with it. Besides, this thesis does not answer the counterthesis.

Asking the Proof Question

Your points of proof should answer the proof question—the question that the thesis provokes. In argument, there are often two proof questions:
- Why don't you believe what your opponent believes?
- Why do you believe what you believe?

For example, the thesis of the essay at the end of this chapter, "Torvald Isn't Such a Bad Guy," is "Torvald's words and actions do not fit the profile of a victimizer, but rather a man who works hard and loves his wife." In response to that thesis, the following two questions arise:
- Why don't you believe (as others do) that Torvald fits the profile of a victimizer?
- Why do you believe Torvald's words and actions fit the profile of a man who works hard and loves his wife?

Designing Your Points of Proof

These two questions lead to two kinds of points of proof: **refutations** and **constructive arguments**. The answers to the first question above are the author's refutations of the counterpoints; the answers to the second question are the author's constructive arguments.

Following are some of the qualities of workable points of proof.

- You must state your own points of proof. Do not quote or paraphrase a source for this task. This is *your* argument, not your source's argument. In the body of the paper, your sources will corroborate your assertions.
- Each point of proof will serve as the central claim of one section of the essay.
- Each point of proof will state a reason, not a fact.
- The point of proof cannot beg the question, as do the statements "First we shall look at Torvald's words. Then we shall look at his actions." Once you have looked at Torvald's words and actions, what conclusions will you come to? The answers to that question will be your points of proof.

Outlining the Argument Essay

While organizing your essay, keep in mind the following guidelines:
- Your thesis must oppose the counterthesis. Both the thesis and counterthesis can not be true.

4-3: Nora dances for her life in *A Doll's House*, performed in 2002 at Minnesota State University, Mankato, and directed by Nina LeNoir. Photographer: Mike Lagerquist.

- It is not always necessary to articulate the counterpoints, especially when the counterthesis is narrow enough not to merit breaking down into subpoints.
- If you have listed counterpoints, organize your refutations in the same order as the counterpoints. In other words, your first refutation should refute the first counterpoint, and so forth.
- Some essays may be more persuasive if the refutations come before the constructive arguments. When this is the case, arrange your points of proof accordingly.
- Constructive arguments are optional. Sometimes an argument is "won" with refutations alone.
- Your strongest point of proof should be your last one

The following outline for Rebecca Penkoff's argument essay, "Torvald Isn't Such a Bad Guy," provides an example. Notice that the organization of the body of the paper matches the organization projected in the list of points of proof in the introduction.

4-4: Torvald Helmer: Villain or conventional man of his time? *A Doll's House*, performed in 1999 at Tarleton State University, was directed by Mark Holtorf. Photographer: Dayle Cox.

Argumentative Essay Outline
"Torvald Isn't Such a Bad Guy"

I. Introduction
   A. Occasion
      1. Background information: *A Doll's House* is a "problem play."
      2. Statement of the issue: Torvald's villainy
      3. Counterarguments
         a. Counterthesis: According to Rosenberg, Torvald victimizes his wife and therefore earns himself the title of villain.
         b. Counterpoints:
            (1) Torvald refuses to support his wife's actions when he discovers her forgery.
            (2) His treatment of Nora reflects his opinion that women are weak and lacking the capabilities to make logical, informed decisions.
   B. Thesis: Torvald's words do not fit the profile of a victimizer, but rather a man who works hard and loves his wife.
   C. Points of proof
      1. Refutations
         a. Refutation of counterpoint #1: Torvald would have to turn his back on everything he believes to be true and good in order to condone Nora's dishonest actions.
         b. Refutation of counterpoint #2: Torvald is justified in his treatment of Nora because oftentimes she proves she needs and depends on her husband's better judgment.
      2. Constructive arguments
         a. Constructive argument #1: Torvald protects and provides for his wife admirably.
         b. Constructive argument #2: Torvald's decision to abide by the rules of society does not make him a villain.
II. Body
   A. Torvald would have to turn his back on everything he believes to be true and good in order to condone Nora's dishonest actions.
   B. Torvald is justified in his treatment of Nora because oftentimes she proves she needs and depends on her husband's better judgment.
   C. Torvald protects and provides for his wife admirably.
   D. Torvald's decision to abide by the rules of society does not make him a villain.
III. Conclusion

Drafting the Body Paragraphs

Well-written body paragraphs for the argument essay contain the same qualities as those for the analytical essay: *unity, adequate development, organization,* and *coherence.* **Refutation paragraphs** are often organized by first stating the counterpoint and the reasons that support it. The paragraph then goes on to make a **refutation statement** and offer support for it.

See, for example, the following excerpt from Rebecca Penkoff's essay:

The issue concerning Torvald's treatment of Nora on a daily basis provides a second point for some critics to name Torvald a villain. The many instances wherein Torvald

> [Restate counterpoint]

refers to Nora as a "skylark" or some other silly animal gives the impression that Torvald sees Nora as a helpless "featherbrain" who is not to be taken seriously, but it would be challenging to take seriously a woman who sneaks macaroons behind her husband's back. Torvald constantly guides Nora and makes all of the decisions, while rarely consulting her, which ultimately leads to Torvald's being tagged a villain. However, Nora

> [Refutation]

reinforces Torvald's treatment of her at every instance. Nora wants to spend the money Torvald will earn from his promotion before they have it and says they can borrow until then. Torvald exhibits responsibility and consideration for the moneylenders in the event he did borrow money and was not able to repay it. Nora shows her lack of consideration for anyone but herself when she replies, "Who would bother about them?" (3).

> [Support for refutation statement]

Another instance of Nora's apparent dependence on Torvald is illustrated when Nora cannot decide on a dress for the ball they are attending. To her husband Nora says, "Torvald, I can't get along a bit without your help" (28). Nora's behavior leads Torvald to believe he is acting exactly as she needs him to act. Therefore, it never occurs to Torvald that he is treating his wife in a derogatory manner. Nora never gives Torvald a hint that she is not happy with the current state of affairs, which is why Torvald cannot be blamed for how he treats her. Torvald thinks he is helping Nora, not hindering her. Furthermore, to his credit, once he sees the errors of his ways, he offers to change: "I have it in me to become a different man" (64).

Templates for Organizing Your Essay

In order to organize your thoughts about your own argument essay, fill in the blanks of the following templates for essay and paragraph outlines. Tailor the templates to the number of counterpoints, refutations, and constructive arguments appropriate for your essay.

My Argument Essay

Title _____

I.   Introduction
   A. Occasion
      1. Background information _____
      2. Statement of issue in contention _____
      3. Counterarguments:
         a. Counterthesis _____
         b. Counterpoints
            (1) _____
            (2) _____
   B. Thesis _____
   C. Points of proof
      1. Refutations
         a. Refutation of counterpoint #1 _____
         b. Refutation of counterpoint #2 _____
      2. Constructive arguments
         a. Constructive argument #1 _____
         b. Constructive argument #2 _____

Use the following template to organize your refutation paragraphs, keeping in mind that the number of items of evidence will depend upon the material available and needed to persuade your reader.

Note the following suggestions when organizing refutation paragraphs:
- If the counterpoint can be stated in one sentence, begin your paragraph with the counterpoint and proceed immediately to refute it.

4-5: Nora and Torvald in happier times. This production of *A Doll's House* at Vanderbilt University was directed by Jon Hallquist in 2001. Photographer: Phillip Franck.

- If evidence for the counterpoint needs to be provided, you might allot a whole paragraph to it and then begin your refutation in a new paragraph. For example, in her essay, Rebecca Penkoff devotes a whole paragraph to explaining counterpoint #1 and begins her refutation in a new paragraph.
- If you have more than one paragraph's worth of support for your refutation statement, break up your evidence into separate paragraphs and begin each paragraph with a topic sentence that states the point of the paragraph.

Body Paragraph: Refutation

Restate the counterpoint
_____

Evidence for counterpoint (optional)
  1. _____
  2. _____
  3. _____

Your refutation statement
_____

Evidence for your refutation (Fill in at least two blanks.)
  1. _____
  2. _____
  3. _____
  4. _____

Paragraphs that offer constructive arguments usually begin with a topic sentence that states the argument. They then supply the evidence for that statement. These paragraphs offer reasons why you, the writer, believe your thesis to be true, in the absence of counterarguments. Use the following template to organize each body paragraph of your constructive arguments, keeping in mind that the number of items of evidence will vary, depending upon the material available and needed to persuade your reader. If you have more than one paragraph's worth of support for one constructive argument, divide your support into as many paragraphs as you need.

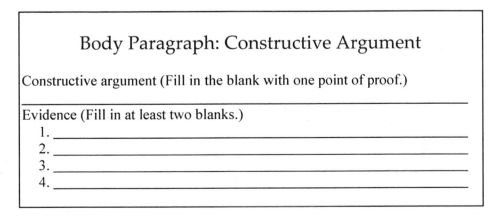

Body Paragraph: Constructive Argument

Constructive argument (Fill in the blank with one point of proof.)
_____

Evidence (Fill in at least two blanks.)
  1. _____
  2. _____
  3. _____
  4. _____

Student Essays

The following essay is about a play that has been stirring up arguments since
its premiere in 1897. Rebecca Penkoff argues with critics who believe that
Torvald Helmer, Nora's husband in Henrik Ibsen's *A Doll's House*, is a
villain. Rebecca adopts a kinder attitude toward Nora's antagonist. However,
she recognizes and addresses the most damning evidence against Torvald,
rather than ignores it or pretends that it is not important. Ignoring or
trivializing your opponent's strongest arguments will only cast suspicion
upon your own argument.

Exercise 4-3

Study Rebecca Penkoff's essay by performing the following tasks:

In the first paragraph:
1. Put a star beside the statement of the issue.
2. Draw a squiggly line under the counterthesis.
3. Circle each counterpoint and number it, for example, "Cpt #1."

In the second paragraph:
1. Underline the thesis.
2. Place brackets around each refutation statement and tell which
    counterpoint it refutes, for example, "Ref of Cpt. #1."
3. Draw a box around each constructive argument and number it, for
    example, "CA #1."

In the body of the paper:
1. Draw a line across the page where each of the four points of proof
    begins development.
2. Underline the sentence that reiterates the counterpoint. Double
    underline the refutation statement.
3. Place brackets around each piece of evidence presented for each
    topic sentence. (These "pieces of evidence" will often consist of
    more than one sentence.)

For the conclusion:
1. State what you think is the controlling idea.

Rebecca Penkoff

Professor Suzanne Hudson

Writing about Theatre and Drama

13 December 2000

Torvald Isn't Such a Bad Guy

Henrik Ibsen's A Doll's House is one of a group of plays he wrote that earned him the reputation as an author of "problem plays." Each of these plays seemed to be written with the intent of illuminating social issues. In A Doll's House, Ibsen shows sympathy for women's frustrations in having to live in a stifling society, but Ibsen also shows that restrictive traditions impact all the members of society. Critic Marvin Rosenberg calls Torvald, Nora's husband in A Doll's House, an "obviously bad man" (192). Along with Rosenberg, many critics claim Torvald victimizes his wife and therefore earns himself the title of villain. The main reason for adopting this attitude is that Torvald refuses to support his wife's actions when he discovers her forgery. Another reason critics label Torvald a villain is that his treatment of Nora reflects his opinion that women are weak and lacking the capabilities to make logical and informed decisions.

However, upon closer examination, Torvald's words and actions do not fit the profile of a victimizer, but rather a man who works hard and loves his wife. First, Torvald would have to turn his back on everything he believes to be true and good in order to condone Nora's dishonest actions. Secondly, although Torvald does treat Nora as though she is not capable of making a decision, he is justified because oftentimes she proves she needs and depends on her husband's better judgment. Furthermore, Torvald protects and provides for his wife admirably. Society has relegated Torvald to a role that he is expected to play without question, but his decision to abide by those rules does not make him a villain.

On the surface, Torvald's angry reaction to Krogstad's letter containing the evidence of Nora's criminal act of forgery serves immediately to make him look cold and selfish, which is why labeling Torvald a villain appears logical. Nora has suffered with her secret for a long time, and rather than berate her as he does, Torvald should be understanding and supporting of his wife. After all, just minutes before Torvald reads the letter, he declared his wish for the opportunity to risk everything to save Nora from a grave danger. Of course, he said that believing that his wife was completely safe. But once Torvald reads the letter, his attitude toward Nora drastically changes. Nora is planning to kill herself to prevent him from assuming the blame for her crime. She says, "When I'm out of the way, you'll be free." He calls her a "miserable creature," and in the heat of the moment cruelly says, "What good would it be to me if you were out of the way, as you say?" (62). He knows his reputation will be ruined whether Nora kills herself or not. This is Torvald's most ignoble, self-incriminating moment.

Looking past the words Torvald speaks in anger and instead focusing on the situation facing him, we see that he is justified in his shocked outburst. His response is the product of a strong moral code, and any other response would make Torvald a hypocrite. Torvald was firing Krogstad for the same crime Nora committed, and he clearly states to Nora that he considers Krogstad's actions completely deplorable: "I literally feel physically ill when I am in the company of such people" (20). For Torvald to hear of his wife's deed from the very man he considers so horrid would be disastrous for Torvald, and Nora knows how Torvald will react. Nora says, "To think of his learning my secret . . . in such an ugly, clumsy way" (23). After he reads the letter, Torvald's cruel dismissal of Nora's offer to commit suicide as pointless is inexcusable, except that she doesn't kill herself, and it is true that even

if Nora were "out of the way," that would do nothing to help
Torvald escape the shame and repercussions that would come.
Also, Torvald would be left grieving for a dead wife, and his
children would have no mother. Unsuspecting Torvald really does
not deserve such a downfall. Also, Nora thinks only of herself
when she expects Torvald to turn his back on society and his
own moral code to dismiss her crime. Torvald says to Nora,
before he reads Krogstad's letter, that he could forgive a
person for a wrong deed, but he qualifies that by saying, "if
he openly confessed his fault and takes his punishment" (28).
Nora could demonstrate some courage and confess her deceit, in
which case Torvald's reaction might be very different. Instead,
Nora chooses to let Torvald find out in the ugliest, clumsiest
possible manner.

The issue concerning Torvald's treatment of Nora on a daily
basis provides a second point for some critics to name Torvald
a villain. The many instances wherein Torvald refers to Nora as
a "skylark" or some other silly animal gives the impression
that Torvald sees Nora as a helpless "featherbrain" who is not
to be taken seriously, but it would be challenging to take
seriously a woman who sneaks macaroons behind her husband's
back. Torvald constantly guides Nora and makes all of the
decisions, while rarely consulting her, which ultimately leads
to Torvald's being tagged a villain. However, Nora reinforces
Torvald's treatment of her at every instance. Nora wants to
spend the money Torvald will earn from his promotion before
they have it and says they can borrow until then. Torvald
exhibits responsibility and consideration for the moneylenders
in the event he did borrow money and was not able to repay it.
Nora shows her lack of consideration for anyone but herself
when she replies, "Who would bother about them?" (3). Another
instance of Nora's apparent dependence on Torvald is
illustrated when Nora cannot decide on a dress for the ball
they are attending. To her husband Nora says, "Torvald, I can't

get along a bit without your help" (28). Nora's behavior leads
Torvald to believe he is acting exactly as she needs him to
act. Therefore, it never occurs to Torvald that he is treating
his wife in a derogatory manner. Nora never gives Torvald a
hint that she is not happy with the current state of affairs,
which is why Torvald cannot be blamed for how he treats her.
Torvald thinks he is helping Nora, not hindering her.
Furthermore, to his credit, once he sees the errors of his
ways, he offers to change: "I have it in me to become a
different man" (64).

The society in which Torvald and Nora conduct their married
lives together places restrictions not just upon the women, but
upon the men as well. As a husband, Torvald's duties include
providing a home for his family and doing so in an honorable
and respectable manner. In both respects, Torvald demonstrates
he is a worthy husband, a man that Nora can be proud of.
Regarding the one episode during their marriage that threatened
their happy home, Nora says Torvald "overworked himself
dreadfully . . . , and he worked early and late" (14), which
led to Torvald's becoming sick. A man working himself to death
for his family bespeaks a noble hero, not a selfish villain. In
order for Torvald to be a respected member of their society, he
had to focus on making money, which he thought Nora wanted,
too. Nora often makes it known that she wants money. She says
to Mrs. Linde about Torvald's promotion, "I feel so relieved
and so happy, Christine! It will be wonderful to have heaps of
money and no worries, won't it?" (12). Torvald cannot be blamed
for thinking that Nora was perfectly content with his focusing
most of his attention towards making heaps of money.

Along with the duty of providing for his family, Torvald is
expected to be the social and moral leader of his family.
Society dictates that a man guide his wife and children in the
proper way to think and act. It is a husband's responsibility
to understand the rules that govern the members of society, and

Torvald takes that duty seriously. During the 1980s, psychologist Lawrence Kohlberg did extensive research concerning moral understanding. He organized moral development into three general levels, with each level having two stages. Torvald belongs in Stage 4 because at this stage, the individual moral standards are based on societal laws, which must be enforced in the same evenhanded fashion for everyone. Moral choices do not depend on close ties to others, but rather each member of society has a personal duty to uphold them. Studies provide evidence that few people move past the Stage 4 level of moral development (Berk 613). Those studies were done in the last few decades in a liberal, free-thinking society. It seems reasonable to assume that it would be much harder to move past Stage 4 in Torvald and Nora's society than it would be today. Torvald's level of morality limits his understanding of marriage to the guidelines society sets, and the blame for Torvald's failure to realize Nora's unhappiness with her restrictive situation must be placed on society, not Torvald.

When taking all the different aspects of Torvald together, it is impossible to consider him a villain. Torvald is just as much a victim of society as Nora. The problem with Torvald is that he does not realize, until Nora confronts him, that there is another way to think. He honestly believes that he is doing everything that society and Nora want him to do. Torvald provides a nice home for Nora and his children, he works hard, and he follows the rules society has deemed appropriate. For Torvald, life is everything it should be until Nora walks out that door. Henrik Ibsen delivers a message with this play, and it is not just that women are the oppressed victims of men. Ibsen seems to want people to realize how repressive society is for both men and women. The rules society places on women are obvious, but men often do not realize that even though they are living in a man's world, many of the rules limit them as well.

Penkoff 6

Nora's walking out the door serves not only as a stand for women's rights, but serves also to enlighten men about how blindly they organize their lives according to society's standards without realizing how it forces them into living shallow existences.

Penkoff 7

Works Cited

Berk, Laura. Infants, Children and Adolescents. Boston: Allyn, 1999.

Ibsen, Henrik. A Doll's House. London: Everyman, 1993.

Rosenberg, Marvin. "Ibsen vs. Ibsen or: Two Versions of A Doll's House." Modern Drama 12.3 (1969): 187-196.

4-6: Torvald's "little skylark." Who wouldn't be happy with such a wife? This 2002 performance of *A Doll's House* at Minnesota State University, Mankato, was directed by Nina LeNoir. Photographer: Mike Lagerquist.

The following essay, by student Debra Blaine, argues from a feminist perspective about what she regards as sexism in Shakespeare's *Taming of the Shrew*.

4-7: In Shakespeare's *Taming of the Shrew,* Kate and Petruchio's marriage is off to a rocky start. In this 2003 Jingju (Chinese opera) adaptation at Denison University, Rouge Tigress and Lion Dog are the squabbling newlyweds. The adaptation was written and directed by Hsing-lin Tracy Chung. Photographer: Cynthia Turnbull.

Debra Blaine

Professor Suzanne Hudson

Theater and Drama 3020

28 July 2003

The Taming of the Shrew: A Romantic Comedy?

Shakespeare's The Taming of the Shrew is usually performed as a lighthearted romantic comedy, but underneath its quick wit and slapstick comedy is a much darker message. Throughout the play Petruchio uses force and threats to make Kate love him, but because there is a happy ending, the real message behind this play is that it is acceptable to abuse women. Kate represents a threat to the dominant gender roles of the time and Petruchio must put her in her place using any means necessary. Kate further reinforces the play's disturbing theme with her final speech, telling us that this treatment is acceptable to her also, because now she is happier and sees the errors of her ways, further reinforcing the male patriarchy. Finally, and the most upsetting part of this play, is that this relationship, which has been the only one full of mental abuse, is telling us that unless men keep their wives in line women will take over, robbing the system of its balance and men of their masculinity.

Kate is a threat to the male patriarchy with her strength and willfulness, which explains Petruchio's abusive actions. Unlike Bianca, Kate isn't interested in finding a man to marry. When Hortensio and Lucentio come to court Bianca, Kate chides them, calling them "fools" (1.1.66), and then physically attacks Hortensio with a lute, leading to the comment that Kate would "sooner prove a soldier" (2.1.152) than a wife. This lack of want, or even need, for male attention and affection upsets the traditional male role of provider and protector. As Karen Newman points out in her article, "The Taming of the Shrew: A Modern Perspective," the traditional roles of women

Blaine 2

and men were in a crisis during Shakespeare's time: "Since
public and domestic authority in Elizabethan England was vested
in men--in fathers, husbands, masters, teachers, magistrates,
lords--Elizabeth I's rule inevitably produced anxiety about
women's roles" (230). Men needed to be reassured about their
dominant place in society, and that is what Petruchio does.
After showing up late and dressed inappropriately for his
wedding, Petruchio takes Kate away as soon as the ceremony is
over proclaiming "I will be master of what is mine own"
(2.3.235).

At first Petruchio's abuse seems fairly innocuous, since
everything is played up for comedy. But once he and Kate
return to his home, he denies her food and sleep, and he
threatens her with captivity until Kate gives in to his every
whim. Petruchio says that he must treat Kate this way because
"till she stoop, she must not be full gorged, / for then she
will never look upon her lure" (4.1.191-192), meaning that
until Kate looks upon him she will be denied even her most
basic needs. Furthermore, when Kate contradicts Petruchio about
the time, Petruchio flies into a tirade saying, "It shall be
seven ere I go to horse / [Whatever] I speak, or do, or think
to do, / You are still crossing it. Sirs let 't alone. / I will
not go today, and ere I do, / It shall be what o'clock I say it
is" (4.4.198-202). Petruchio continues this threat of captivity
to get Kate to do what he wants, no matter how ridiculous: "It
shall be moon, or star, or what I list, / Or e'er I journey to
your father's house" (4.5.7-10). He uses this threat again to
make Kate kiss him on the street:

> Petruchio: [K]iss me Kate, and we will.
> Kate: What, in the midst of the street?
> Petruchio: What, art thou ashamed of me?
> Kate: No sir, God forbid, but ashamed to kiss.
> Petruchio: Why, then, let's home again. (5.1.146-151)

It is through this constant bullying and threats that
Petruchio ends up with the best wife of all the men in Padua as
the audience sees in the end. When all the men place a bet on
whose wife will come when called, Kate is the only one who
comes. However, Kate is not coming because she loves her
husband and wants to come to him, but because she has learned
that if she ever wants to eat, sleep, or leave her house again
she had better come to him. What Petruchio is really doing is
reasserting his dominant position in society. He is showing to
Kate, and to the audience, that even if a man can't be lord and
master over all of England, he can still be lord and master
over his own home.

What is more disturbing than Petruchio's treatment of Kate
is Kate's acceptance of her treatment. With her final speech
that ends the play, the balance of power has been restored and
the traditional role of man as provider and protector has been
reasserted:

> Thy husband is thy lord, thy life, thy keeper
> Thy head, thy sovereign, one that cares for you
> And for thy maintenance commits his body
> To painful labor both by sea and land
> To watch the night in storms, the day in cold,
> Whilst thou liest warm at home, secure and safe
> (5.2.162-167).

The way that Kate's final speech, in which she proclaims
what it is to be a proper wife, is delivered has been much
debated. But whether it is delivered ironically or
sarcastically or straightforward is irrelevant, because we can
see that Kate is happy with her husband and with her treatment
by him, and that she is better off than when she was a shrew.
We can see this in the way that Kate defends Petruchio to
Hortensio's wife (5.2.22-34), and that she kisses him in front
of all the people at the feast (5.2.196). This says to the men
that it is good to abuse your wife because if she is smart, she

will see the error of her ways and be all the better for the abuse.

Finally, the most offensive part of the play is its happy ending. Kate and Petruchio's relationship is stable and happy while the other two, which were not abusive relationships, are not happy or stable. Lucentio and Hortensio pursued their wives without abuse, and in the end they are left with shrewish, disobedient wives. In fact, Petruchio laughs at Hortensio and his new wife: "Now, for my life, Hortensio fears his widow" (5.2.19). Shakespeare is poking fun at these two men; he is showing them as unable to command their wives and therefore stripped of their manhood. They have lost their position in the hierarchy to their wives and are now miserable. Petruchio and Kate's relationship in the end is the best, probably in all of Shakespeare's plays. In this lies the main problem with The Taming of the Shrew, that women must be kept down, be it through physical or mental abuse, in order to maintain happiness in the home and in society.

The Taming of the Shrew could just as easily be performed as a tragedy. Its only real accomplishment is to uphold age old gender roles and promote violence toward women. But perhaps what is the bigger tragedy is that it is still loved and performed today.

Works Cited

Newman, Karen. "The Taming of the Shrew: A Modern Perspective."
    The Taming of the Shrew. Ed. Barbara A Mowat and Paul
    Werstine. New York: Washington Square-Pocket, 1992. 229-
    238.

Shakespeare, William. The Taming of the Shrew. Ed. Barbara A.
    Mowat and Paul Werstine. New York: Washington Square-
    Pocket, 1992.

Revising and Editing Your Essay

Use the following checklist to be certain that your paper is ready for submission. Consult the Handbook at the end of this book for guidance in issues of word choice, sentence structure, and punctuation.

Revision and Editing Checklist

- ☐ Thesis statement is clear and present. It makes an argumentative statement—a statement with which a rational, educated person might disagree. The thesis is narrow and specific enough to be adequately supported in the space of the paper but general enough to need support.

- ☐ The introduction contains specific details. It leads the reader to the thesis; it does not mislead the reader about the subject of the essay.

- ☐ The introduction contains a counterthesis and counterpoints, and it clearly identifies the people who represent them.

- ☐ Points of proof are clear and present. Each point answers the proof question. Each point is narrow and specific enough to be supported adequately in one to three paragraphs and general enough to need support.

- ☐ Points of proof include refutations of all the counterpoints.

- ☐ Essay adheres to the plan set out in the points of proof.

- ☐ Body paragraphs are unified, adequately developed, organized, and coherent.

- ☐ Conclusion solidifies the paper's main point without resorting to mere repetition of the thesis and points of proof. Conclusion is unified and developed and does not bring up any new issues.

- ☐ Sentences are well constructed. There are no run-ons or fragments.

- ☐ Sentences are correctly punctuated.

- ☐ Words are correct and well chosen.

- ☐ All quotations use acknowledgment phrases.

- ☐ Sources are correctly cited in text.

- ☐ Title is appropriate.

- ☐ Paper is properly formatted.

Notes

[1] Sophocles, *Antigone. The Oedipus Plays of Sophocles*, trans. Paul Roche (New York: New American Library, 1958) 179.

[2] "A Contemporary Reaction to *Mrs. Warren's Profession*," *The Bedford Introduction to Drama*, ed. Lee A. Jacobus, 4th ed. (Boston: Bedford/St. Martin's, 2001) 860.

[3] George Bernard Shaw, [New York] *Sun, The Bedford Introduction to Drama*, ed. Lee A. Jacobus, 4th ed. (Boston: Bedford/St. Martin's, 2001) 861.

[4] Molière, *Tartuffe*, trans. Richard Wilbur, *Plays for the Theatre,* ed. Oscar G. Brockett and Robert J. Ball, 8th ed. (Belmont: Thomson/Wadsworth, 2004) 210.

[5] Robert Brustein, "Waiting for Hamlet," *New Republic* 4 Nov. 1967:25.

[6] Robert Brustein, *Dumbocracy in America* (Chicago: Dee, 1994) 23.

[7] Marvin Rosenberg, "Ibsen vs. Ibsen or: Two Versions of *A Doll's House,*" *Modern Drama* Sept. 1969: 192.

5

Writing the Performance Review

Vladimir and Estragon, the protagonists of Samuel Beckett's *Waiting for Godot*, agree at one point in their conversation to "abuse each other." They face each other and shoot insults back and forth: "Moron!" "Vermin!" "Sewer-rat!" "Cretin!" and, finally, with relish, "Cr-r-itic." Perhaps Beckett had good reason for insulting theatre critics—they have annoyed most of us at one time or other—but surely not *all* critics have earned the comparison to sewer rats. At some time in your college or professional writing career, you may be called upon to write a performance review. This chapter is intended to assist you in writing the review that will mark you as an informed, fair, and balanced critic, not the kind who earned Beckett's contempt.

5-1: Lucky dances as well as he thinks in this performance of *Waiting for Godot* at Belmont University, directed by Lynn Eastes in 2004.
Photographer: Rick Malkin.

The Nature of the Performance Review

Performance reviews are fun to write. First, the reviewer gets to spend an evening at the theatre—a treat in itself—and then gets to pass judgment on the performance in a freer form than is common in academic writing and in colorful language, meant to entertain the reader. One has the impression that the theatre critic is entertaining him or herself as well.

Professional drama critics, whose opinions are published in newspapers and magazines, sometimes find themselves in a powerful position—able to turn theatregoers either toward or away from a theatre's door with the drop of a well turned phrase. Wielding such clout can be a heady experience. Or it can get the critic into serious trouble with readers. As critic John Simon writes, "[M]asses of people will not comprehend such discrimination, feel threatened by it, and resent it bitterly."[1] An actress once smashed Simon himself on the head with a dinner plate at Sardi's, a popular restaurant in New York's famous theatre district. The privilege of sitting in judgment of other people's work and talent must not be taken lightly. Remember that the word *criticism* in this context does not mean "condemnation"—it means "evaluation or analysis of a work of art."

Ensure that your opinion is worthy of respect. Formulate it intelligently and honestly. Resist the temptation, even though it arises from an appropriate sense of modesty, to refer to your criticism as "just my opinion," as if your opinion didn't matter. It does matter because theatre matters.

Purpose

Generally speaking, your purpose is to *describe, interpret,* and *evaluate.* In so doing, your review could perform any or all of the following services:

- *Aid the consumer*: Many readers of reviews are trying to decide whether to spend their money on theatre tickets. Your review could help them decide whether the performance is worth the expense.

    Perhaps your readers want to know whether the play is humorous or serious, prudent or risqué, slow- or fast-paced, so that they can make an informed decision about whether to take their in-laws or their children or their business associates to the theatre. By the same token, if a review informs the reader that "This production of *The Taming of the Shrew* is set at a 1950s drive-in movie," the reader who dislikes the trend toward nontraditional productions of Shakespeare's plays will know to avoid this one.

Your review may provide the background information necessary for a reader to appreciate the performance. If, for example, the review informs the reader about Bertolt Brecht's alienation effect, then that reader will not be caught unawares at the theatre when she finds herself unable to identify with the characters.

- *Judge the degree of a performance's success*: Readers interested in the theatre arts, whether or not they are planning to attend the play, want an informed evaluation of the production. Theatre lovers cannot, obviously, attend every production, but they like to stay current.

- *Cultivate the reader's tastes*: Readers of reviews often want to refine their opinions, so they look to the experts for help. We need not always agree with the critic, but the very act of disagreeing forces us to examine our own standards and makes us more reluctant to settle for mediocrity.

- *Give enjoyment*: Some people read performance reviews simply because the lively style in which they are written makes for entertaining reading. For this reason, many of the most successful drama critics—Robert Brustein, John Lahr, and Frank Rich, for example—have published anthologies of their reviews; readers appreciate the creative expressions and figurative language that characterize them.

- *Offer suggestions to performers and producers*: Many a performance has been improved because of a reviewer's insights.

- *Advocate support for theatre.* The last thing the critic wants to do is run a theatrical company out of business. Any critic worth her salt wants more theatre, not less. The mean-spirited critic who sneers at everything shoots herself in the foot. Putting on a play is hard; these people are trying to bring art to us, and we must not only exhibit the appropriate appreciation but also drum some up in the community.

Audience

What sort of people read reviews? How much detail and background information will they need? What tone should you adopt in order to earn your readers' respect? These are some of the questions you should keep in mind as you write your review. Here are a few assumptions you might make about your readers:

- Envision your readers as reasonably well educated adults with reasonably refined tastes who read the newspapers. They could be sipping coffee while reading your performance review in the Sunday morning newspaper. They are not your college instructor or your classmate. They may be familiar with the play you are reviewing but have not likely seen this particular production. While it may be true that your instructor will read and evaluate your review, he or she will likely be adopting the mindset of a Sunday morning newspaper reader.

- Your readers expect you to provide information about the most remarkable aspects of the production. The critic who neglects to mention that *Nicholas Nickleby* is eight and one-half hours long, with less than an hour-long dinner break, has failed her reader. If all the cast members of *A Midsummer Night's Dream* are women, and they are not shy during the love scenes, one would expect the reviewer to mention that.

- Your readers share your love of theatre but will not accept your evaluation without proof. You will have to support your assertions by supplying evidence. For example, critic Richard Hornby, in a review of a 1987 production of *King Lear*, claims the production was "hamstrung by David Hare's inept direction." In support of this claim, Hornby offers the example of "wretched blocking" when Lear brought in Cordelia's body: "Hare had [Anthony] Hopkins [who played Lear] place her on a table and then sit down behind it for his final speech, effectively disappearing from half the audience."[2] No matter what your claim, be prepared to supply proof, as Hornby does, and you, too, will command respect as a critic.

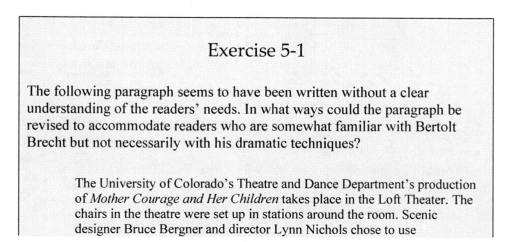

Exercise 5-1

The following paragraph seems to have been written without a clear understanding of the readers' needs. In what ways could the paragraph be revised to accommodate readers who are somewhat familiar with Bertolt Brecht but not necessarily with his dramatic techniques?

> The University of Colorado's Theatre and Dance Department's production of *Mother Courage and Her Children* takes place in the Loft Theater. The chairs in the theatre were set up in stations around the room. Scenic designer Bruce Bergner and director Lynn Nichols chose to use

environmental seating, which put the audience on stage with the actors. This effect helped to alienate the audience from the play. The alienation effect was created by Bertolt Brecht. It is a way of removing the audience from the play and making them feel that they are watching actors playing parts, and creating a feeling of separation from the actors. Brecht used the alienation effect to cut any connections one may have with the actor(s). By removing the feeling, the play is able to be viewed objectively, and the message is clearer. The scenery in *Mother Courage* creates a barrier. The five pillars are large, bulking, and right in the way in the scenes. This adds to the alienation effect because the comfort zone is taken away. Sitting back, relaxing, and watching the play is not an option when trying to dodge pillars. This works well with the overall theme of the play.

Tone

What attitude should you adopt as you write a review? approving? disapproving? raving? ranting? sincere? sarcastic? The content of the review determines in large part what "tone of voice" readers will "hear" as they read.

- Assume the voice of authority. Do not volunteer the information in your review that you are a novice at writing reviews. You are not being asked to misrepresent yourself here; you are being asked to become an authority. Ideally, you should study not only the particular work you are to review, but also the artist's body of work, his or her biography, and reviews of his or her work. Realistically, few critics, even professional ones, know everything about a work before they evaluate it. They learn as much as they can, and then, when writing, assume the voice of authority.

  Omit the fact, in your review, that you have read the play. For one thing, it goes without saying. For another, such an admission gives the impression that your only experience with the play is that you have read it, not that you have seen it.

- Have appropriate expectations. It would be unfair to complain that the acting in a community theatre or college production is "amateurish." The actors are, after all, amateurs. Still, some of them will not live up to appropriate expectations, and others will exceed them. Some set designs, even on a shoestring budget, will be ingenious. Some directors will make magic with the barest resources. You probably cannot expect Broadway production values, but you can expect people to do their best.

- Be honest. You may be right or wrong about the play, but the important thing, if you want to be credible, is to deliver a carefully considered opinion.

Style

For some readers, *how* a critic writes is just as interesting as *what* he or she writes. Drama critics, perhaps more than writers of any other kind of essay, employ figurative language—alliteration, analogy, allegory, allusion, assonance, rhyming, rapping, irony, metaphor, simile, hyperbole, and onomatopoeia, to name a few. Why? Because using these devices helps a reader to "see" what the reviewer has seen. Following are a few suggestions for keeping the reading interesting.

- Use vivid language. Your readers want you to put them in the action. In the following excerpt, drama critic Carolyn Clay describes a 2004 production of *A Midsummer Night's Dream*:

  > In [Martha] Clarke's vision, we are dreaming, primarily in black and white, of a kingdom of air and earth where sexuality takes shapes both delicate and carnal, embracing even its oft-heralded connection to the grave. Here sprites singing eerie songs . . . somersault slowly through space to land in a field of ash, and Oberon, the ultimate voyeur, watches amused as Titania happily copulates with a snorting ass. Crickets sound, as do Chopin nocturnes, and daybreak seems a long time coming to this shadowy swamp of love's confusion.[3]

- Instead of adjectives and adverbs, rely on concrete nouns and simple, active verbs as Carolyn Clay does in the above excerpt: *sprites somersault*; *Oberon watches*; *Titania copulates*; *crickets sound*.

- Avoid the verb *to be*; it lacks energy. Nouns exist but they do not perform when forms of *be—am, is, are, was, were, been, being—* occupy the prose.

- Avoid clichés—*clean as a whistle, clear as a bell, thin as a rail*.

- Whether you are dazzled or disgusted by a play performance, do not rely upon adjectives like *terrific, amazing, awful*, or *horrible*. Be explicit. Describe in concrete terms the elements that have made the event superior or inferior.

- Similarly, avoid vague phrases such as *does a good job* (or *an excellent job*, or *a terrible job* or *a miserable job* or any variation thereof).

- Do not bore the reader with tales of the ordinary, as in "I climbed the stairs, took my seat, and opened my program. Then the lights went down and the play came to life."
- Use your verb tenses wisely.

Generally, write in **present tense** when describing characters or events in the play, as in this example by drama critic Mary McCarthy:

> Fortunately, however, for everyone, there is a goddess in [*The Importance of Being Earnest*]. The great lumbering dowager, Lady Augusta Bracknell, traveling to the country in a luggage-train, is the only character thick and rudimentary enough to be genuinely well-born.[4]

Use the **past tense** for historical background and other events that occurred offstage in the past, as in McCarthy's description of an audience member's arrival:

> The irony of the pastoral setting was apparently not lost on the Marquess of Queensberry, who arrived at the first [performance of *The Importance of Being Earnest*] with a bunch of turnips and carrots.[5]

Use the **present perfect tense** (with the helping verbs *have* or *has*) for an action that started in the past and is continuing in the present, as in this passage by McCarthy:

> [Orson] Welles has cut [*Julius Caesar*] to pieces; he has very nearly eliminated the whole sordid tragic business of the degeneration and impotence of the republican forces; he has turned the rather shady Cassius into a shrewd and jovial comedian whose heart is in the right place; he has made Caesar, whose political stature gave the play dignity and significance, into a mechanical, expressionless robot; he has transformed the showy, romantic, buccaneering Antony into a repulsive and sinister demagogue.[6]

Use the **past perfect tense** (with the helping verb *had*) to denote the first of two past actions, as in this observation by McCarthy:

> [Macbeth] could never have been a good man, even if he had not met the witches; hence we cannot see him as a devil incarnate, for the devil is a fallen angel.[7]

- Name names. Do not write, "the actress who plays Hedda Gabler" but instead "Anna Greenberg, who plays Hedda Gabler." Name the set designer, costume designer, playwright, and other principals rather than refer to them generically.

- Distinguish between character and actor. The character says the words; the actor delivers those words by means of enunciation, pitch, tone, volume, and accent. The character has a personality; the actor conveys that personality by means of posture, gesture, stride, and facial expression. Frank Rich, in a review of a 1988 production of *Richard II* for *The New York Times*, distinguishes clearly between the character of Richard and the actor who plays Richard, Derek Jacobi:

  > When Richard imagines himself as "a mocking king of snow, standing before the sun of Bolingbroke, to melt myself away in water drops," Jacobi dissolves to the floor as rapidly as Margaret Hamilton melted away in *The Wizard of Oz*.[8]

- Show respect for the artists by referring to them by their last names. The first time you name an artist, use his first and last names, such as Bernard Kravitz. From then on, refer to that person as Mr. Kravitz, or simply Kravitz, but never Bernard. For a female artist, after the first reference, use Ms., as in Ms. Greenberg, or her last name only, but never her first name only.

- Paragraphs written for magazines, journals, and academic papers are usually longer than those written for newspapers. The narrow columns of the newspaper format necessitate shorter paragraphs. Another element peculiar to newspaper style is that titles of plays are set in quotation marks rather than italicized, as they are in academic writing.

- It is conventional in a performance review to use sources but not to document them (with footnotes or parenthetical source citations).

Planning and Drafting Your Performance Review

The following pages contain guidance in the process of writing about a play production, from preparing to attend the play to revising and editing your review.

Preparing for the Play

- Before you go to the theatre, read the play if it has been published. Do not worry that this previewing will take the fun out of the theatre experience. Reading the play beforehand does not take the fun out of viewing it any more than knowing the words to a song takes the pleasure out of hearing it performed at a concert. Moreover, your job is to educate yourself as well as possible so that you can write authoritatively.

- Before you see the play, read some critical essays. You need to know what the experts view as the play's strengths and weaknesses. *The Merchant of Venice*, for example, is well known as a problem play because Shakespeare's portrait of Shylock seems noticeably anti-Semitic. Many directors are unwilling to believe that Shakespeare, who has proven himself a deeply committed humanist in thirty-six other plays, could have intended to perpetuate the prejudice against Jews that was commonplace in his time. These directors continually grapple with the problem of presenting a Shylock who does not insult the values of modern audiences. The astute critic is aware of such problems beforehand and watches for the director's handling of them.

Attending the Play

- At the theatre, get a copy of the program. It will provide you with commentary on the play and some biographical information—names and backgrounds of the actors, director, set designer, and other principals.

- Take notes during the production. You will not be able to write much in the dark, but you should jot down quick reminders of the things you find remarkable. Do not try to write in complete sentences— these are merely memory joggers. Be unobtrusive in your note taking. The actors can see you and can be distracted by rattling papers and flailing elbows. During intermission, flesh out your notes.

Organizing Your Notes

- Immediately after you leave the theatre, begin transcribing your notes, and add everything else you are thinking about the production. Do not waste time worrying about spelling, punctuation, grammar, or organization. Simply throw all of your observations and impressions onto the page as quickly as possible. Some of your best ideas will get away if you become distracted by concerns best saved for later. You might even use a tape recorder to capture all those first impressions and reactions.

- Decide which elements you will emphasize. A review may touch upon any or all of several theatrical elements, but most discuss in depth only a few of them. Following is a list of some of the elements often discussed in reviews.

Playwright	Actors	Props
Plot	Director	Music
Script	Set	Dancing
Theme	Lighting	Costumes
Mood, tone	Sound	Makeup
Characters		

- Organize your notes into categories, for example, *actor*, *director*, *set*, and perhaps *miscellaneous*. Many writers use scissors and tape to cut and paste their notes before they pile them into categories.

Drafting the Introduction

If the introduction does not catch the reader's attention in the first couple of sentences, it has not done its job. Early in the review, the reader wants to know some specifics: what play is being reviewed, who wrote it, where it is being performed, and perhaps the names of the director and the principal actors. Second, the reader wants to read imaginative writing. This second requirement dictates that the writer embed the specifics in interesting sentences. The first two sentences of a review by *The New York Times* critic Frank Rich demonstrate:

> To hear his wife tell it, Troy Maxson, the middle-aged Pittsburgh sanitation worker at the center of *Fences*, is "so big" that he fills up his tenement house just by walking through it. Needless to say, that description could also apply to James Earl Jones, the actor who has found what may be the best role of his career in August Wilson's new play, at the 46th Street Theater.[9]

In another example, Ben Brantley of *The New York Times* weaves the specifics into the first few sentences of a 2004 review of *Agamemnon*:

> Women! Yuck! Ptooey!
> That's the way the menfolk gathered around the House of Atreus seem to feel about the opposite sex in the Aquila Theater Company's version of Aeschylus' "Agamemnon." In this stiff, achingly atmospheric production, which opened last night at the John Jay College Theater, a fellow can't even say the word woman without a rattle of contempt creeping into his voice.[10]

5-2: Puck promises to "put a girdle round the earth in forty minutes" in *A Midsummer Night's Dream*, performed by the University of Alabama at Birmingham Department of Theatre in 1999, directed by Karma Ibsen. Photographer: Kelly Allison.

The introduction to your review should be governed by a **controlling idea**—a subject that is developed throughout the introductory remarks and that leads to a **thesis statement**—an evaluative statement about the production as a whole, which the review will validate. The thesis statement is often the last sentence of the introduction.

There is no "correct" length for an introduction. In the following examples, you will see some long introductions, broken into manageably-sized paragraphs, and some short ones. Following are several review introductions, written by professional drama critics, that use different types of controlling ideas. Each introduction also contains a thesis statement.

The First Impression

In this type of introduction, the idea is to freeze-frame those first few moments of the production. Describe those moments in detail and then connect the idea to a thesis. In the following excerpt, David Richards of the *Washington Post* moves from a description of the first moments of Lily Tomlin's one-woman show, *The Search for Signs of Intelligent Life in the Universe* to an evaluation of the production as a whole:

> At the beginning of her new one-woman show, Lily Tomlin ticks off a litany of worries she can't get out of her head—that "evolution works on the Peter Principle," that "God has Alzheimer's disease and has forgotten we exist" and that the audience in the Plymouth Theatre is watching her only because "you couldn't get tickets for what you really want to see."
>
> But Tomlin needn't waste another fretful thought on her audience. "The Search for Signs of Intelligent Life in the Universe," as she calls this resourceful, wise and howlingly funny show, is the first SRO smash of the Broadway season. All the poor souls outside the theater, desperately trying to get in, are what she should be worried about.[11]

The Question and Answer

Alexis Soloski, writer for New York's *Village Voice,* finds a creative way into her material by asking a provocative question.

> What if you included all the formal requirements of the early-'80s stag picture— hot girls, hirsute guys, appalling puns, risible acting, nonsensical plot, synthesizer music—and excised the raison d'être, actual sex? You'd have writer-director William Osco's excruciating *Alice in Wonderland*, an inexplicit yet unrelentingly icky transposition of his 1977 flick to the off-Broadway stage.[12]

The Challenge

John Simon begins his 1994 review of a production of Euripides's *Medea* with a statement about the difficulty of staging the play:

> Any new production of *Medea* must come to grips with the fact that although Euripides speaks as one of us, much of his technique strikes us as dated, though less so than that of his fellow Greek dramatists. This *Medea*, originally produced

at London's Almeida Theatre, has many features to its credit, most notably that
its director, Jonathan Kent, is aware of this *aporia* (as the Greek would call it) or
hot potato (as we would): Euripides today is both necessary and impossible. So
Kent pawkily tries to steer a course between these infernal Symplegades (or a
rock and a hard place).[13]

Theatrical History

Some plays have been performed often enough to have accumulated a history
of their own. A brief summary of that history can provide material for an
introduction, as it does in John Lahr's review of a 1994 production of
Hamlet:

> *Hamlet* is a play that tests the best actors of each generation, and also each
> generation's sense of itself. Over the last thirty years, in England, no fewer than
> three *Hamlets* have served as such cultural bellwethers. In 1965, during the
> Vietnam War, David Warner gave us an untidy undergraduate Hamlet who was
> frustrated by Denmark's military-industrial complex. In 1980, as Britain's
> economy went into a weird free fall, Jonathan Pryce's *Hamlet* was possessed by
> the ghost of his father, who spoke through him in a frightening supernatural
> flirtation with madness. And now, in the neutral, post-Thatcher nineties, Ralph
> Fiennes has pitched his drop-dead matinee-idol profile and the modesty of his
> sensitive soul into a postmodern *Hamlet* whose refusal to risk interpretation
> reflects Britain's current bland and winded times.[14]

The Social/Historical Context

Some reviews more explicitly focus on the social and historical context in
which the plays were written. The following introduction by Robert Brustein
begins with a discussion of the trend in the United States toward cultural
diversity. Brustein's introduction is longer than most, and the material more
opinionated politically. When you are making decisions about length and
content, consider your readers. Brustein wrote this review for *The New
Republic*—a magazine whose readers are likely to appreciate the political
slant.

> The contemporary surge in racial, sexual, and ethnic consciousness-raising
> popularly known as "cultural diversity" has resulted in a tremendous outpouring
> of works by minority artists. Some of these are of genuine significance. Others
> have importance mainly as calling cards—demands for seats at a national
> banquet from which a lot of hungry people have long been excluded. And since
> our liberal culture—amorphous, uncertain, and continually in the process of
> defining itself—is more than eager to welcome new guests to the table,
> invitations are sometimes extended merely on request.

It is a practice that can lead to confused standards. White male critics are being asked to subscribe to a relativist code which decrees that, not being members of minority groups, they are disqualified from making judgments on minority art (unless, of course the judgments are positive—separatists rarely refuse praise, prizes, and subsidies from the people they claim can't comprehend their work). It's disarming, in all senses of the word, to say we don't share common experiences that are measurable by common standards. It's also defensive nonsense. But the growing number of truly talented minority artists with more universal interest, like Anna Deavere Smith, John Leguizamo, Suzan-Lori Parks, George C. Wolfe, and others, suggests that we may soon be in a position to return to a single value system.

Two recent off-Broadway productions reinforce this hope: José Rivera's *Marisol* at the New York Public Theater, and OyamO's *I Am a Man*, which recently concluded a run at the Classic Stage Company. Both are written by dramatists of genuine power and imagination whose perceptions go beyond sectarian racial or ethnic agendas.[15]

The Analogy

An introduction can also use an analogy—a comparison—as its controlling idea as Robert Brustein does in the following example:

> In my profession, nothing is more alienating than going to a smash hit and not being able to share the good time everyone seems to be having. Contrary to opinion, it's no fun for a reviewer to be in disagreement with an audience. It's about as satisfying, in fact, as entering a foreign country without a passport. There you are, morose and crestfallen, surrounded by hordes of natives who not only understand the language but greet it with roars of laughter, screams of approval, and standing ovations. Deafened by all these noises recently at the Palace Theatre, I felt very lonely indeed in the presence of *La Cage aux Folles*.[16]

Expectations Unfulfilled

Perhaps, like Brustein at *La Cage aux Folles*, you expected one response to the play but had another. The description of your response could fuel an introduction, as it does Juliet Wittman's introduction to her review of *The Vagina Monologues*:

> I walked into the Denver Center's Stage Theatre harboring the darkest of suspicions. I'd read all about *The Vagina Monologues*—who hasn't?—but somehow I'd managed to miss the show on its previous visits to Colorado. It sounded like a lot of other allegedly feminist phenomena that bother me. Take breast cancer (yeah, please!): A movement that began as women coming together for mutual strength and comfort, in the hope of discovering some facts

about cause and some funds for a cure, burgeoned over the years into a mass outbreak of kitsch, sentimentality and self-congratulation. . . .

So when I read that *The Vagina Monologues* had morphed from a play into a mission, that it travels from city to city recruiting local women as performers and that playwright Eve Ensler uses it to raise money to prevent violence against women, my response was skeptical.

From the sound of things, *The Vagina Monologues* didn't seem particularly thrilling as art, either. The "let's question ordinary people about a particular topic and then shape their words into a play" thing has been done and done, from *Chorus Line* to *Quilters* to *The Laramie Project*.

And let's get personal. I wasn't so keen to sit in an auditorium with hundreds of other women and a sprinkling of men and spend the evening thinking about my vagina. I mean, for God's sake, I'm English.

I was wrong on all counts. Turns out women really do have amazing things to say about their vaginas—raunchy, poetic, funny and surprising things— because their vaginas represent a very deep part of themselves. And when you select intelligently from their words, it does add up to a revelatory evening. So after an hour or so in the audience—oh, how I hate to admit this—I was feeling good about my woman-ness and powerful in a kinda sexy, life-affirming way and sensing a kinship with the other people in the room. It was the female version of being at one of those patriotic, flag-waving rallies, except that you weren't revving up to kill anyone. Quite the opposite, in fact.

Exercise 5-2

For each of the preceding professionally written examples of introductions, underline the thesis statement: the sentence that states an evaluation of the production as a whole. Notice its placement in the paragraph. Why do you think each thesis is placed where it is placed?

There are hundreds, perhaps thousands, of possibilities for developing your introduction. But you must select only one. You might build your introduction around a quotation. You might compare playwrights or compare plays. The main point is *control*. Let the introductory material focus on a single subject, preferably one that will *not* reappear later in the paper.

One of the main purposes of the performance review is to entertain. The predictable introduction offers the necessary information (play, playwright, and venue), several unrelated assertions ("The acting was good, the set was interesting, but the sound was terrible") and such a generic evaluation of the play that it could easily have been composed by someone who had never seen it. The imaginative introduction, however, will make the reader want to read on.

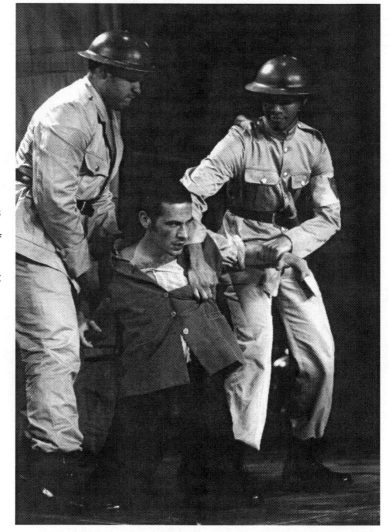

5-3: Swiss Cheese is exposed as a thief and arrested in this 2002 performance of *Mother Courage and Her Children* at the State University of New York, Stony Brook, directed by Chris Dolman. Photographer: Maxine Hicks.

Exercise 5-3

Following are three introductory paragraphs for performance reviews. Which one is the most creative? Which one exhibits concentration on a single idea? Which one ends with an evaluation of the production as a whole? Explain your responses.

1. When I walked into the theater to find my seat I saw the set right in front of me. There was no curtain to be seen, just a stage ready to be acted upon. I was there to see Anton Chekhov's *The Cherry Orchard* put on by the University Theatre Department. Soon enough the play came to life. This four-act play stars many up-and-coming actors like the delightfully charming Jana Mahler, who plays Anya.

2. I looked forward to experiencing the Vermont Shakespeare Festival's production of *The Taming of the Shrew*. Prepared to enjoy this play, I was disappointed that I was unable to join in the good times enjoyed by my fellow theatergoers. The eight-thirty performance promised an exciting Friday night but developed into a disappointment filled with overly flamboyant actors and messy directing. This production distracts the audience with excessive on-stage problems and leaves the audience with little substance.

3. When I first entered the Loft Theatre at the University of Colorado, to see the Theatre and Dance Department's production of *Mother Courage and Her Children*, I was taken aback by the actors, in costume, wandering about the theater, speaking to the audience members in their everyday personas while helping them find their seats and answering questions about Brecht. As I ambled around the space, I felt disoriented in a theatre I have occupied numerous times. The black, cushioned, and most notably comfortable chairs I have so often sunk into were nowhere in sight; in their place were clusters of wooden benches and hard-backed chairs. The theatre had taken on an unfamiliar vastness, an essence of impermanency. As the lights dimmed and the actors approached their performance space, I was still unsettled. I felt part of an inescapable dream in which time was altered and the characters were constantly changing. This feeling remained with me throughout the show, which held my attention from the minute I entered the theatre to hours after the show had ended.

Drafting the Body Paragraphs

Each body paragraph of a performance review should be about an element of the play (see the list in the section "Organizing Your Notes") and should accomplish three goals: *describe, evaluate*, and *support*. For example, a paragraph about the set of a certain production should describe that set, tell whether it is effective, and tell why it is or is not effective. In addition, each body paragraph should exhibit the same characteristics of body paragraphs in other kinds of writing: *unity, adequate development, organization,* and *coherence*. Following are examples of body paragraphs from several reviews, each of which offers a vivid description of one element of a play, an evaluation of that element, and support for that evaluation.

Playwright

Your readers may benefit from some biographical information about the playwright. Such information is surely warranted when the playwright is not widely known, but even when the playwright is more established, the review writer may see a reason to provide it, as Hilton Als has in his review for *The New Yorker* of a 2003 revival of Harold Pinter's *The Caretaker*:

> No other contemporary playwright has explored the nasty ways in which fathers and sons construct each other—and then smash the models—with such vibrancy and intellectual perspicacity. *The Caretaker* was Pinter's fourth full-length play to be staged. (He was twenty-nine when it was first produced, in London in 1960.) With it, he established himself as a powerful force in the British theatre. He offered an alternative to the kitchen-sink drama, which critics and audiences had come to accept as the only version of reality. (One of the main props here, in a fantastic set by John Lee Beatty, is an unused and cumbersome kitchen sink.) Pinter's work was, instead, an exploration of the nightmare landscape of the mind—the mind that lies to itself about what is real and tries to reshape the world around it. Pinter described the inner life of the colonialist without an empire.
>
> Pinter wrote his early plays while touring the provinces as an actor. Attuned to the absurd and absurdist tales he picked up on the road—the emotional connections missed in a shabby teahouse; the dank wooden stairs that creak under the weight of the suspicious landlady as she eyes life through her tenants' keyholes—he later incorporated these memories into his work adding to them his genius for delineating the political without becoming ideological. Structurally, he borrowed from Beckett, whose prose the younger playwright admired without reservation. Rather than setting up a dramatic pretense (murder, mayhem) Pinter reveled in his characters' horrifying and horrifyingly funny swipes at one another's consciousness.[17]

Keep in mind that the biographical details should be pertinent to the review at large. For example, your readers would gain little from mundane details of the life of William Shakespeare—such as where and when he was born and the names of his wife and children—in a review of *Antony and Cleopatra*.

Script

If the play is newly written and produced, your readers are probably not familiar with its plot or basic premises. In the following paragraphs, David Richards, writing for the *Washington Post*, describes and evaluates one of the early performances of *A Tuna Christmas*, written by Jason Williams, Joe Sears, and Ed Howard. The emphasis here is upon the script, not the production.

> [*A Tuna Christmas*] is a follow-up to *Greater Tuna*, the account of life in the third-smallest town in Texas. . . . Tuna certainly hasn't changed its stripes. It remains a hotbed of political conservatism, redneck manners, religious fundamentalism, bouffant hairdos and rampant bad taste.
>
> The populace is caught up in the annual Christmas yard display contest, sponsored by Radio Station OKKK. The little theater group has plunged headlong into rehearsals for "A Christmas Carol" by Charles Dickens, despite the possibility that the electricity may be cut off on opening night. Didi Snavely's used weapons store ("If we can't kill it, it's immortal") is doing a brisk trade in gifts and favors. And all over town, people are wishing one another, well, ill. Tuna never was a haven for brotherly love, and the holidays haven't exactly warmed it up.
>
> The new script—written by Williams, Sears and Ed Howard—doesn't have the satisfying dawn-to-dusk unity that *Greater Tuna* did. It spreads the action out over three days and allows what was already a hearty spirit of exaggeration to get out of hand now and again. But the ingredients still make for an immoderately funny evening. Sears and Williams know this world well. If they're quick to point out its shortcomings, they are never mean-spirited.[18]

Theme

The **theme** is a statement about the nature or meaning of the human experience that the play is expressing. Very often, the "theme paragraph" of a review expresses what the playwright intended, not necessarily what the production accomplished—in other words, it is about the play's message. Mark Steyn, writing for *The New Criterion* in December 2003, writes about the theme of the musical *Wicked*, especially as compared to its counterpart, *The Wizard of Oz*:

[In the film version of *The Wizard of Oz*] the wizard may be a charlatan, but, if Dorothy and her friends believe he can give them courage, brains, etc., then they'll find what they always had within themselves: that's a hopeful message. *Wicked* upends that Oz: hope is for suckers, and happiness is fake, a tyrannous illusion. The Wicked Witch, an outsider "misunderstood" because of the color of her skin, is the real good witch. Galinda the Good is a scheming bitch with no flair for witchcraft. The wizard is not merely a fraud but a megalomaniac fascist ruling a totalitarian state that permits no dissent. Galinda becomes a flack for the Wizard's brutal regime, while Elphaba signs on with the resistance as a militant animal-rights activist, the whole Wicked Witch thing being a front for a rebel with a caw.[19]

Mood or Tone

What tone does the play strike? Is it somber and heavy? upbeat? sentimental? Mike Steele, writing for the [Minneapolis] *Star Tribune*, describes the tone of *Fame, the Musical*:

> *Fame, the Musical* has been attracting a teenage audience, and it's not hard to see why. The show is cheesy and cheerful, earnest and unsophisticated, bounding along on the energies of a handsome, high-octane cast of willing and eager youngsters.
>
> Based on the 1980 movie and the TV series that premiered in 1982, this story of kids at New York's School of the Performing Arts panders to the young. It flatters them with hopelessly dweeby teachers at the mercy of teen wisdom. It takes teen angst seriously. It preaches that the mind can't hold a candle to the glands. [20]

Plot

The **plot** is, simply, the story line. E. M. Forster wrote that "the king died and the queen died" is not a plot, but "the king died and the queen died of grief" *is* a plot—a series of events *connected by causation.*[21] If the play you are reviewing has seldom been produced you will probably need to summarize the plot so that your audience can follow your analysis. Otherwise, such a summary is rarely necessary. Richard Hornby's plot summary in his review of David Henry Hwang's *M. Butterfly* was necessary because the play was new in 1988 when the review was written.

> *M. Butterfly* is an odd play based on a real-life incident: A French diplomat [Rene Gallimard] was recently convicted of passing secrets to the Chinese government via his mistress of twenty years, a performer of Beijing Opera. At

the trial, the mistress turned out to be a man, which seemed to surprise the diplomat as much as it did the public.

. . . At the trial, "Butterfly" now finally dressed as a man, is naturally asked how he was able to pull off such a stunt for such a long time. He replies that he characterized himself as shy (which Gallimard adored), never undressing in the man's presence; that in their sexual relations he "did most of the work"; and, most important, he was able to fool Gallimard because the man wanted to be fooled, his romanticism about women and the orient caused him to live in a world of fantasy in which reality was simply rejected. It all seems a bit far-fetched, but then again, drama is notorious for requiring major suspensions of disbelief, and the playwright's premise here provides an interesting vehicle for exploring our culture's attitudes toward gender and race.[22]

Actor

One of the main challenges in writing about acting is to separate the character from the actor. Another is to convey the actor's techniques for performing the role. Characters *say* the words; actors *deliver* them. Your reader wants to know what posture, gesture, facial expression, what voice pitch, quality, and inflection influenced your evaluation. Below is a well-developed description and evaluation of Stacy Keach's performance as Richard III in a 1990 review by David Richards, writing for *The New York Times*. Notice the specific examples Richards uses to support his evaluation.

But back to Mr. Keach, who has opted to give us a monstrously misshapen Richard and, in fact, could probably step into the role of Quasimodo without so much as a change of makeup. The character, of course, has never pretended to grace. He's scarcely been on stage a minute—and in Mr. Keach's case, had time to scramble down from a metal catwalk, winking at spectators as he goes—than he has informed us that he is "rudely stamped" and "cheated of feature." Since Nature has so ill-equipped him for fair deeds, his reasoning goes, it is only natural that he should distinguish himself in foul exploits.

Mr. Keach and his equally vigorous director, Michael Kahn, are not content to leave it at that, though. They've expanded the opening monologue to include some of Richard's lines from "Henry VI, Part 3." This allows Mr. Keach to tick off the deformities one by one—the arm "like a wither'd shrub," the "envious mountain on my back," the "legs of an unequal size." As if that were not enough, he is, he further boasts, disproportioned "in every part"—the lascivious leer leaving little doubt about just what part he really means.

Then comes that gesture I mentioned. Having proudly exhibited himself as the unappetizing lump that he is, Mr. Keach throws his arms wide—like a vaudevillian who's successfully executed a cheap trick—smiles a broad smile and lets out a triumphant hiss, as if to say "Tah-dah!" Yes, Richard is a tyrant in the making. But he's also an unapologetic showman, raring to make a spectacle of himself. The manic glint in Mr. Keach's eyes and the brief eruption of razzle-dazzle are rife with the promise of bloody entertainments to come. Whatever we may think of the monarch's morals, we are bound to appreciate him for his unabashed theatricality.

Glee infuses every warped and crooked inch of Mr. Keach's performance. Let him successfully woo Lady Anne—over the corpse of her father-in-law, no less—and he explodes in uncontrollable laughter. Amazed that she could find him "a marv'lous proper man," he promptly covers himself with congratulatory kisses. Hatching his lethal plots, he adopts a tone that suggests they are no more than clever pranks, and there's enough leftover boyishness in his face so that he almost gets away with it.

When the young Prince of Wales, his rival for the throne, arrives in London, Richard is there to welcome him with a colorful gift. Up pops a jack-in-the-box to the Prince's manifest disinterest. Even though Richard intends to have the boy murdered, he is genuinely crestfallen that the offering has fallen flat. How can anyone not like a good surprise, he seems to be wondering? (What, after all, are the reversals and betrayals he's been busy fomenting, if not surprises raised to a deadly power?) Moments later, the Prince and his brother are packed off to the Tower of London, and the gates in Derek McLane's steel and wire set clang shut. Mr. Keach can't contain himself: he waves bye-bye, as he would to toddlers on their way to school, and then permits himself a delicious chortle. If he weren't promoting so much bloodshed, wreaking so much misery, he would make an adorable troll, perched on the right garden wall.

Only in the end does the revelry drain out of him. The laughing mouth drops open dully, the eyes take on a fishlike glaze and you're left with a hollow man, reeling. Mr. Keach, quite splendid at the devious merriment, makes a grand transformation to the numbness of the lurching dead. It's a wild performance, encouraged at every bend, I dare say, by Mr. Kahn, who wields buckets of blood and a severed head with trick-or-treat flair. For some, it may smack too much of "Grand Guignol," but there's no contesting that director and actor are keeping the stage of the Folger in a state of zesty turmoil.[23]

Director

It is often difficult to know how much of what happens onstage is attributable to the director. A striking gesture may have come from the director, but it also may have been written by the playwright or conceived by the actor. Other times, happily for the critic, the director's imprint is obvious, as was Peter Brook's in a landmark 1970 production of *A Midsummer Night's Dream*, reviewed by Clive Barnes.

Brook's first concern is to enchant us—to reveal this magic playground. He has conceived the production as a box of theatrical miracles. It takes place in a pure-white setting. The stage is walled in on three sides and the floor is also white. Ladders lead up the walls and on the top are scaffolds and rostrums from which actors can look down on the playing area like spectators at a bullfight.

The fairy characters—Oberon, Titania, and Puck—are made into acrobats and jugglers. They swing in on trapezes, they amaze us with juggling tricks, Tarzan-like swings across the stage, all the sad deftness of clowns.

Shakespeare's quartet of mingled lovers, now mod kids humming love songs to loosely strummed guitars, are lost in the Venetian woods. The trees are vast metal coils thrown down from the walls on fishing rods, and moving in on unwary lovers like spiraling metallic tendrils. And in this wood of animal desire the noises are not the friendly warblings of fairyland, but the grunts and groans of some primeval jungle. . . .

[Brook] makes it all so fresh and so much fun. After a riotously funny and bawdy courtship of Titania by Bottom, the two leave the stage to, of all wonderful things, Mendelssohn's Wedding March, and all hell breaks loose, with confetti, paper streamers, and Oberon himself flying in urbane mockery across the stage.

And Brook uses everything to hand—he is defiantly eclectic. It is as though he is challenging the world, by saying that there is no such thing as Shakespearean style. If it suits his purpose he will use a little kathakali, a pop song, sparklers borrowed from a toyshop, dramatic candles borrowed from Grotowski. It is all splendid grist to his splendid mill. Shakespeare can be fun, Shakespeare can be immediate, Shakespeare can most richly live.[24]

Scenic Design

The artists who design the set of any theatrical performance are concerned with conveying its theme and mood. A bare-bones set may be the correct choice for some productions—indeed, a British Broadcasting Corporation (BBC) version of *Hamlet* exhibits no "scenery" as such, but only an arrangement of plain, heavy-looking blocks. The actors soliloquize on the blocks, or meditate on them, or swordfight on them, or ignore them altogether. The starkness of the set is effective in a production intended to emphasize Hamlet's fundamental appeal. On the other hand, an elaborate set, such as the one utilized in director Stephen Daldry's revival of playwright J. B. Priestley's *An Inspector Calls*, may better advance the theme or mood. Kevin Kelly writes for the *Boston Globe*:

An astonishing scenic coup gets the production under way and sets the show's dark and desperate tone. To the ominous crescendo of police sirens and Stephen Warbeck's blood-quickening film noirish music (performed live), a Yorkshire street urchin (Christopher Marquette) scrambles out from a gash in the stage decking that protrudes roughly beyond the proscenium. Lolling in the front curtain's luxuriant gold fringe for a moment, the boy slowly raises the curtain on a storm—the wettest, windiest and most realistic I've ever witnessed in a theater—that's raging across a bleak plain of rain-darkened cobblestones.

Perched on stilts in the middle of the tempest is a turreted Victorian house, ludicrously tiny for the guests laughing and toasting each other inside. You see their knees through the first-story windows and their necks through the second.

What Priestley envisioned was a 1912 dining room where an engagement dinner for a socially aspiring young woman (Jane Adams) and her excessively rich fiancé (Aden Gillett) is under way. Daldry and his inspired designers (sets by Ian MacNeil, lighting by Rick Fisher) have used the play's drawing-room conventions to trap an entire social class inside a decorated box. The house is part fortress and part flimsy bird cage, soon to be buffeted by forces beyond the insulated imagining of these straw giants.[25]

Music/Dancing

When mezzo-soprano Marilyn Horne made her debut in *Norma* at the Metropolitan Opera in 1970, singing the role of Adalgisa with soprano Joan Sutherland playing Norma, opera critics responded with praise. In the following paragraphs, *Time*'s reviewer first defines *bel canto* and then, through analogy, describes the sound of these two women's voices.

> The essence of *bel canto* is making the vocally difficult sound delectable. Long, lung-stretching phrases, rococo trills, breathtaking leaps of voice slide into the air and ear with soft, summery ease and grace. The quintessential *bel canto* role is Norma, the most taxing female part in all opera. Giuditta Pasta, the first singer to try the part after Bellini created it in 1831, found it so difficult that the violins had to play out of tune to disguise her failures.
>
> Last week New York's Metropolitan Opera offered a new *Norma* production with Joan Sutherland in the title role. Hardly had she finished her first duet with mezzo-soprano Marilyn Horne (as Adalgisa) than the audience began to cheer and occasionally stamp and yell. The enthusiasm was fully justified. Sutherland's voice warmed toward a soaring, languorous tenderness. Horne, making one of the greatest Met debuts, showed a vocal reach and richness that exceeded nearly everybody's grasp. In "Mira, O Norma," closing Act III, the two together floated along like two strings of a violin being stroked by the same bow. The way their voices blended and interwove produced moments of sheer delight—moments to justify opera and fleetingly suggest that the shaky conspiracy called civilization may actually be worth all the trouble.[26]

Costumes

Often, costumes are so important in a production that they deserve the amount of attention that John Lahr gives them in his review of *The Lion King*:

> In the opening number, "Circle of Life," [Julie] Taymor submerges the audience in a mythic universe; it's like being in a dream awake. Here the stage picture

aspires to the sacred as much as to the spectacular. The air fills with the sound of African drumming, marimbas, and balophones, and the saffron sun rises out of the gray daybreak, as the animals make their slow, reverent, astonishing appearance. They are ingenious, beautifully painted constructions, made from materials like fiberglass, rope, clay, and foam rubber, which are harnessed to the actors and guided by them. This poetic interplay between puppeteer and puppet, where the human being is always visible within the animal, is Taymor says, "a cubistic event, because the audience experiences the art from several perspectives." On close inspection, for instance, the giraffe's torso turns out to be a man on stilts, bent forward at a forty-five-degree angle in order to operate the front legs, which are attached to his arms; leaping gazelles are conjured up in miniature on a carousel of rotating wheels that is pushed across the stage; Scar's mask is positioned above and behind the actor's head, and it can tilt forward almost two feet in front of his face to intensify his intrusive menace; and, perhaps best of all, the cheetah-whose back legs are strapped to the legs of its handler, Lana Gordon, while the front of the torso is controlled by her head and hands—glides stealthily across the savanna. Are the animals human or are the humans animal? As in a naïve painting, the boundaries blur after a while into a teeming, surreal anthropomorphic universe.[27]

Drafting the Conclusion

The conclusion is of utmost importance in a review. It is your last chance to convince your reader of your insight and to give your reader a sense of satisfaction. So save some ammunition for the conclusion.

When it comes to writing conclusions, like introductions, there are too many possibilities to cover completely here. However, many of the best conclusions observe the following advice:

- Use concrete imagery
- Offer something other than repetition of points already covered
- Give the reader a sense of closure
- Reiterate, without repeating, an overall evaluation of the production.
- Develop a controlling idea

Without a controlling idea, conclusions can become a hodgepodge of general, abstract, repetitious and unrelated statements, which would be a shame to tack onto an otherwise scintillating review. Following are some examples of controlling ideas for concluding paragraphs.

Audience Reaction

The conclusion can describe the audience's reaction to the performance, as David Richards does in the following conclusion to a review of *Having Our Say*, a theatrical adaptation of the best-selling memoir in which Sadie and Bessie Delany, two African-American women in their nineties, look back over their lives.

> No one, however, questions the hold that the Delanys exert on an audience's affections. Spectators talk to them, cheer them, whoop and holler and generally carry on as if the Booth Theatre were a Southern Baptist church on Sunday. Midway through *Having Our Say*, Bessie gets an approving roar when she proclaims, with her characteristic feistiness: "I am the kind of Negro that most white people don't know about. Or maybe they just don't want to know about."
>
> For more than a century, time has been on the Delanys' side, but in this instance, it is likely to prove Bessie wrong.[28]

Recommendation

The conclusion can tell the readers what kinds of audience members are likely to enjoy the performance and why, as Brooks Atkinson does in a 1930 review of a revival of the Greek comedy *Lysistrata*:

> Although *Lysistrata* is a robust comedy, it is not sophisticated. Instead of cracking jokes, it pummels and grimaces, or splashes jars of water on a parcel of feeble old men. And, although the pace of the performance is slow and uneven, and lacking rhythm, it is a tempo not unsuited to the festival quality of the humors.
>
> Those who expect a neat, brisk show will be disappointed. But those who still like to snort over the earthy japery of elementary comedy will find that the congenial version of *Lysistrata* has laughing matter of rare quality.[29]

Final Impression

Just as a theatrical review might begin with a first impression as the curtain rises, so might it end with a description of the final scene and the impression it leaves. John Lahr uses this idea to control the conclusion of his review of Shakespeare's *A Winter's Tale*, produced and directed by Ingmar Bergman:

> On that note of grace, Time (Kristina Adolphson) rises from the front row of the orchestra section and, having opened Act II, now ends the play. She is a

regal, white-haired lady in a formal black dress with a red train. She holds a cheap brass alarm clock and now sets it on the lip of the stage. As she moves upstage to leave, she looks back over her shoulder at us, and a smile plays briefly across her face. The clock's hands are at five minutes to twelve. For Shakespeare in *The Winter's Tale*, for the seventy-six-year-old Bergman, and for us in the theatre, Time is almost up. In this eloquent production, imbued with the calm authority of genius, Bergman leaves us with the ticking of the clock and the urgency of forgiveness and blessing.[30]

Prediction

The conclusion is often a good place to predict the future of a playwright, a play, a director or actor, or even the future of theatre itself. In the following conclusion, Jack Kroll, writing for *Newsweek*, predicts the future of *Hamlet*:

> Watching the gifted [Ralph] Fiennes wrestling with the sacred monster of Hamlet, you sympathize with his task. For nearly half a millennium Hamlet has been our prince, the symbol of humanity caught between earth and heaven. But culture is changing, racing farther from the Shakespearean universe. Bernard Shaw said: "We are growing out of Shakespeare." It may not be growth, but technological transformation and spiritual diminution. We need a Hamlet that reclaims him as our own. Or else it may really be good night, sweet prince.[31]

Quotation

You might use a quotation as the basis for a conclusion. The quotation might come from the playwright, from the play itself, or from some well-known historical or literary figure. In a 2002 review of Eve Ensler's *Necessary Targets*, Nancy Franklin, writing for *The New Yorker*, builds a conclusion around a quotation.

> In the introduction to the published version of "Necessary Targets" (which is not identical to the version produced at the Variety Arts), Ensler writes, "When we think of war, we think of it as something that happens to men in fields or jungles. We think of hand grenades and Scud missiles. . . . As long as there are snipers outside of Sarajevo, Sarajevo exists. But after the bombing, after the snipers, that's when the real war begins." Ensler didn't discover this truth, but, in bearing witness to Bosnian women's suffering and loss, she brings it home.[32]

The Miscellaneous Collection

Not every element of a production can be treated to a separate body paragraph, so sometimes the conclusion is a good place to collect details that require only one or two sentences each. This kind of conclusion, however, runs the risk of becoming disorganized and pointless. One way to prevent this mistake is to organize the miscellaneous details. For example, group the elements you do not like, followed by the ones you do like. Head each group with a topic sentence, or assertion, that makes a generalization about the group collectively, as Robert Brustein does in the following conclusion to his review of *Einstein on the Beach.*

> Not all the elements of this monumental work are equally dazzling. A feminist parody by the judge in the second "trial" scene seems rather out of place; I don't understand the relevance of the Patty Hearst sequence; and I'm unsure of the cogency of a long episode in a train caboose involving a man and woman in 1920s dress clothes (the Einsteins on honeymoon?) that culminates with the woman wielding a pistol. Still, even these lacunae compel attention because the control is so confident and the material so evocative. Robert Wilson is an artist who paints magnificent images in motion, and Philip Glass is a composer who drives musical nails into your soul. Together with a dedicated cast and the magical lighting of Beverly Emmons, they have fashioned a piece that launches the theatre into new dimensions of the unknown, propelling our imaginations into the expanding universe of art.[33]

Creating a Title

It is often easiest to compose a title for your review after you have finished writing it. If you are writing for a newspaper, your editor will probably give your review a title that fits the constraints of newspaper style and space. Otherwise, you must write your own. Remember that your essay is a work of art in its own right and needs its own title. Therefore, your review of *Hamlet* will not be titled "*Hamlet*" nor anything so mundane as "A Review of *Hamlet.*"

You might mine your essay for a particularly apt turn of phrase. In a review of Ibsen's *Ghosts*, Walter Kerr writes, "The result is that the play itself—or at least this production of it—grows evermore lightweight."[34] He uses part of that sentence in his review title, "A *Ghosts* That Grows Evermore Lightweight." Try, perhaps, some wordplay; "It Isn't Easy Being Queen" is the title of Ben Brantley's review of Aeschylus's *Agamemnon.* Sometimes a familiar phrase works well as a title, as in John Lahr's review of *The Lion King*, "Animal Magnetism." Another possibility is a question: "Where is Britney Spears When You Really Need Her?" You might employ the ever-popular colon, as in "*The King and I*: A Puzzlement." Give your title some thought. It should both interest potential readers and indicate the gist of the review.

Student Performance Reviews

Following are two student-written performance reviews. The first, "A Fallen Orchard Rises to the Occasion" by Jordan Young, gives the University of Colorado's Theatre and Dance Department performance of Chekhov's *The Cherry Orchard* a favorable assessment. Note, as you read, the voice of authority in which the essay is written, as well as the examples offered in support of each assertion.

Exercise 5-4

Study the following performance reviews by performing the following tasks:
1. Label the introduction according to its controlling idea.
2. Underline the thesis statement.
3. Label each body paragraph according to its topic.
4. Draw a squiggly line under each topic sentence.
5. Place brackets around each piece of supporting evidence. (One piece of evidence could be expressed in more than one sentence.)
6. Label the conclusion according to its controlling idea.
7. Circle the words and phrases that you find particularly vivid.
8. Mark places that you would amend, and be prepared to explain why.

5-4: A pensive group on an outing in the countryside near Gayev's estate. This performance of *The Cherry Orchard* at Brandeis University was directed by Liz Terry in 2004. Photographer: Mike Lovett.

Jordan Young

Writing about Theatre and Drama

Professor Suzanne Hudson

10 Dec. 2003

A Fallen Orchard Rises to the Occasion

The University of Colorado at Boulder's Department of Theatre and Dance has undertaken the monumental task of mounting <u>The Cherry Orchard</u>. The choice to produce Chekhov is an ambitious one for an educational theatre program. Chekhov's writing presents many problems for the young actor, among them attention to rhythms of the play, dealing with silence, and most significantly, communicating multiple levels of meaning and broad shifts in emotion simultaneously. CU's production rises admirably to the occasion under the caring and studied direction of James Symons.

CU's production successfully presents one of the overriding themes of the play: the turbulent and confusing change overtaking the world in general and Russia in particular during the late 19th century, immediately preceding the Bolshevik Revolution. This theme is most clear in the second half of the show when we see the interactions of the three examples of the changing social landscape of Russia represented by Lopahkin, Petya, and Pischtik. All three of these characters understand that the world is changing, and those who refuse to embrace this change will be left behind as Madam Ranevsky is. However, how these three characters embrace this change differs significantly.

Eric D. Pasto-Crosby, who turns in one of the most engaging performances of the evening, presents Lopahkin as a caring friend to the Ranevsky family. He is endearing in his comically forced civility as he attempts to convince Ranevsky that her only hope is to sell her beloved cherry orchard. The audience laughs at his persistent and businesslike, yet fruitless,

attempts to help Ranevsky. However, when he appears in the
third act with his collar unbuttoned and a newfound self-
assuredness to announce he has himself purchased the orchard,
we see Lopahkin as the quintessential capitalist. He has
accepted his position in the world as someone who, through hard
work and perseverance, is able to buy and sell his way to an
important social position. When he stands in the nearly vacant
Ranevsky house in the fourth act with Yasha waiting upon him
with a tray of champagne, there is the glimmer of a smirk on
his face as he allows himself to enjoy his rise to prominence.
When he turns to face the household with the news that it is he
who now owns the orchard, Pasto-Crosby holds the audience in
the palm of his hand.

Jeffrey Sasz plays Petya, the perpetual student and primary
mouthpiece for Marxism in the play. He is costumed like a young
Lenin with drab, modest clothing and a pronounced beard. Sasz
brings the youthful earnestness of a young student radical to
Petya. He has read the fiery musings of those calling for
change and perhaps participated in their rallies, but does not
really know how to apply these changes to his own life. Petya
does not "practice what he preaches." He may represent what
went wrong with the Bolshevik Revolution. He is fervent about
his desire for and acceptance of change, yet he does not
consider the social ramifications of such radical upheaval. He
has not applied the changes he advocates to himself. Sasz
performs admirably, balancing the earnestness of the student
radical with the occasional bumbling ineptitude of the career
student who can never quite get it together.

Matthew Americo Zambrano turns in an inspired performance
of the character of Pischtik. Pischtik could easily descend
into parody or caricature, yet Zambrano plays Pischtik with the
sort of subtle honesty that allows the audience to laugh at his
foibles and eccentricity, while empathizing with his desire to
live as he wants. Pischtik represents the third example of life

in the changing world. He accepts and participates in the
changing world, but is not concerned with elevating his social
status or overthrowing political structures. He is like
Goldilocks's third bowl of porridge. He's just right. Pischtik
is only concerned with living a simple life in which he can
care for himself and his family. Pischtik suggests that between
the capitalist Lopahkin and the Marxist Petya there is a middle
ground.

 While's CU's production is undeniably engaging, it is clear
that the difficulty of Chekhov's style prevents a full
realization of <u>The Cherry Orchard</u>. Young actors learning their
craft often struggle with Chekhov. Chekhov's writing presents
perhaps the most naturalistic portrayal of human life onstage
of any of the early modern realists. His characters are engaged
on multiple levels and with multiple emotional states at once.
Young actors are taught to pick a single objective and pursue
it. Chekhov's characters, like people in real life, are nearly
always pursuing more than one objective, resisting emotional
impulses, talking around issues, and quick to change the
subject. Furthermore, Chekhov has a unique rhythm. It is an
undulating, circular rhythm that brings the audience back to
where it began, apparently without rising action or climax.
Chekhov often requires periods of silence and inactivity. It is
difficult for young actors to allow a play to breathe at its
own pace. Their tendency is never to allow a moment of "dead
air" onstage. Emily Hagburg and Annika Speer are two actors
who, along with Pasto-Crosby, Sasz, and Zambrano, are
successful. Hagburg's Anya allows the entire gamut of her
emotions to run across her face within single lines. Speer's
Dunyasha switches instantaneously between pursuing what she
herself wants and what is expected of her by her employers.

 The most successful design elements of this production are
the set and costume designs. Bruce Bergner's raked and slightly
rotated stage and steep vertical lines create a sense of

expansiveness within a small playing space. The raked stage is particularly well utilized by Symons. It allows a great variety of movement and stage pictures. Symons suggests much of the play's thematic qualities through his use of Bergner's design. The raked stage allows characters in close proximity to appear to be far apart, suggesting the difficulty of effective communication amongst the characters.

Janice Benning's costumes were likewise essential in the elucidation of Chekhov's themes and character development. The costumes vary from the opulent extravagance of Ranevsky's gowns to the modest, stern quality of Varya's dresses to the peasant functionality of Pischtik to the intentionally drab Petya. The choice to unbutton Lopahkin's collar in the second half of the evening is brilliant, as he himself allows his true self to become unfettered.

Chekhov is a difficult playwright to produce for a variety of reasons, particularly the difficult task of bringing his characters to life in a fully realized manner. While CU's production suffers from forcing unseasoned actors into characters that virtuosos would struggle with, the overall production does justice to Chekhov's writing and is well worth the price of admission.

The following student-written performance review, "Mother Courage: The Great Survivalist" by Kim Compton, evaluates a production of Bertolt Brecht's *Mother Courage and Her Children*.

5-5: With Kattrin, her mute daughter, by her side, Mother Courage screams silently at the news of her son's death in this 2003 performance of *Mother Courage and Her Children* at the University of Colorado, directed by Lynn Nichols. Photographer: Steven McDonald.

Kim Compton

Writing about Theatre and Drama

Professor Suzanne Hudson

29 Oct. 2003

Mother Courage: The Great Survivalist

When critics reviewed Bertolt Brecht's play Mother Courage and Her Children in 1941 after its premiere in Switzerland, they viewed Mother Courage, performed by Therese Giehse, as a tragic character with whom the audience sympathized. Unhappy with Giehse's sentimental interpretation of Mother Courage, Brecht rewrote parts of the play to achieve a more unsympathetic character. The 1949 production starring Brecht's wife, Helene Weigel, served as a model production for future attempts. Instead of becoming Mother Courage, she played the role as an actress who is angry at her own character. In the University of Colorado's production of Mother Courage, three actresses recreate the character. The end result is a less hard and angry depiction of Mother Courage than Weigel performed. Even though this production does not follow the 1949 model with 100 percent accuracy, it still is an excellent interpretation of Brecht's anti-war message.

Mother Courage portrays the life of a family trying to survive the Thirty Years War. The title character provides for her three children—-Eilif, Swiss Cheese, and Kattrin—-by selling goods from her wagon. A businesswoman to the core, Mother Courage is the only family member to live through the entire play due to cruel business tactics and a lack of sympathy for others. Conversely, each of her children has virtues that eventually lead to their untimely deaths. Eilif is too brave, Swiss Cheese too honest, and Kattrin too caring. Mother Courage's business comes before all else. She is willing to let a peasant bleed to death before she will donate her linens for bandages, and her excessive bargaining results in the loss of her son's life. After all three children are dead,

Compton 2

Mother Courage joins the soldiers seeking new business opportunities. Through Mother Courage's business, Brecht illustrates that war as a business can profit those involved but will certainly take back what has been earned, plus interest.

Mother Courage is performed in the Loft Theatre of the University Theatre building. Stage designer Bruce Bergner uses the space, usually a theatre in the round, to create environmental seating. Groups of seats, such as benches, chairs, and one recliner, are clumped about the space so that the action will move through and around the audience. The seating may be uncomfortable for some; however, this compact arrangement makes the audience focus on the message of the play. Because the actors are so close to the audience members, it is hard to ignore the tragedy war fuels in Mother Courage's life.

Director Lynn Nichols employs three actresses to fill the role of Mother Courage in a successful attempt to achieve Brecht's alienation effect. The alienation effect creates a distance between the audience and the characters so that the main focus is the message of the play. Throughout the performance the actresses switch roles, forcing the audience to break any emotional connection with the character. The current Mother Courage stands center stage, face-to-face with the actress who will now take the part. Mother Courage gives this actress her belt, signifying the transfer of roles. Nichols has instructed each actress to play Mother Courage in her own style. The actresses' different perspectives on Mother Courage reinforce the realization that Courage is only a character being played by actresses.

The three actresses' styles produce mixed results. Jessie Anne Fisher's portrayal comes closest to recreating Helene Weigel's model version. Fisher has a strong stage presence and uses her deep voice to depict the hard, greedy side of Mother

Courage. She shows little sorrow over the death of her daughter and even saves a few extra coins for herself instead of using them for Kattrin's burial. Fisher portrays Mother Courage's unwavering attitudes toward war and business by playing the character both at the beginning and the end of the play, creating a complete circle. Even though Mother Courage has lost all of her children, she remains unchanged in the end.

Courtney Prusse, the second actress to play Mother Courage, depicts the character much like Giehse in the play's debut. In the scene in which Swiss Cheese is killed, she presents the caring, motherly side of Mother Courage, acting with more compassion than Brecht intended. Even though Mother Courage is upset over her son's situation and finally his death, portraying the character as overly sensitive, as Prusse does with tactics like a silent scream, eases the formation of an emotional bond with the audience. In the absence of the other two actresses, Prusse's performance would be so powerfully tragic that the audience would inevitably sympathize with Mother Courage, the very reaction of audiences to Giehse that caused Brecht to rewrite portions of the script. The only thing that saves Prusse's performance is that the actresses switch parts, again breaking the audience's connection with the character.

Jessie Laura Butler, the third actress to play Mother Courage, adds a sexy, flirtatious side to the character. Butler's performance creates an interesting dynamic in the layers of Mother Courage. The coarse sexuality of Butler's movement and inflection echo the character's harsh business nature. Butler does not make Mother Courage into a sweet, love-struck girl but instead creates a straightforward, unrefined woman. The straightforward attitude that Butler demonstrates in flirtatious conversation with the men around her wagon is the same attitude Fisher uses while doing business in her scenes.

Brecht's 1949 model of <u>Mother Courage</u>, as well as his
instruction manual, serves to guide contemporary performances
of the play. Brecht realized that the play can be performed
using other staging techniques. He did not want to limit
artistic freedom in writing the manual. Brecht did, however,
note that the play, if staged without his new techniques of
alienation and epic theatre, may backfire. He contended that if
crucial moments in the play were omitted, the play's meaning
would change. The techniques outlined in the model that Brecht
developed and utilized in <u>Mother Courage</u> are difficult to
accomplish. The University of Colorado production has its high
and low points in achieving these effects, but it by no means
backfires. Overall, the cast and crew create the desired result
by striking the core of Brecht's anti-war message. Seeing
Brecht's compelling message come to life on the stage is a
powerful experience.

Revising and Editing Your Review

This last step is a crucial one. Your words are not sacred, and you are not obligated to preserve them if they are not doing their job. Use the Handbook at the back of this textbook for guidance in the elements of word choice, sentence structure, and punctuation.

Revision and Editing Checklist

☐ The introduction is unified; it develops one controlling idea.

☐ The introduction contains a thesis—a statement that evaluates the production as a whole. There is only one statement in the introduction that could be taken for a thesis.

☐ The body paragraphs describe, evaluate, and offer adequate support for your evaluation.

☐ The body paragraphs are unified, adequately developed, organized, and coherent.

☐ The actors, directors, set designers, and other principals are named. Their first and last names are used the first time they are mentioned, and their last names are used from them on.

☐ A careful distinction is made between the characters and the actors.

☐ The conclusion is unified; it develops one controlling idea.

☐ The conclusion reiterates, without repeating verbatim, the thesis.

☐ The review assumes the voice of authority.

☐ The review offers explicit reasons and supporting details for the opinion it expresses.

☐ The review makes it clear that the expectations of the performance are appropriate.

☐ The review uses verb tenses correctly.

☐ The review uses vivid language, avoiding as much as possible forms of the verb *be*, clichés, and overworked, unimaginative phrases, opting instead for concrete nouns and simple, active verbs.

☐ The review has a creative title.

☐ The review contains no sentence fragments, run-ons, or awkward sentence constructions.

☐ Sentences are properly punctuated.

☐ Each word is carefully chosen and correctly spelled.

Notes

[1] John Simon, *Uneasy Stages* (New York: Random, 1975) xi.

[2] Richard Hornby, "The London Theatre, Summer 1987," *Hudson Review* (Winter 1988): 642.

[3] Carolyn Clay, "Flight of Fancy: Martha Clarke's Dark *Dream*," *Boston Phoenix* 25 Jan. 2004 <http://www.providencephoenix.com/theater/tripping/documents/03537179.asp>.

[4] McCarthy, *Mary McCarthy's Theatre Chronicles 1937-1962*, (New York, Farrar, 1963) 109.

[5] McCarthy 110.

[6] McCarthy 18-19.

[7] McCarthy 242.

[8] Frank Rich, "Derek Jacobi—Ruler of the Stage," *New York Times* 22 Dec. 1988:C11

[9] Frank Rich, "Family Ties in Wilson's 'Fences,'" *New York Times* 27 Mar. 1987:C3.

[10] Ben Brantley, "It Isn't Easy Being Queen (Murders and Power Grabs!)," *New York Times* 13 Feb. 2004: E1+.

[11] David Richards, "Tomlin, the One-Woman Wonder: Her New Show is the Toast of Broadway," *Washington Post* 1 Oct. 1985: E1.

[12] Alexis Soloski, "Down the Rabbit Hole with a Salaciously Unsatisfying Twist," *Village Voice* 4-10 Feb. 2004: <http://www.villagevoice.com/issues/0405/soloski.php>.

[13] John Simon, "Review of *Medea*," *The Bedford Introduction to Drama*, ed. Lee A. Jacobus, 4th ed. (Boston: Bedford/St. Martin's, 2001) 158.

[14] John Lahr, *Light Fantastic: Adventures in Theatre* (New York: Dial, 1996) 329.

[15] Robert Brustein, *Dumbocracy in America* (Chicago: Dee, 1994) 190-91.

[16] Robert Brustein, "Musicalized Propaganda," *New Republic* 19 & 26 Sept. 1983: 26.

[17] Hilton Als, "Sons and Lovers," *New Yorker* 17 Nov. 2003: 160+.

[18] David Richards, "Christmas Cheer in 'Tuna,'" *Washington Post* 22 Dec. 1989, D1.

[19] Mark Steyn, "PETA Politics, Dreamworks Score," *New Criterion* Dec. 2003: 64.

[20] Mike Steele, "*Fame* Is a High-Energy Lightweight," [Minneapolis] *Star Tribune* 12 Feb. 1999: 7E.

[21] E. M. Forster, *Aspects of the Novel* (New York: Harcourt, 1927) 86.

[22] Richard Hornby, "New Life on Broadway," *Hudson Review* (Autumn 1988): 512.

[23] David Richards, "Three Faces of Richard III in a One-Man Display of Evil," *New York Times* 7 Oct. 1990: sec. 2:5. Copyright © 1990 by The New York Times Co. Reprinted by permission.

[24] Clive Barnes, "Review of *A Midsummer Night's Dream,*" *The Bedford Introduction to Drama*, ed. Lee A. Jacobus, 4th ed. (Boston: Bedford/St. Martin's, 2001) 323.

[25] Kevin Kelly, "Nothing Is As It Seems in Stunning 'An Inspector Calls,'" *Boston Globe*, 3 Oct. 1994: 30.

[26] "Marilyn at the Met," *Time* 16 Mar. 1970: 69.

[27] John Lahr, "Animal Magnetism," *New Yorker* 24 Nov. 1997: 126.

[28] David Richards, "The Delany Sisters, Having Their Day," *Washington Post* 14 May 1995: G1.

[29] Brooks Atkinson, "Review of *Lysistrata,*" *The Bedford Introduction to Drama*, ed. Lee A. Jacobus, 4th ed. (Boston: Bedford/St. Martin's, 2001) 323.

[30] John Lahr, *Light Fantastic: Adventures in Theatre* (New York: Dial, 1996) 366-67.

[31] Jack Kroll, "Fiennes's Hamlet Is a Hot Ticket," *Newsweek* 15 May 1995: 62.

[32] Nancy Franklin, "War Stories, Revisiting the Ruins of Bosnia," *New Yorker* 11 Mar. 2002: 90.

[33] Robert Brustein, "Expanding Einstein's Universe," *New Republic* 28 Jan. 1985: 25.

[34] Walter Kerr, "A *Ghosts* That Grows Evermore Lightweight," *New York Times* 5 Sept. 1982: sec. 1: 13.

┌─────────┐
│   6   │
└─────────┘

Writing the Research Paper

The Nature of the Research Paper	
Planning Your Research Paper	*Choosing and Narrowing a Topic* *Researching the Topic* Templates for Planning Your Research Paper
Drafting Your Research Paper	*Paraphrasing vs. Plagiarizing* *Incorporating Quotations*
Citing Sources MLA Style	*Models for Parenthetical* *Source Citations* *Models for Works Cited Entries*
Student Research Paper	*"Guilty or 'Knot': The Virtue* *of Vigilante Justice"* *by Chris Gluckman*
Revising and Editing **Your Research Paper**	Revision and Editing Checklist

Writing research papers affords several rewards: the fun of digging around in the library, the stimulation of reading about topics we find absorbing, the satisfaction of synthesizing diverse bits of information into a commentary that is uniquely our own. Through research papers, we engage in dialogue with the community of thinkers and writers who, like ourselves, are stimulated intellectually by theatre and drama. And there is the opportunity to become an expert in some small corner of the field. Researching, compiling information, citing and documenting sources: these tasks are inevitably time consuming. Yet the result is quite satisfying.

The Nature of the Research Paper

Research paper is a general term for any of several types of papers that use sources. **Term paper** is the more specific name for a paper that is required to fulfill the requirements of an undergraduate course. A **thesis** is a paper required in a graduate course. A **dissertation** is a longer paper written in pursuance of a doctoral degree.

The research paper is different from the critical essay in that it relies more on sources. Many papers published in journals such as *Modern Drama* are research papers. Characteristically, the writers of these papers refer to each others' comments and observations as they pursue a particular idea about theatre, thus expanding the discussion. You might use your sources in several ways: as corroboration of your ideas, as a springboard for new ideas, or as an opinion against which to argue. In short, you will capitalize on ideas in previously published papers to advance your own.

Planning Your Research Paper

Much of the process of planning a research paper matches that of planning the analytical and argument essay, discussed in chapters 3 and 4. Rather than repeat those steps, this chapter will dwell on elements of planning specific to the research paper.

Choosing and Narrowing a Topic

Before you decide on a topic for your research paper, you need a clear understanding of your assignment. A major consideration is the **mode of discourse** in which you are expected to write. Will your research paper be descriptive, analytical or argumentative? Your thesis statement must reflect your paper's main point as well as its mode of discourse. Compare the following examples:

Descriptive Thesis	David Mamet's *Oleanna* has caused much consternation among feminists.
Analytical Thesis	David Mamet's minimalist techniques reinforce *Oleanna*'s message that propaganda is a dangerous weapon.
Argumentative Thesis	*Oleanna* intentionally promotes antifeminist backlash.

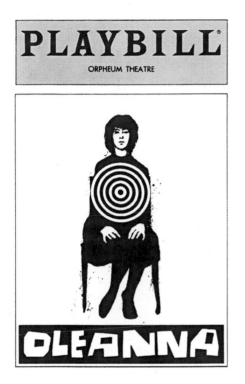

6-1: Who is the victim in David Mamet's *Oleanna*? The woman or the man?

When the play opened in 1992 at the Orpheum Theatre in New York, two *Playbills* were printed.

The *descriptive thesis* promises an impartial paper. The *analytical thesis* promises a paper that will show how the elements of the play work to convey a particular meaning, but it will not try to settle a dispute. The *argumentative thesis* promises to take a position in some controversy that the play has engendered.

A research paper may also combine the modes of discourse. For example, you might describe a playwright's life and influences objectively and then analyze her work by speculating about the reasons for her choices or the public's reaction to her plays.

Once you have settled on a general topic, you will probably find that it needs narrowing. For example, the topic of David Mamet's use of language is too broad for a ten to twelve-page research paper. But a paper that compares the broken, stuttering language of the victims in *Oleanna* and *Glengarry Glen Ross* to show the connection between jargon and power could be narrow enough to pursue in some depth.

Researching the Topic

Once you have chosen and narrowed your topic, you will collect as many relevant books and articles as time allows. Your library, including its electronic databases, is likely to be your best resource; the World Wide Web will probably prove second best.

Searching the Library

To collect books and articles that are not available in full text online, you will need to pay a visit to your local or college library. For extensive instructions and advice on library research, consult *The Oxford Guide to Library Research* by Library of Congress reference librarian Thomas Mann. Remember two things: (1) allot more time than you think you need because tracking down relevant sources takes time; (2) when in doubt, ask a librarian.

Finding Books

To find books, use the library's computer catalog. If you know the author or the exact title you are looking for, search by author or by title. Otherwise, search by word (or keyword); that is, type in a word or phrase that may be contained in the title or the description of the book. For example, if you are looking for a book on kabuki theatre, you would type *kabuki* in the "word" box. The computer will then generate a list of books on that topic as well as each book's **call number** so that you can find it on the library's shelves. If there are too many choices, you can limit your search by adding another keyword or phrase, such as *performance*.

Finding Periodical Articles

Finding periodical articles can be a bit more involved than finding books. **Periodicals** include **magazines**, which are written for general audiences, and **journals**, which are written by and for authorities in a particular discipline. You might find an article on your topic in a magazine such as *Newsweek* or in a journal such as *Modern Drama*. To find periodical articles, use print indexes or electronic databases.

> **Print indexes:** A **periodical index**, in this context, is a book that lists articles that have been published in magazines and journals on any of thousands of topics. The more widely used print indexes for theatre research are The *Humanities Index, MLA (Modern Language Association) International Bibliography*, and the *Reader's Guide to Periodical Literature*.

> You can use your library's computer catalog to obtain the call number of the index volumes and their location in the library. The volumes are organized by year, and each volume is organized alphabetically according to keywords. In the front of each volume is a key to the abbreviations.

> If you see an article listed in the index that looks potentially useful, you must then locate that article. For example, if the *Reader's Guide to Periodical Literature* lists an article printed in the April 1996 issue of *Theatre in America* on a kabuki-style performance of Ibsen's *Peer Gynt* at the Tyrone Guthrie Theatre, your next step is to locate the library's collection of issues of that magazine. Ask the computer for that periodical's call number, and go find it on the shelves. Once you have located the bound volumes of the magazine, you will easily find the correct issue and the desired article. If your library does not collect the periodical you need, you can find out which libraries do and request a copy of the article via interlibrary loan.

> **Electronic databases:** Another way to search for articles on your topic is through your library's electronic databases. Each database contains lists of books, articles, and other resources such as audiotapes and videocassettes. Some contain the full text of the articles as well. Most college libraries give students and faculty an access code and password so that they can search from their home computers. Some textbooks also include a subscription to an online database. *The Essential Theatre*, 8th

edition, by Oscar G. Brockett and Robert J. Ball, for example, is packaged with a subscription to *InfoTrac*®, a comprehensive database for periodical articles.

InfoTrac and other electronic databases use keywords, such as *Peer Gynt* and *kabuki*. Some of the articles listed in the database will be available in full text online. If they are not online, you will need to go to the library to obtain them.

Finding Newspaper Articles

If it is appropriate for your topic, you might expand your search to include newspaper articles. Like periodical articles, newspapers are indexed in both print indexes and electronic databases.

Print indexes: Some of the more widely used newspaper indexes include the *New York Times Index*, the *Los Angeles Times Index*, and the [London] *Times Index*. Using a call number, locate the volumes of the index on the shelves of your library. Indexes for newspapers are organized in the same way as indexes for magazines and journals. Use a keyword, *kabuki* for example, to find articles on that topic in that newspaper.

Electronic databases: In order to conduct an electronic search for newspaper articles on your topic, seek, via your library's computer, an electronic database that includes newspapers, such *Lexis-Nexis Academic Universe*. Using that database's search screen, search by keyword, title, or author. Many of the articles you locate will be available in full text online. Others you will need to find in the library, either in hard copy or on microfiche or microfilm.

Exercise 6-1

Using *InfoTrac*, locate the article "The Language of Understanding" by Arthur Holmberg. Print and read the article, which analyzes David Mamet's *Oleanna*, and then answer the following questions:

1. One female student accuses David Mamet of political irresponsibility. Paraphrase Mamet's answer to the student.

2. Paraphrase Mamet's answer to the question, "What is the function of theatre in society?"

3. How does Holmberg support his assertion that "Mamet's use of language gives the play rich texture"?

4. According to the article, Mamet suggests that two groups of people patrol universities these days. What two groups are they? Do you agree?

5. What primal fears does the play tap into, according to Holmberg?

Searching the World Wide Web

The World Wide Web is another possible source of information on your topic, but be aware that the results of a World Wide Web search are often unsatisfactory. One reason is that many articles retrieved from the Web have not gone through the filtering processes of editing, peer review, and library selection. Also, there are far too many sources to sort through easily.

To begin a Web search, type in the name of the search engine you want to use in the search box and hit Enter. *Google* is probably the most popular search engine at this writing. When the homepage of the search engine is on your screen, type the keyword in the search box and hit Enter. The more words you enter, the narrower your search becomes, and the shorter the list of relevant Web sites becomes.

Put phrases and names in quotation marks. For example if you put the words *Sexual Perversity in Chicago* in quotation marks, the search engine will look for those words as a group instead of individually. Most of the links will be to Web sites with articles on David Mamet's play of that title. A search without the quotation marks will bring up a *very* different list of Web sites, most of which will not advance your college education.

The ability to evaluate a Web site is essential. To do that, you first need to know who created the site and their purpose. In the Web site address, or the **URL** (uniform resource locator), the suffix *.edu* denotes an educational organization; these sources may well be worthy of your attention. Web sites with *.com* in the URL are usually selling goods or services, but they can provide relevant information. The suffix *.org* denotes a noncommercial organization. Many of these Web sites offer useful, objective, and accurate information; however, many private organizations have an agenda: their purpose is to persuade their readers to adopt their position.

Following are a few Web sites that provide useful and reliable information for academic research in theatre and drama as well as links to other such sites:

- About.com <http://www.about.com>
- BUBL LINK <http://bubl.ac.uk/link/>
- Humbul Humanities <http://www.humbul.ac.uk/>
- Jam! <http://www.canoe.ca/Theatre/>
- Performing Arts Links <http://www.theatrelibrary.org/links>
- Theatre Communications Group <http://www.tcg.org>
- Theatre Links-Suite 101.com <http://www.suite101.com>
- Theatrenet <http://www.theatrenet.co.uk/>
- The WWW Virtual Library for Theatre and Drama <http://www.vl-theatre.com>
- World Wide Art Resources <http://wwar.com/categories/Theater>

Templates for Planning Your Research Paper

To plan your research paper, use the template in chapter 3 if the paper will be written in an analytical mode of discourse. Use the template in chapter 4 if your research paper will be written in the argumentative mode. Remember that the templates are only a starting point for organizing your ideas and information, not a rigid mold. You will need to tailor these outlines to your own paper, offering as many points of proof, refutations, and pieces of evidence as necessary to prove your thesis.

Drafting Your Research Paper

Having researched your topic, taken notes, planned, and outlined your paper, you are ready to begin writing. As you write, keep in mind the following general advice:

- Synthesize sources of information to create your own unique view of the topic.
- Incorporate the words of authorities who have written on the topic.
- Use your sources to corroborate your ideas, which you have written in your own words by means of your thesis and points of proof.
- Do not let your sources speak for you.
- Assume the voice of authority. You have read extensively and have assimilated much information on your topic. You are qualified to present a unique point of view.

- Give credit for borrowed words and ideas to their originators. The following pages will discuss this important point further.

Paraphrasing vs. Plagiarizing

Much of your research paper will consist of information gleaned from your sources and then paraphrased. To **paraphrase** is to relate your source's ideas in your own words and style and to give your source credit for those ideas *in text*.

To **plagiarize** is to commit one or more of the following mistakes:

- copying a passage word for word without using quotation marks or naming the source
- merely substituting synonyms for some words in the original passage
- merely rearranging the sentence structure in the original passage
- presenting someone else's ideas or writing as your own

Consider the following examples. The original passage comes from an article titled "The Language of Misunderstanding," written by Arthur Holmberg in *American Theatre*.

Original Passage from Source

> On an archetypal level, Mamet's play—a sexual minuet of violence—deals with the unending struggle for power between male and female. Deep within, men and women mistrust each other, and the relationship between them can never be easy, owing to primal fears: the male fear of castration and the female fear of male force and rape.

Plagiarism

> Mamet's play, a dance of sex and violence, deals on an archetypal level with the power struggle between men and women. Internally, they don't trust each other, and the relationship between them is uneasy because of the male's primal fear of castration and the female's primal fear of rape.

This paraphrase qualifies as plagiarism because it matches the original far too closely. The writer has made some word substitutions, but the paraphrase is illegitimate on at least four counts:

- the sentence structure is almost exactly that of the original;

- the style has been lifted from the original passage, best demonstrated by the comparison between the play and a minuet in the original and the paraphrase's comparison between the play and a dance;

- some words and phrases are copied exactly but not placed in quotation marks;

- the writer has presented Arthur Holmberg's idea about the play's archetypal appeal as his own.

The challenge in paraphrasing sources is to convey their meaning accurately without unintentionally copying their structure or style. Following is one way to incorporate Holmberg's idea and to give proper credit for it.

Legitimate Paraphrase/Quotation

> According to Arthur Holmberg, author of an article about David Mamet titled "The Language of Misunderstanding," Oleanna strikes a nerve because it demonstrates the basic fears that drive the battle of the sexes: "the male fear of castration and the female fear of male force and rape" (95).

Incorporating Quotations

Many writers make the mistake of overquoting their sources. You should use a quotation only in certain circumstances:

- when the source's phrasing is so well written that you could not possibly convey the message in any other words; or

- when it is important that the reader see the original words of the source.

If quoting is warranted you must *weave* the quotations into your paper, not insert them awkwardly. Each quotation should be accompanied by an **acknowledgment phrase** that tells who is being quoted and offers an explanation of the relevance of the quotation. Simply tacking a source citation onto the end of a quotation, as in the following example, is not sufficient.

Unacknowledged Quotation: Incorrect

> In Mamet's plays, "Sentences refuse to complete themselves; they run on, loop back, start over, peter out, or suspend flight mid-air as the other character butts in" (Holmberg 94).

The reader does not know who is being quoted in the preceding example, only that the quotation was taken from page 94 of Holmberg's article. You must identify the person being quoted *in the text*.

Acknowledged Quotation: Correct

```
Arthur Holmberg, author of an article about David Mamet
titled "The Language of Misunderstanding," aptly
describes the failure of communication among Mamet's
characters: "Sentences refuse to complete themselves;
they run on, loop back, start over, peter out, or
suspend flight mid-air as the other character butts in"
(94).
```

The first time you quote a person, provide that person's first and last name and credentials. For example, in the preceding acknowledgment phrase, Arthur Holmberg is identified as the author of the cited article about David Mamet. If the person is mentioned again, you may refer to him or her by last name only.

Citing Sources MLA Style

There are several documentation systems, but the one currently most accepted for arts and humanities papers is the MLA (Modern Language Association) system. The system entails in-text parenthetical notes, or source citations, that correspond to a list of works cited. The following condensed instructions may be comprehensive enough for your paper on drama, but if they are not, refer to the *MLA Handbook for Writers of Research Papers*, 6th edition, by Joseph Gibaldi. Although the entire MLA handbook is not available online, many colleges and universities offer online summaries of the system, including OWL at Purdue <http://owl.english.purdue.edu/handouts/research/r_mla.html>.

Models for Parenthetical Source Citations

The basic idea is that the brief citation in the text should point the reader to the first word on the left margin of the works cited entry. For example, the parenthetical note (Holmberg 94) at the end of a sentence directs the reader to the entry beginning with the word "Holmberg," on the works cited page, which is organized alphabetically. There, the reader will find complete publication information.

You should cite

- quotations
- any facts that are not widely available
- statistics, and
- paraphrased or borrowed ideas

Standard source citation: Enclose in parentheses the author's last name and the page number(s).

> The title of the play refers to a folksong about a utopia called Oleanna, where the powerless become the powerful (Jacobus 1640).

Following are variations on this standard format.

Author is named in the text: Do not name the author again in parentheses.

> Gerald Weales, theatre critic for Commonweal, writes, "The characters in David Mamet's Oleanna have names—John and Carol—but they might as well have been called professor and student or man and woman or accused and accuser, or simply victim 1 and victim 2" (15).

Character in a play is quoted: If it is clear from the context which play is the source of the quotation, you do not include the playwright's name in parentheses with the page number.

> Carol says, "It is a sexist remark, and to overlook it is to countenance continuation of that method of thought" (1109).

Play has numbered lines: Use arabic numerals unless your professor prefers that you use roman numerals to designate act and scene (for example, IV.iv.202).

> When Kate contradicts Petruchio about the time, Petruchio flies into a tirade saying, "It shall be what o'clock I say it is" (4.4.202).

If the play has numbered lines but is not broken into acts and scenes, write *line* (or *lines*) before the line number(s) only in the first parenthetical source citation. Having established that lines, not page numbers, are being referenced, use only the line numbers thereafter.

First reference:

> Antigone explains to Kreon why she has has no respect for his power as king or his decree that her brother be left unburied: "[A]ll your strength is weakness itself against / The immortal unrecorded laws of God" (lines 60-61).

Subsequent reference:

> In a typical display of masculine insecurity, Kreon asks, "Who is the man here, / She or I, if this crime goes unpunished?" (82-83).

Author of source is unidentified: Use a short version of the title, beginning with the word by which the title is alphabetized (not *a*, *an*, or *the*) in the list of works cited. Enclose the shortened titles of the articles and Web pages in quotation marks.

> David Mamet's Oleanna implies to some that sexual harassment is a figment of the female imagination ("He Said" 6).

Quotation's source is secondhand: Although quotations ideally come from their original source, sometimes only an indirect source is available.

> Mamet claims, "I have no political responsibility. I'm an artist. I write plays, not political propaganda. If you want easy solutions, turn on the boob tube" (qtd. in Holmberg 94).

List of works cited includes more than one work by the same author: If the work is not named in the text, include the name (or a shortened version) in the parenthetical citation.

> Hamlet is the second-most cited figure in Western consciousness; Jesus is the first (Bloom, Shakespeare xix).

Separate multiple references for the same assertion with a semicolon.

> Oleanna has been barraged with criticism, chiefly
> from feminists who claim that the play promotes
> the notion that sexual harassment is a figment of
> the female imagination and that violence against
> women in response to false accusations is not only
> justifiable but an event to be cheered (Mufson
> 111-13; "He Said" 6).

Source has two or three authors: Give the names in the same order that they are listed on the title page of the work and in your list of works cited.

> David Mamet's Glengarry Glen Ross explores the
> disintegration of honor in American business (Brockett
> and Ball 13).

> Kabuki theatre reveals much of Japanese culture not
> expressed in the No or the puppet theatre (Huberman,
> Pope, and Ludwig 252).

Source has more than three authors: Use the abbreviation *et al.* after the name of the first author.

> The classical arrangement of an argument places
> refutations at the end. Modern writers, however, have
> found it useful to place refutations at the beginning
> (Hodges et al. 513).

List of works cited includes two authors with same last name: Add the first initial or, if the first initials are the same, the full first name.

> After the fall of the Roman empire, bishops in the Roman
> Catholic Church suppressed theatre as a godless form of
> entertainment (R. Woolf 201).

> Women are remarkably absent from the history books
> written by G. M. Trevelyan and John Aubrey, whereas they
> are prevalent characters in the dramatic works of the
> time (V. Woolf 1378-80).

Source has no pagination, such as a speech or a personal interview: Include in the text, rather than in a parenthetical reference, the name of the person that begins the corresponding entry in the works cited list.

> In a speech to the Yale student body, Frank Rich
> surmised that David Mamet's Oleanna is an impassioned
> response to the Clarence Thomas/Anita Hill sexual
> harassment face-off that occurred in 1992 in Washington,
> D.C.

Electronic source without pagination: Use the paragraph or section numbers if they are given in the Web site. If they are not, identify the source as it is identified in the list of works cited: by the author or, if that is not available, by the name of the Web site.

```
Law professor Marina Angel claims that Susan Glaspell's
one-act  play,  Trifles,  "raises  basic  jurisprudential
questions regarding the legitimacy of rebellion by those
closed out of a legal system" (sec. IIC, par. 16).
```

Source is a classic dramatic work: After the full title is first given in the text, include its abbreviation in parentheses, and use that abbreviation in subsequent parenthetical citations of the work.

Aeschylus	*Ag.*	*Agamemnon*
	Eum.	*Eumenides*
	Or.	*Oresteia*
Aristophanes	*Lys.*	*Lysistrata*
Euripides	*Bac.*	*Bacchae*
	Hip.	*Hippolytus*
	Med.	*Medea*
Molière	*Mis.*	*Le misanthrope*
	Tar.	*Tartuffe*
Shakespeare	*Ado*	*Much Ado about Nothing*
	Ant.	*Antony and Cleopatra*
	AWW	*All's Well That Ends Well*
	AYL	*As You Like It*
	Cor.	*Coriolanus*
	Cym.	*Cymbeline*
	Err.	*The Comedy of Errors*
	F1	First Folio edition (1623)
	F2	Second Folio edition (1632)
	Ham.	*Hamlet*
	1H4	*Henry IV, Part 1*
	2H4	*Henry IV, Part 2*
	H5	*Henry V*
	1H6	*Henry VI, Part 1*
	2H6	*Henry VI, Part 2*

	3H6	*Henry VI, Part 3*
	H8	*Henry VIII*
	JC	*Julius Caesar*
	Jn.	*King John*
	LLL	*Love's Labour's Lost*
	Lr.	*King Lear*
	Mac.	*Macbeth*
	MM	*Measure for Measure*
	MND	*A Midsummer Night's Dream*
	MV	*The Merchant of Venice*
	Oth.	*Othello*
	Per.	*Pericles*
	Q	Quarto edition
	R2	*Richard II*
	R3	*Richard III*
	Rom.	*Romeo and Juliet*
	Shr.	*The Taming of the Shrew*
	TGV	*The Two Gentlemen of Verona*
	Tim.	*Timon of Athens*
	Tit.	*Titus Andronicus*
	Tmp.	*The Tempest*
	TN	*Twelfth Night*
	TNK	*Two Noble Kinsmen*
	Tro.	*Troilus and Cressida*
	Wiv.	*The Merry Wives of Windsor*
	WT	*The Winter's Tale*
Sophocles	*Ant.*	*Antigone*
	OR	*Oedipus Rex,* or
	OT	*Oedipus Tyrannus*

```
Shylock protests against anti-Semitism when he asks, "If
you prick us do we not bleed?" (MV 3.1.59-60); Kate
asserts her independence in the face of male authority:
"What, shall I be appointed hours, as though belike I
knew not what to take and what to leave? Ha!" (Shr.
1.1.103-04). Yet both capitulate in the end.
```

Special Punctuation Considerations When Citing Sources

In general, put a parenthetical citation at the end of a sentence, clause, or quotation so that it will not interrupt the flow of the text.

Sentence ending with a period: The period follows the parenthetical note:

```
According to Christine Macleod, Carol will later use this
newfound linguistic freedom to redefine the term rape,
to give it a meaning specific to her specialized area of
discourse (209).
```

```
Willy tells his boys, "You take me, for instance. I
never have to wait in line to see a buyer. 'Willy Loman
is here!' That's all they have to know, and I go right
through" (320).
```

Sentence ends with a question mark or exclamation mark: Keep the end punctuation mark as set in the original; follow the parenthetical note with a period.

```
Willy is struck with the realization that Biff loves
him: "Isn't that—isn't that remarkable? Biff—he likes
me!" (355).
```

Quotation is indented: The note should follow the final period of the quotation.

```
In his essay "The Flaw of Oedipus," the critic Laszlo
Versenyi writes:

    Oedipus revealed to, and equated with, himself
    finds himself essentially unequal to the task,
    unequal to being what he now knows himself to be.
    Man the knower cannot live without knowing, yet
    he cannot live having found out. (25)
```

Models for Works Cited Entries

The list of works cited is an alphabetical list of the sources you have cited in your paper. As you assemble this list, keep in mind the following format guidelines:

- The works cited page begins on a new page at the end of the paper and is double spaced throughout.

- The first line of each entry is at the left margin; subsequent lines of the entry are indented one-half inch.

- Titles of books, journals, magazines, newspapers, plays, films, and television series are either underlined or italicized, but not both. MLA advises underlining.

- If the publisher is in the United States, give the name of the city but not the state. Names of cities outside of the United States may be accompanied by an abbreviation of the country, such as Manchester, Eng.

- Names of publishers are shortened to one word whenever possible.

- *UP* is the abbreviation for University Press.

- Disregard the articles—*a, an,* and *the*—when alphabetizing works cited; use the second word for alphabetical placement, but do not move the article to the end of the title.

- Abbreviate the months, except for May, June, and July.

- For periodicals, dates are given in this order: day month year, with no commas.

- If a newspaper or periodical title begins with an article (*a, an, the*), do not use the article in the works-cited entry. Thus, it is <u>New York Times</u>, not <u>The New York Times</u>.

On the following pages are examples of works-cited entries for various kinds of sources.

Books and Plays

A book with one author:

> Eliot, T.S. <u>Murder in the Cathedral</u>. New York: Harcourt, 1935.

A book with multiple authors: The name of the first author is reversed, but the names of subsequent authors are given in the normal order.

> Brockett, Oscar G., and Robert J. Ball. <u>The Essential Theatre</u>. 8th ed. Belmont: Wadsworth, 2004.
>
> Huberman, Jeffrey H., Brant L. Pope, and James Ludwig. <u>The Theatrical Imagination</u>. 2nd ed. Belmont: Wadsworth, 1996.

A play in a collection or anthology: For ranges of page numbers, the second number includes only the last two or three digits, depending on how many are different from the first page number.

> Mamet, David. <u>Oleanna</u>. <u>American Drama: Colonial to Contemporary</u>. Ed. Stephen Watt and Gary A. Richardson. Fort Worth: Harcourt, 1995. 1096-116.

An essay in a collection or anthology:

> Finke, Laurie A. "Painting Women: Images of Femininity in Jacobean Tragedy." <u>Performing Feminisms</u>. Ed. Sue-Ellen Case. Baltimore: Johns Hopkins UP, 1990. 223-36.

A translation:

> Dürrenmatt, Friedrich. <u>The Visit</u>. Trans. Patrick Bowles. New York: Grove, 1962.

> Pirandello, Luigi. <u>Six Characters in Search of an Author</u>. Trans. John Linstrum. <u>The Wadsworth Anthology of Drama</u>. Ed. W. B. Worthen. 4th ed. Boston: Wadsworth, 2004. 688-708.

An introduction, preface, foreword, or afterword: After the name of the author of the part, identify the kind of part. If the author is also the author of the work, give only the author's last name after *By*.

> Braun, Richard Emil. Introduction. <u>Antigone</u>. By Sophocles. Ed. and trans. Richard Emil Braun. New York: Oxford UP, 1973. 3-18.

An article in an encyclopedia or other reference work: If the article is signed, give the author's name before the title.

> "Molière." <u>Encyclopaedia Britannica</u>. 1991 ed.

Two or more works by the same author: Give the author's name in the first entry only. Thereafter, use three hyphens to signify that the name is the same as that in the preceding entry. Order these works by title.

> Brustein, Robert. <u>Dumbocracy in America: Studies in the Theatre of Guilt, 1987-1994</u>. Chicago: Dee, 1994.

> ---. <u>The Siege of the Arts: Collected Writings 1994-2001</u>. Chicago: Dee, 2001.

Articles in Periodicals

An article in a magazine:
> Mendelsohn, Daniel. "Theatres of War." <u>New Yorker</u>
> 12 Jan. 2004: 79-84.

An article in a journal in which each issue begins on page 1: Include the volume and issue number (e.g. 36.1) after the journal title.
> Resnikova, Eva. "Fool's Paradox." <u>National Review</u>
> 36.1 (1993): 54-56.

An article in a journal with pages numbered continuously throughout the volume: Omit the issue number.
> Macleod, Christine. "The Politics of Gender, Language
> and Hierarchy in Mamet's 'Oleanna.'" <u>Journal of</u>
> <u>American Studies</u> 29 (1995): 199-213.

An article in a newspaper:
> Richards, David. "The Jackhammer Voice of Mamet's
> 'Oleanna.'" <u>New York Times</u>, 8 Nov. 1992, sec 2:1+.

Note that "sec 2:1+" means that the article begins on page 1 of section 2 and is continued on a nonconsecutive page, not on page 2.

An unsigned article:
> "He Said . . . She Said . . . Who Did What?" <u>New York</u>
> <u>Times</u>, 15 Nov. 1992, sec. 2:6.

A review:
> Als, Hilton. "Arrested Development." Rev. of <u>Aunt Dan</u>
> <u>and Lemon</u>, by Wallace Shawn. Clurman Theatre, New
> York. <u>New Yorker</u> 5 Jan. 2004: 87-88.

Miscellaneous Nonprint Sources

An interview that you conducted: Identify the type of interview as *Personal interview, Telephone interview*, or *E-mail interview*.
> Kerr, Walter. Personal interview. 18 Oct. 1985.

A performance:
> <u>Uncle Vanya</u>. By Anton Chekhov. Trans. Ronald Hingley.
> Dir. Jonathan Kratzke. Perf. Pierre Hill, Kramden

```
Dropinski, and Richard Trabold. Shadow Playhouse,
    Ft. Meyers. 22 March 2004.
```

A lecture or speech: If the speech has a title, include it in quotation marks after the speaker's name.

```
Potts, Lee. Lecture. Acting 1000 class. University
    of Colorado-Boulder. 16 April 2001.
```

Electronic Publications

When citing online sources, you will probably offer two dates: the first date is the one in which the work was originally published; the second is the date on which you retrieved the work from a website. Present the URL (uniform resource locater) in angle brackets followed by a period. If the URL exceeds one line, begin a new line, ideally, after a slash. Do not insert a hyphen to signify continuation on the next line.

Online play: If available, include the year of first publication or performance after the title.

```
Shaw, Bernard. Pygmalion. 1916. 1 May 2004.
    <http://www.bartleby.com/138/index.html>.

Sophocles. Antigone. Trans. R. C. Jebb. 442 BCE.
    5 Mar. 2002. <http://classics.mit.edu/Sophocles/
    antigone.html>.
```

Article originally published in a scholarly journal, reproduced in an electronic periodical database: Instead of an extremely long URL, you can provide the URL of the database's search page. The date before the URL refers to the date on which you found the article.

```
Angel, Marina. "Criminal Law and Women: Giving the
    Abused Woman Who Kills a Jury of Her Peers Who
    Appreciate Trifles." American Criminal Law Review.
    33.2 (1996). 229-348. 24 June 2000 <http://
    web4.infotrac.galegroup.com/>.
```

Article originally published in a newspaper, reproduced in an electronic periodical database:

```
Rosen, Marjorie. "Playwrights Who Lunch." New York
    Times. 4 May 2003, late ed.: sec. 2:7. 6 June 2004
    <http://web.lexis-nexis.com/universe/>.
```

Article originally published in a magazine, reproduced in an electronic periodical database:

> Henry, William A. "Works: Three New American Plays."
> Rev. of <u>Oleanna</u>, by David Mamet. Orpheum Theatre, New
> York. <u>Time</u>. 2 Nov. 1992. 3 Apr. 2001 <http://
> web4.infotrac.galegroup.com/>.

Exercise 6-2

Assume that the following passages are taken from the same research paper. Parenthetical notes have been omitted, but information about their sources is given in brackets following each passage. First, write the list of works cited that would appear at the end of the paper (assuming that these are the paper's only sources). Second, insert parenthetical notes in the passages.

1. Sophocles believed that his dramatic style had peaked when he wrote <u>Oedipus at Colonus</u>.

   [You paraphrased this fact from page 64 of a book titled *Understanding the Psychology of Sophocles*. The book was written by William J. Grabowski and Larry John Greskamp. It was published in 1998 in Chicago, Illinois, by Hudson Press.]

2. Paul Roche believes there is a recurring theme in Sophocles's plays: "In the last play, the <u>Antigone</u>, Sophocles returns to the theme of the first [*Oedipus Rex*] and shows us again what happens when the ostensibly good man succumbs to pride."

   [You found this quotation on page x in the introduction to a collection of Sophocles's plays titled *The Oedipus Plays of Sophocles*. The editor and translator of the play, Paul Roche, also wrote the introduction. The book was published by the New American Library, Inc., in New York in 1958. The introduction spans pages ix–xviii.]

3. In the prologue, Ismene says, "[W]e are women, born unfit to battle men; / and we are subjects, while Kreon is king. / No, we must obey. . . ."

[This quotation is from lines 74, 75 and 76 of *Antigone*, written by Sophocles in 443 BCE. This version of the play was published in New York by the Oxford University Press in 1973. The editor is William Arrowsmith. The translator is Richard Emil Braun. This is the first quotation in your paper that is taken from the text of *Antigone*.]

4. According to Aristotle, an evil person who passes from favorable to unfavorable circumstances does not produce the tragic effects of pity and fear.

[You have paraphrased this from Aristotle's *Poetics*, which you found last Thursday online at the Internet Classics Archive <http://classics.mit.edu/Aristotle/poetics>. You found the information in section 2, part XIII. Aristotle wrote *Poetics* in 350 BCE. This version has been translated by S. H. Butcher.]

5. What did Protagoras mean when he said, "Man is the measure of all things?"

[You found the quotation of Protagoras on page 234 of *Classic Drama*, a journal with continuously numbered pages throughout the volume, in an article titled "A Historian's View of the Oedipus Plays." The article was published in volume 23, issue 2 in June 1992. The article spans pages 219-254. The author of the article is Susan McArthur.]

Student Research Paper

The following research paper is written in the argumentative mode. It differs from analysis mainly in that it argues against an existing opinion. Notice that those views, or counterarguments, are set out in the introductory paragraph. The second paragraph contains the author's thesis and points of proof.

6-2: "We all go through the same thing," says Mrs. Hale in this 2003 production of *Trifles* at Messiah College, directed by Kasi L. Krenzer Marshall. Photographer: Melissa Engle.

Chris Gluckman

Prof. Molly LeClair

Introduction to Theatre

6 May 2002

Guilty or "Knot": The Virtue

of Vigilante Justice

Susan Glaspell's one-act play, <u>Trifles</u>, first performed in 1916, is a tightly wound drama about two women who solve a murder and then conspire to hide the evidence from the law. The murderer is Minnie Wright, an abused woman who has hanged her husband from the rafters of their bedroom in retaliation for his strangling her pet canary. The women's ethical dilemma-- whether or not to conceal the evidence--has launched many healthy discussions about the validity of prosecuting women who use violence against their abusive spouses, not in self-defense during a struggle, which is clearly justifiable, but in an act of aggression while their husbands' backs are turned or while they sleep.

Alan Dershowitz, renowned defense attorney, argues that abuse is no excuse for murder. He points out that not all victims of abuse resort to violence (5-6); they use other options, such as seeking safe shelter. Also, Dershowitz says that to excuse such retaliation is to sanction vigilantism, a dangerous step toward anarchy (4-5).

And yet, given the play's historical context, one can justify the women's decision to conceal the evidence and thus protect Minnie from prosecution. Minnie did have other options, including seeking shelter at her neighbors' home, but her demeanor at the time her husband's body was found indicated insanity. And Mrs. Wright definitely took the law into her own hands when she planned and executed the murder of her husband, but in this case, justice is better served without the interference of the law: Minnie would not have gotten a fair trial because her jury would have been constituted entirely of men who would have no regard for mitigating circumstances. Furthermore, the options open to Minnie would have relegated her to a life of destitution, the likes of which no one is likely to survive.

In his book, <u>The Abuse Excuse and Other Cop-outs, Sob Stories, and Evasions of Responsibility</u>, Alan Dershowitz writes, "Nowhere in the civilized world do self-defense laws justify the killing or maiming of a <u>sleeping</u> spouse by a woman who has the option of either leaving or calling the police" (28-29). In <u>Trifles</u>, Minnie Wright has killed her husband while he slept, and surely she would have found shelter and sympathy at Mrs. Hale's house.

But the abuse has apparently driven Minnie insane. John Wright had kept her isolated: Mrs. Hale says their home is a "lonesome place" because it's "down in a hollow and you don't see the road" (56). John Wright wouldn't acquire a telephone because, he said, "folks talked too much anyway," and all he asked was "peace and quiet" (50). Minnie's clothes were shabby, which made her too ashamed to join in the women's social activities, such as the Ladies Aid. Mrs. Hale shivers as she describes John: "a hard man. . . . Like a raw wind that gets to the bone" (57). Minnie had no children, and that could well have been John's decision, or the result of his abuse. Minnie's only company had been a canary that sang, and John, apparently in a fit of rage, given the broken door and separated hinge of the cage, had broken its neck.

Mrs. Hale and Mrs. Peters appreciate the effects of isolation. "If there'd been years and years of nothing, then a bird to sing to you, it would be awful--still, after the bird was still" remarks Mrs. Hale (58). Mrs. Peters agrees: "I know what stillness is. When we homesteaded in Dakota, and my first baby died--after he was two years old, and me with no other

then--"(58). And Mrs. Peters appreciates the horror of
witnessing the murder of a beloved pet. When she was a girl, a
boy had taken a hatchet to her kitten. "If they hadn't held me
back," she says, "I would have--hurt him" (58).

Isolation is a powerful torture, which is why prisoners so
fearfully dread solitary confinement. Apparently it had driven
Minnie over the edge because when Mr. Hale found her sitting in
her kitchen the morning after John's murder, she looked "queer"
and "kind of done up" (50). She sat in her rocking chair,
pleating her apron, not looking at Mr. Hale as he asked her
what had happened, laughing bitterly, nodding. Perhaps she was
telling the truth when she claimed not to know who killed John.
Someone came into their bedroom, slipped a rope around his
neck, and strangled him, and Minnie says she didn't wake up
because she "sleep[s] sound" (51)--a story so preposterous that
only an insane person, or someone who has blocked the
experience from her consciousness, would have told it.

Why didn't Mrs. Hale and Mrs. Peters turn the evidence over
to the men? Wouldn't the men be able to see it not only as
evidence that Minnie murdered John but also as evidence that
she had done it as the result of years of pent-up rage at her
abuser? Wouldn't a jury take these mitigating factors into
account? Probably not. Juries of the early 20th century, when
the play takes place, were made up entirely of men. The United
States Constitution does not guarantee "a jury of one's peers"
in those exact words. And yet the term is often used in legal
deliberations as a matter of interpretation. At the July 4,
1876, centennial celebration of independence in Philadelphia,
Susan B. Anthony read the following statement:

> The right of trial by jury of one's peers was so
> jealously guarded that States refused to ratify the
> original constitution until it was guaranteed by the
> [S]ixth [A]mendment. And yet the women of this nation

have never been allowed a jury of their peers--being
tried in all cases by men, native and foreign, educated
and ignorant, virtuous and vicious. Young girls have
been arraigned in our courts for the crime of
infanticide; tried, convicted, hanged--victims,
perchance, of judge, jurors, advocates--while no woman's
voice could be heard in their defense. (qtd. in Angel
sec. III-C)

The drama of Glaspell's play hinges upon the difference in
the ways that women and men solve problems. The men's approach
is methodical. Minnie is either guilty or not; their
"either/or" thinking pattern is reflected in the county
attorney's recurring, condescending question about Minnie's
quilt: "Well, ladies, have you decided whether she going to
quilt it or knot it?" (57). The women's thinking pattern is
less rigid, complicated by what Suzy Clarkson Holstein
describes in her essay titled "Silent Justice in a Different
Key" "the messier pattern of day-to-day life and shared
responsibilities and experience" (par. 15). This ethic based,
as psychologist Carol Gilligan phrases it, upon a
"psychological logic of relationships" rather than a "formal
logic of fairness" (73) is what necessitates a jury that
contains women.

As Dershowitz points out, all victims of abuse have options
other than murder. But let's examine Minnie's options. Calling
the police to intervene was not a viable option for Minnie. She
had no telephone. Besides, in her day, wife abuse was legally
sanctioned by the "rule of thumb," the right of a husband to
beat his wife with a rod no thicker than his thumb (Angel sec.
III-B). If the laws against physical abuse were so weak,
certainly the laws against emotional abuse were even weaker.
How seriously would the sheriff take her concerns if she had

come to him with a dead canary, expressing the fear that she
would be next?

Minnie could have left her home and gone . . . where? There
was no such thing as a battered women's shelter, so she would
have to live with friends or relatives. Mrs. Hale certainly
would have provided temporary shelter, but it is not realistic
to expect anyone to provide permanent housing for her. There
was no chance that Minnie would eventually gain a legal right
to her own house. Personal property belonged to the husband
absolutely. Married women could not enter into independent
contracts, sue anyone, sell anything, or hold jobs without
their husbands' permission (Bardaglio 31).

Divorce? Minnie would never have been able to obtain one.
Grounds for divorce included infidelity and desertion, neither
of which was relevant in Minnie's case, and cruelty, which
Minnie would have had difficulty proving. In A Treatise on the
Law of Domestic Relations, written in 1895, James Schouler
writes,

> [W]e subject ourselves by marriage to a law of family.
> . . . And although the voluntary act of two parties
> brings them within the law, they cannot voluntarily
> retreat when so minded. To an unusual extent, therefore,
> is the law of family above, and independent of, the
> individual. (qtd. in Grossberg xv)

Minnie Wright would not have survived without shelter,
money, or health care. She was hopelessly trapped in a loveless
marriage with a cruel man. It's no wonder she killed him. And
Mrs. Hale and Mrs. Peters were right to protect her from the
law. History and fiction are full of famous lawbreakers--
Antigone, Harriet Tubman, and Rosa Parks, to name only three.
Sometimes justice can be gotten only when the law is broken.

Works Cited

Angel, Marina. "Criminal Law and Women: Giving the Abused Woman
    Who Kills a Jury of Her Peers Who Appreciate Trifles."
    American Criminal Law Review. 33.2 (1996). 229-348. 24 June
    2000 <http://web4.infotrac.galegroup.com/>.

Bardaglio, Peter W. Reconstructing the Household: Families,
    Sex, and the Law in the Nineteenth-Century South. Chapel
    Hill: U of North Carolina P, 1995.

Dershowitz, Alan M. The Abuse Excuse and Other Cop-outs, Sob
    Stories, and Evasions of Responsibility. Boston: Little,
    1994.

Glaspell, Susan. Trifles. How to Write about Theatre and Drama.
    By Suzanne Hudson. Fort Worth: Harcourt 2000. 49-60.

Grossberg, Michael. Governing the Hearth: Law and the Family in
    Nineteenth-Century America. Chapel Hill: U of North
    Carolina P, 1985.

Holstein, Suzy Clarkson. "Silent Justice in a Different Key:
    Glaspell's 'Trifles.'" The Midwest Quarterly 44 (2003). 7
    May 2004 <http://web4.infotrac.galegroup.com/>.

Revising and Editing Your Research Paper

Use the following checklist to be certain that your paper is ready for submission. Consult the Handbook at the end of this book for guidance in issues of word choice, sentence structure, and punctuation.

Revision and Editing Checklist

☐   Thesis is clear and present. It is written in the appropriate mode of discourse. The thesis is narrow and specific enough to be adequately supported in the space of the paper but general enough to need support.

☐   Points of proof are clear and present. Each point answers the proof question. Each point is narrow and specific enough to be supported adequately in one to three paragraphs and general enough to need support. If the paper is argumentative, points of proof include refutations of counterpoints.

☐   The introduction contains specific details. It leads the reader to the thesis; it does not lead the reader to believe the essay will be about something it is not about. If the essay is argumentative, the introduction contains a counterthesis and counterpoints, and it clearly identifies opponents.

☐   Essay adheres to the plan set out in the points of proof.

☐   Body paragraphs are unified, adequately developed, organized, and coherent.

☐   The conclusion solidifies the main point without merely repeating the thesis and points of proof. Conclusion is unified and developed. The conclusion does not bring up new issues.

☐   Sentences are well constructed. There are no run-ons or fragments. Sentences are correctly punctuated.

☐   Words are correct and well chosen.

☐   All quotations use acknowledgment phrases.

☐   Sources are correctly cited in text.

☐   Paraphrases and summaries are legitimate, not unintentionally plagiarized.

☐   Title is appropriate.

☐   Paper, including the works cited page, is properly formatted.

Handbook

Word Choice	*Verbs*
	Pronouns
	Wordiness
	Tone
	Vivid Words
Sentence Structures	*Sentence Fragments*
	Run-on Sentences
	Awkward Sentence Constructions
Punctuation	*Comma*
	Semicolon
	Colon
	Dash
	Apostrophe
	Quotation Marks
	Ellipsis Dots
	Brackets

No matter how interesting and insightful the content of your essay or research paper, your reader's interest will flag if there are distracting errors in word choice, sentence structure, and punctuation. This section of *Writing about Theatre and Drama* is designed as a reference manual to help you avoid such errors. Throughout this handbook, incorrect sentences are marked with an **X**.

Word Choice

According to Mark Twain, "The difference between the right word and the almost right word is the difference between lightning and the lightning bug."[1] But how do we know what the right word is?

Verbs

One way to improve your writing is to choose your verbs carefully. **Verbs** are words that express an action or a state of being.

Active versus Passive Verbs

Use active rather than passive verbs whenever possible. Active constructions create direct, vigorous sentences. Passive constructions, although useful when you do not want to emphasize the actor, tend toward wordiness and awkwardness. In an **active construction**, the subject of the verb is doing the acting. In a **passive construction**, the subject is being acted upon.

To spot the passive voice in your paper, look for the following:

- sentences with forms of the verb *be* (*am, is, are, was, were, being, been*) followed by a past participle (usually, verbs ending in *ed, en,* or *t)*
- phrases beginning with *by*

Active: The oracle **predicts** Oedipus's fate.

Passive: Oedipus's fate **is predicted** by the oracle.

Strong Verbs versus Weak Verbs

Choose simple, active verbs. Replace, wherever possible, phrases using forms of *be, have,* and *do* with another verb. In addition, rather than qualify a verb with an adverb, search for a more precise verb:

Weak	Strong
is symbolic of	symbolizes
is representative of	represents
does a dance	waltzes
has a hunch	suspects
walks slowly	ambles
knows somehow	intuits

H-1: Oedipus appears, having punished King Laius's murderer, in this 1990 production of *Oedipus Rex* at the University at Albany, State University of New York, directed by Jarka Burian. Photographer: Andi Lyons.

Verb Tenses

Generally, write in the **present tense** when you are recounting words or actions that happen during the course of a play:

```
Teiresias tells Oedipus the awful truth.
```

Use the **present perfect tense** (with the helping verb *have* or *has*) when recounting an event that occurred previous to an event written in the present tense:

```
When the play begins, Oedipus has solved the riddle of the
sphinx.
```

Use the present perfect tense, also, to relate ongoing action:

```
Oedipus has served as a wise and gentle ruler of Thebes.
```

Use the **past tense** when offering historical background:

```
Sophocles wrote Oedipus the King about the year 430 BCE.
```

Use the **past perfect tense** (with the helping verb *had*) when recounting an event previous to an event written in the past tense:

```
Sophocles had written more than 120 plays by the time he
wrote Oedipus at Colonus.
```

Subject-Verb Agreement

A verb must agree with its subject in number: if the subject is singular, the verb must be singular; it the subject is plural, the verb must be plural. (Most verbs ending in *s* are singular: *thinks, writes, has, is, was*). In the following examples, the subjects are underlined once; the verbs are underlined twice:

```
Oedipus vows to find Laius's murderer.
```

Long phrases between the subject and its verb can cause errors in agreement.

X The question of whether people determine their own fates or are helpless victims of uncontrollable forces need to be answered.

Subject-verb disagreements often occur when the subject is a singular, indefinite pronoun, such as the following:

one	anyone	everybody	something
no one	anybody	everything	each
nobody	anything	someone	either
nothing	everyone	somebody	neither

X Not one of Oedipus's efforts to trick fate have succeeded.

Pronouns

A **pronoun** is a word that takes the place of a noun. A **first-person** pronoun (such as *I, me, us, we*) refers to the speaker. A **second-person** pronoun (*you*) refers to the person being spoken to. A **third-person** pronoun (*he, she, it, they, them*) refers to the person or thing being spoken about.

Avoiding "I"

While it is not unequivocally wrong to use first-person pronouns in formal writing, it is a mistake to focus more upon yourself than upon your topic, as is the case in the following sentence:

> **X** Now that I have read some critical essays on Eugene O'Neill's <u>The Iceman Cometh</u>, I realize that the play is about characters who cannot face the truth about themselves.

Pronoun Case

With a compound subject or object, the easiest way to be sure you are using the correct pronoun is to mentally cross off all the words in the phrase except the pronoun in question and read the sentence without them:

> Cora's pipe-dream is that ~~Chuck and~~ **she** will buy a farm in New Jersey.

> When Pearl hints that Rocky is a pimp, Rocky gives ~~Margie and~~ **her** a hard stare.

Choose *who* or *whoever* when the pronoun will serve as the subject for a verb:

> **Who** is the biggest self-deceiver in <u>The Iceman Cometh</u>?

Choose *whom* when the pronoun will serve as an object:

> **Whom** does Harry Hope think he is deceiving?

Following are two ways of simplifying the choice between *who* and *whom*:

- Convert a question into a statement:

  > Harry Hope thinks he is deceiving **whom.**

- Substitute *he* or *him*. If *he* fits, choose *who*; if *him* fits, choose *whom*.

  > Harry Hope thinks he is deceiving **him.**

Pronoun-Antecedent Agreement

Pronouns usually refer to some specific noun. That noun is the pronoun's **antecedent**. In the following sentence, *Harry Hope* is the antecedent of the pronoun *his*:

```
Harry Hope has stayed inside the saloon ever since his
wife's death.
```

A pronoun must agree with its antecedent in three ways:
- number (singular or plural)
- gender (masculine, feminine, or neuter)
- person (first, second, or third)

Mistakes occur most often when the antecedent is singular and the pronoun is plural, as in the following sentence:

```
X  Every man in Harry Hope's saloon has their illusions.
```

The indefinite pronouns listed on page 221 are singular. Pronouns that refer to them must also be singular. The following sentences suffer from pronoun-antecedent disagreement:

```
X  In Harry Hope's saloon, everyone hides behind their
   illusions.
X  Neither of the men is able to accept the truth about
   their life.
```

The sentences above could be repaired either by changing the antecedents to plural words, or changing the pronouns to singular words:

```
In Harry Hope's saloon, the customers hide behind their
illusions.

In Harry Hope's saloon, everyone hides behind his or her
illusions.

The men are not able to accept the truth about their lives.

Neither of the men is able to accept the truth about his
life.
```

Unclear Pronoun References

A pronoun must refer to someone or something specific. The pronouns *this* and *it* are most often the culprits in an unclear reference, as in the following example:

> **X** Hickey is not a hero according to Arthur Miller's definition because he is not nobler than the forces that bring him down. He is not a hero according to Aristotle's definition because he doesn't arouse our sympathy or admiration. **This** is why we cannot classify The Iceman Cometh as a tragedy.

The pronoun *This* in the last sentence above refers to ideas in the sentences that precede it, not to any specific word. Such a vague use of *this* is usually regarded as a mistake in formal writing. You might correct the last sentence in the passage above as follows:

> Our inability to classify Hickey as a tragic hero prevents us from classifying The Iceman Cometh as a tragedy.

H-2: "All I want is to see you happy," says Hickey, the hardware salesman who comes to "save" the denizens of Harry Hope's saloon in this 1979 production of *The Iceman Cometh* at Lewis University, directed by Harold McCay. Photographer: Harold McCay.

Wordiness

Your writing should be free of unnecessary words. Wordiness is not related to sentence length. Many long sentences are terse; many short sentences are wordy. To proofread for wordiness, look for redundancies and unnecessary prepositional phrases:

Redundant	Better
red in color	red
shaped like an octagon	octagonal
over-exaggerate	exaggerate
the month of August	August
basic fundamentals	basics (or fundamentals)

Unnecessary Prepositional Phrases	Better
come to the conclusion	conclude
in the event that	if
due to the fact that	because
in today's society	today
In the script, it says	The script says
In the article, it says	The article says

Proofread for repetitiousness:

X *A Raisin in the Sun* is about **pride and self-respect.**

X Mama is **bossy and domineering.**

X The play's **universality and its appeal to audiences everywhere** are its strengths.

Passive and weak verbs cause wordiness, as does the *There is/are* construction:

X Walter **is forgiven** by Mama.

X Walter **is** under the impression that material wealth will make him a man.

X **There is** growth in the Younger family's sense of dignity.

Another step you can take to eliminate wordiness is to delete the word *very* and its synonyms, such as *extremely*, *greatly*, and *quite*, every time they occur. If you are left with a weak word or phrase, change it to a strong one. For example, change *extremely large* to *massive* or *huge*, *very many* to *numerous*, and *very many times* to *often* or *frequently*. Never write *very*

H-3: Mama's gift from her grandson is a new hat for gardening in her new backyard in this performance of *A Raisin in the Sun* at the University of Iowa in 1999, directed by Harriette M. Pierce. Photographer: Reggie Morrow.

unique. If a thing is unique, it is one of a kind and cannot be made more so with the addition of *very*.

Remove all announcements of your intentions and statements of purpose. You can make your point with announcing it:

X In this essay I will show that . . .
X The purpose of this essay is to . . .

Tone

If you are writing or speaking informally, you may say anything you want. If you are writing or speaking formally, however, there are correct and incorrect choices. If *whom* is correct, use it when the occasion calls for formality, even if, to your ear, it sounds stilted.

Avoid words or phrases that dictionaries label informal, slang, colloquial, archaic, illiterate, nonstandard, obsolete, or substandard. The word *butt*, for example, is a coarsened form of *buttocks* and is not considered polite language. Such words lower the tone of your essay.

Vivid Words

Avoid clichés and overworked phrases such as *all in all, to make a long story short, easier said than done, better late than never.*

Choose vivid, specific words. You could write, "*Aida* is pretty to look at, with lots of tropical colors and objects," or you could emulate Hedy Weiss, who writes:

> The imagery is riveting—from the blood red sails of the Egyptian navy's ships that carry Nubian slaves who are the spoils of war along the river Nile, to the starkly silhouetted palm trees reflected in the glassy water, to the sight of the statuesque women sinuously carrying their laundry basins atop their heads.[2]

Which description is more interesting? Which description gives the reader a clearer sense of the play?

Sentence Structures

When constructing sentences, heed the advice of Henry David Thoreau: "A sentence should read as if its author, had he held a plough instead of a pen, could have drawn a furrow deep and straight to the end."[3]

Sentence Fragments

Sentence fragments are word groups that pose as complete sentences but are missing one or more essential elements—usually a subject or a verb. Although fragments are deliberately used at times for creative effect—especially in plays wherein characters speaks informally, they are usually mistakes in formal writing.

Length is not the issue when it comes to fragments. A very short word group may be a complete sentence, and a very long word group may be a fragment.

Fragments are often easy to identify in isolation. When they are positioned, however, inside a paragraph, they are harder to spot because the paragraph sounds correct when read quickly. For example:

> **X** Willy Loman is a salesman who gets by on nothing but
>   appearances. A smile and a shoeshine. That's all he
>   needs to make a sale.

To repair a fragment, either incorporate it into a nearby sentence, or give it the subject or verb needed to complete it.

A frequent cause of fragments is to mistake a dependent clause for an independent clause. **Dependent clauses**, also called **subordinate clauses**, are word groups that contain a subject and a verb but cannot stand alone as sentences. For example:

> **X** Although Biff, the princely high school football hero,
>   tries desperately to live up to his father's dreams.

The fragment above is a dependent clause because it begins with the word *although*, which is a **subordinate conjunction**. Other common subordinate conjunctions are *if, when, whenever, even though, unless, because, after, whereas, wherever,* and *since*. For a sentence to be complete, the dependent clause must be attached to an independent clause that completes the idea.

Another frequent cause of fragments is to mistake a participle for a verb. **Participles** are verb forms that are used as adjectives:

> **X** For example, Willy, **encouraged** by his brother, Ben, to
>   keep dreaming of striking it rich.

Sentence fragments, together with run-on sentences, send a clear signal that the writer is not in control of his or her sentences. Finding and correcting them is worth the effort.

Run-on Sentences

Run-on sentences, like fragments, are a common mistake. Run-ons consist of two or more independent clauses that have been incorrectly joined. There are two types of run-on sentences: fused sentences and comma splices.

Fused sentences are composed of two or more independent clauses joined without the benefit of any punctuation:

> **X** Torvald thinks Nora is a wastrel she spends money faster
>   than he earns it.

Comma splices are composed of two or more independent clauses joined by only a comma:

> **X** Torvald thinks Nora is a wastrel, she spends money
> faster than he earns it.

Of the many ways to repair a run-on sentence, the following are four of the easiest:

1. Separate the two independent clauses into separate sentences:

    > Torvald thinks Nora is a wastrel. She spends money
    > faster than he earns it.

2. Separate the two independent clauses with a comma plus a **coordinating conjunction** (*but, or, yet, for, and, nor, so*):

    > Torvald thinks Nora is a wastrel, for she spends money
    > faster than he earns it.

3. Separate the two independent clauses with a semicolon:

    > Torvald thinks Nora is a wastrel; she spends money
    > faster than he earns it.

4. Convert one of the independent clauses into a dependent clause:

    > Torvald thinks Nora is a wastrel because she spends
    > money faster than he earns it.

A frequent cause of run-on sentences is to connect independent clauses with adverbs like *however* instead of coordinating conjunctions:

> **X** Nora is tired of performing tricks, however, she dances
> the tarantella for Torvald.

Another common cause of run-on sentences is to force the pronoun *it* or *its* into the same sentence as the noun to which it refers:

> **X** Nora worries about the letter, its presence in the
> mailbox drives her to distraction.

Awkward Sentence Constructions

Constructing graceful sentences is a skill that requires practice. Cleanth
Brooks and Robert Penn Warren offer their advice: "[The writer ought] to
learn to recognize rhythmic defects in his own prose as symptoms of poor or
defective arrangement of sentences and sentence elements."[4]

Misplaced and Dangling Modifiers

A **misplaced modifier** is an adjective, adverb, or modifying phrase or clause
that is in the wrong place in the sentence.

> **X**   Godot never comes, much to the disappointment of
>   Vladimir, whatever he represents.

In the above sentence, "whatever he represents" modifies (or describes)
Godot, not Vladimir, and so should be placed next to *Godot*.

A **dangling modifier** is a more subtle problem. In this construction, the
word the modifier is supposed to modify is missing from the sentence,
leaving the modifier "dangling."

> **X**   While reading Beckett's <u>Waiting for Godot</u>, the
>   characters Estragon and Vladimir become conflated.

The sentence above says that Estragon and Vladimir become conflated while
they read *Waiting for Godot*, which is impossible, of course. The characters
are in the play; they don't read the play. The writer of the above sentence is
probably trying to avoid the use of the pronoun *I* but in so doing has created
another problem. The above sentence could be corrected as follows:

> While reading Beckett's <u>Waiting for Godot</u>, one tends to
> conflate the characters Estragon and Vladimir.

Or:

> Readers of Beckett's <u>Waiting for Godot</u> tend to conflate the
> characters Estragon and Vladimir.

Faulty Predication

Faulty predication is the term for a sentence that claims someone or
something is being or doing something unlikely or impossible.

> **X** Beckett's <u>Waiting for Godot</u> believes that emotional interdependency can be either healthy or destructive.
>
> **X** An example of cruelty is Pozzo, who whips and curses Lucky.

The second sentence above says that a person is an example of cruelty. Actually, the acts of whipping and cursing are examples of cruelty. You might correct the sentence as follows:

> Pozzo's whipping and cursing of Lucky exemplify cruelty.

Faulty Comparison

One common fault in making comparisons is the **incomplete comparison**.

> **X** Pozzo and Lucky are more exaggerated characters.

More exaggerated than what? The comparison needs to be finished.

Another mistake is to compare things that can't be compared.

> **X** The tie that binds Estragon and Vladimir exists but is less visible than with Pozzo and Lucky.

The sentence above compares a noun (*tie*) to a prepositional phrase (*with Pozzo and Lucky*). The sentence might be corrected as follows:

> The tie that binds Estragon and Vladimir exists but is less visible than the tie that binds Pozzo and Lucky.

Faulty Definition

The most common type of **faulty definition** incorrectly defines a concept or object as a time or a place.

> **X** Theatre of the absurd is when characters live in an unfathomable universe.
>
> **X** Theatre of the absurd is where characters live in an unfathomable universe.

Avoid the "is when" or "is where" construction unless the thing you are defining really is a time or a place. The sentence above could be corrected as follows:

```
Theatre of the absurd is a style of drama featuring
characters who live in an unfathomable universe.
```

Another source of faulty definitions is the "is because" construction:

```
X   The reason Estragon and Vladimir continue to wait for
    Godot is because they don't like the alternative.
```

Instead of *because*, the word should be *that*.

Unnecessary Shifts

Be consistent in the use of pronoun person. For example, do not shift from third person to second person.

```
X   Audiences of the 1950s did not know what to think about
    Waiting for Godot. Was it a masterpiece or an empty bit
    of drivel? You couldn't be sure at first.
```

It is a mistake to shift verb tense, voice, or mood midway through a sentence or paragraph.

```
X   Estragon struggles with his boots, and Vladimir asks,
    "It hurts?" Later, Estragon asked, "It hurts?"
```

Mixed Constructions

Sometimes beginning writers start a sentence one way and end it another way. For example, the following sentence begins as a statement and ends as a question.

```
X   Vladimir asks the boy if he has a message from Godot and
    what is the message?
```

Avoid shifting between indirect and direct discourse. In direct discourse, the writer addresses the reader directly.

```
X   Vladimir agrees that if Godot comes tomorrow they'll be
    saved, but just in case, bring a good bit of rope.
```

In the following mixed construction a prepositional phrase (beginning with *By*) incorrectly serves as the subject of the verb *reveals*.

X By comparing Lucky's speech in <u>Waiting for Godot</u> to the
monologues in James Joyce's <u>Ulysses</u> reveals that Beckett
was validating an earlier literary innovation.

Simply deleting the word *By* would correct the sentence above.

Lack of Parallel Construction

Parallelism adds elegance and rhythm to our sentences. The idea is to
present two or more similar items in the same grammatical form. The
following sentences could be improved by parallel construction.

X Lucky is beaten, cursed, and has a sore on his neck from
the rope. [two passive verbs and one active verb]

X The philosophical dilemma dramatized in <u>Waiting for
Godot</u> is not so much whether we have free will as the
decisions that we make. [one noun clause and one simple noun
modified by an adjective clause]

Punctuation

In his humorous "Notes on Punctuation," Dr. Lewis Thomas writes,
"Exclamation marks are the most irritating of all. Look! they say, look at
what I just said! How amazing is my thought! It is like being forced to watch
someone else's small child jumping up and down crazily in the center of the
living room shouting to attract attention."[5] We must punctuate both correctly
and wisely.

Comma

Four basic rules, if followed, will usually result in the correct use of the
comma.

Rule 1

Use a comma after an introductory modifying phrase or adverb clause:

Despite the play's flaws, Christopher Marlowe's <u>Doctor
Faustus</u> remains influential.

Do not place a comma after a noun clause or phrase serving as the subject of a verb. It is a mistake to separate a subject from its verb with a comma:

> **X**   What Marlowe created in his tale of the ambitious
>   doctor, is an archetypal figure of western civilization.

Rule 2

Use commas between words, phrases, and clauses in a series of three or more. Use a comma before the word *and* that precedes the final item in the series:

> In order to be saved, it is necessary for Doctor Faustus to
> renounce magic, curse Mephistophilis, believe in God's
> mercy, and repent.

Rule 3

Use a comma before a coordinating conjunction—*but, or, yet, for, and, nor, so* (remember the acronym BOYFANS)—that links independent clauses. An independent clause can stand alone as a complete sentence:

> The Good Angel warns Faustus of God's wrath, and the Bad
> Angel extols the power of magic.

It is a mistake to place a comma before a coordinating conjunction that is not linking independent clauses:

> **X**   Doctor Faustus has been compared to Everyman because of
>   its morality drama format, and to Macbeth because of its
>   theme that power corrupts.

Rule 4

Set off nonessential words, phrases, and clauses with commas. A word, phrase, or clause is nonessential if the sentence retains its complete meaning without the word, phrase, or clause:

> Faustus, nevertheless, agrees to bind himself to Lucifer
> after twenty-four years.

> Robin, a hungry clown, knows better than to sell his soul
> to the devil for a shoulder of mutton.

Clauses beginning with *that* are essential and are not set off with commas:

```
The power that Faustus uses to fool the horse-courser is
the squandered power of a dissipated magician.
```

Clauses beginning with *which* are nonessential and are set off with commas:

```
Faustus's power, which he squanders at the end of the play
in pranks like fooling the horse-courser, has not satisfied
him.
```

Clauses beginning with *who*, *whom*, or *whose* can be essential or nonessential. If the adjective clause refers to a specific person, it is nonessential and should be set off with commas:

```
Doctor Faustus, who seeks knowledge, learns that knowledge
for its own sake is an empty acquisition.
```

If the adjective clause does not refer to someone specific, the clause is essential and should not be set off with commas:

```
Anyone who seeks knowledge should be warned that knowledge
for its own sake is an empty acquisition.
```

When quoting, consider the acknowledgment phrase—the phrase that tells who is speaking or writing—as nonessential, and set it off with commas.

```
Doctor Faustus says, "[A]ll is dross that is not Helena."
```

Consider *yes*, *no*, mild interjections, terms of direct address, interrogative tags, and sharply contrasting elements as nonessential.

```
Yes, Doctor Faustus sold his soul to the devil.
No, he was never able to redeem himself.
Well, Doctor Faustus wasn't so smart after all.
Doctor Faustus, are you listening?
Doctor Faustus went to hell, didn't he?
Doctor Faustus, not Robin, was the fool.
```

Semicolon

Use a semicolon to separate independent clauses not joined by a coordinating conjunction. Think of the semicolon as a weak period, not as a strong comma:

```
The central conflict in Doctor Faustus is not between
characters; it is within the mind of Faustus himself.
```

Colon

A colon separates a summary or series from an independent clause:

```
Doctor Faustus is entertained by the seven deadly sins:
Pride, Covetousness, Envy, Wrath, Gluttony, Sloth, and
Lechery.
```

In accordance with this rule, it would be a mistake to place a colon after a word group that is not an independent clause:

```
X   Robin promises to buy Dick all kinds of drinks, such as:
    wine, sherry, muscadine, malmsey, and "whippincrust."
```

Another use of the colon is to follow an independent clause acknowledging a quotation's source:

```
Faustus admires Helen of Troy: "Oh thou art fairer than the
evening air / Clad in the beauty of a thousand stars."
```

Dash

Think of the dash as a strong comma; it signals a longer pause than that signaled by the comma. The dash has two main uses. The first is to set off a short summary after an independent clause:

```
Doctor Faustus finally meets the angel who was thrown from
heaven for his insolence--Lucifer.
```

The second use of the dash is to set off an interrupting phrase that contains commas:

```
Three devils--Lucifer, Belzebub, and Mephistophilis--appear
to Doctor Faustus.
```

Most computers do not have a dash on the keyboard. To make a dash, type two hyphens (--). Do not use a space before or after a dash. Many computer programs will convert the two hyphens to a dash automatically.

Apostrophe

Apostrophes have two main uses. The first is to create contractions such as *don't, can't, they're,* and *it's.* Contractions are two words condensed. The apostrophe stands for the omitted letters. Avoid using contractions in formal writing.

The second use of the apostrophe is to show possession. The following examples show how to make nouns possessive.

- If the possessive noun is singular, add *'s*:

```
The doctor does not heed the angel's advice.
Doctor Faustus's mistake cost him dearly.
```

- If the possessive noun is plural and does not end in *s*, add *'s*:

```
In many productions, the roles of the seven deadly sins
are women's roles.
```

H-4: Faustus cannot be restrained from signing with his blood a vow to serve Lucifer in this 2003 production of *Doctor Faustus*, performed at Baylor University, directed by Steven Pounders. Photographer: Jason Raddin

- If the possessive noun is plural and ends in *s*, simply add an apostrophe:

```
The Seven Deadly Sins' appearances startle Faustus.
```

The personal possessive pronouns—*hers, ours, theirs, yours, whose, its*—do not contain apostrophes.

Quotation Marks

Copy quoted material exactly, including the internal punctuation. Some adjustments may be made, however, to the end marks and to initial capitalization.

Double Quotation Marks

Place double quotation marks around direct quotations.

```
Doctor Faustus says, "Che serà serà."
```

Do not put quotation marks around indirect quotations or paraphrases—often signaled by the word *that*.

```
Doctor Faustus is being a fatalist when he says that what
will be will be.
```

Place quotation marks around the titles of songs, short stories, essays, poems, and articles in newspapers and magazines. **Underline** or **italicize** titles of plays, books, magazines, newspapers, journals, movies, television programs, works of art, and foreign words. In short, put quotation marks around the titles of smaller works, and underline or italicize the titles of larger works.

```
A review titled "Abbott's Best Yet" in the June 1960 issue
of National Play Review compares Damn Yankees to Doctor
Faustus.
```

Quotation marks may enclose words intended in a special or ironic sense. Use this option sparingly.

```
Doctor Faustus, the "studious artisan," squanders his
twenty-four years of power in trivial pursuits.
```

Single Quotation Marks

Use single quotation marks for quoted material inside other quoted material.

> According to Gerald Pinciss, author of <u>Christopher Marlowe</u>,
> "When Faustus remarks, 'Oh this cheers my soul!' Marlowe
> implies the opposite meaning."

Capitalization with Quotation Marks

Capitalize the first word of a complete quotation but not the first word of a partial quotation (that is, a quotation that is not a complete sentence).

> Faustus thanks Mephistophilis for the book of instructions
> and says, "This will I keep as chary as my life."

> Faustus thanks Mephistophilis for the book of instructions
> and says he will keep it as "chary as my life."

Notice there is no punctuation separating the partial quotation from the rest of the sentence.

Other Punctuation Marks with Quotation Marks

Commas and **periods** always go inside the closing quotation marks, whether they are part of the quoted material or not.

> Wagner brags that he can teach Robin to turn himself into
> "a dog or a cat or a mouse or a rat or anything."

> "I'll teach thee to turn thyself to a dog or a cat or a
> mouse or a rat or anything," brags Wagner to Robin.

Notice that the period at the end of the first sentence above has been changed to a comma in the second sentence, which ends with the acknowledgment phrase.

Question marks and **exclamation marks** are placed inside the closing quotation marks when they are part of the quoted material.

> In a moment of panic, Faustus cries, "I'll burn my books!"

Question marks and exclamation marks are placed outside the closing quotation marks when they are not part of the quoted material.

> Doesn't Mephistophilis warn Faustus that life is hell on
> earth when he says, "Why this is hell, nor am I out of it"?

Colons, **semicolons**, and **dashes** are placed outside the closing quotation marks.

> When hell opens up before him, Faustus cries, "I'll burn my
> books!"; then he exits with the devils.

Quotations are usually separated from their attribution by a comma. However, if the attribution information is an independent clause, it is followed by a **colon**.

> Faustus expresses a philosophy of fatalism when he says,
> "Che sera, serà."

> Faustus reveals his philosophy of fatalism: "Che sera,
> sera."

Forward slashes separate two or three quoted lines of poetry incorporated into your text. (Longer passages should be indented and copied line for line without slashes.) Space before and after the slash.

> Mephistophilis shows no pity when Faustus's twenty-four
> years are spent: "What, weep'st thou! 'Tis too late,
> despair, farewell! / Fools that will laugh on earth, most
> weep in hell."

Indent quoted passages of four or more lines. See the research paper in chapter 6 to see how indented material should look on the page. Notice that the indented material is double-spaced, the left margin is indented one inch, the right margin is not indented at all, and there are no quotation marks around indented material.

Ellipsis Dots

Ellipsis dots show that you have omitted material from a quoted passage. Use three dots when omitting material in the middle of a quotation. Space once before the first dot and once after each dot.

> Faustus believes that all is utterly lost: "Faustus hath
> lost both Germany and the world, yea heaven itself
> . . . and must remain in hell forever!"

Use three ellipsis dots after the original passage's end punctuation mark when leaving out material at the end of a sentence.

```
Faustus regrets his bargain, but he still doesn't repent:
"O, would I had never seen Wittenberg, never read a
book. . . ."
```

```
Faustus believes that all is utterly lost: "Faustus hath
lost both Germany and the world, yea heaven itself! . . ."
```

With a parenthetical reference note, the above passages would appear as follows:

```
Faustus regrets his bargain, but he still doesn't repent:
"O, would I had never seen Wittenberg, never read a book
. . ." (99).
```

```
Faustus believes that all is utterly lost: "Faustus hath
lost both Germany and the world, yea heaven itself!
. . ." (102).
```

Brackets

Brackets signify clarifications in quoted material. Use them to add clarifying words or substitute clear words for unclear ones.

Original Passage

FAUSTUS: But is there not <u>coelum igneum et crystallinum</u>?

Brackets used to add clarifying words

```
Faustus, seeking understanding of astronomy, asks, "But is
there not coelum igneum et crystallinum [a heaven of fire
and a crystalline sphere]?"
```

Brackets used to substitute clear words for unclear ones

```
Faustus, seeking understanding of astronomy, asks, "But is
there not [a heaven of fire and a crystalline sphere]?"
```

Brackets can also indicate a change in capitalization of a quotation for the purpose of maintaining grammatical and mechanical integrity in your sentence:

Original Passage

> Faustus: Here will I dwell, for heaven is in these lips
>   And all is dross that is not Helena.

Quotation

> When it comes to Helen of Troy, Faustus is given to overstatement: "[A]ll is dross that is not Helena."

Notes

[1] Mark Twain, *Good Advice on Writing*, eds. William Safire and Leonard Safir (New York: Simon, 1992) 210.

[2] Hedy Weiss, " 'Aida' Is Gorgeous but Tone Still a Problem," *Chicago Sun Times* 26 Aug. 2002, 48.

[3] Henry David Thoreau, *Good Advice on Writing*, eds. William Safire and Leonard Safir (New York: Simon, 1992) 222.

[4] Cleanth Brooks and Robert Penn Warren, *Good Advice on Writing*, eds. William Safire and Leonard Safir (New York: Simon, 1992) 214.

[5] Lewis Thomas, "Notes on Punctuation," *The Rinehart Reader*, eds. Jean Wyrick and Beverly J. Slaughter, 3rd ed. (Fort Worth: Harcourt, 1999) 470.

Cover

The cover photograph is from a 2003 Denison University Theatre adaptation of William Shakespeare's *The Taming of the Shrew*. Hsing-lin Tracy Chung wrote the adaptation and directed it in the style of *Jingju,* or traditional Chinese opera. Actors: James Ramsey as Little Sister and Tariq Vasudeva, Dominic Dodrill, Matt Orlins, and David McDonald as her suitors. Costume designer: Cynthia Turnbull, chair of the Department of Theatre; scenic and lighting designer: Peter Pauzé; hair and makeup designer: Sarah Lentz. Photographer: Cynthia Turnbull. Thanks to Marilyn Sundin, department secretary, for coordinating efforts to publish the photograph.

Chapter One

1-1: *Hamlet*, by William Shakespeare, produced by the Colorado Shakespeare Festival, Boulder, Colorado, in 1995. Director: Patrick Kelly; costume designer: Jeanne Arnold; scenic designer: D. Martyn Bookwalter. Festival director: Dick Devin; public relations/marketing: Mell McDonnell. Actors: Christopher Burns as Laertes, Joel G. Fink as Polonius, and Florencia Lozano as Ophelia. Photographer: Martin Natvig.

1-2: *Trifles*, by Susan Glaspell, performed at the University of Wisconsin, Oshkosh, in 2001. Director: Richard Kalinoski; set designer: Roy Hoglund, coordinator, Theatre Program. Actors: Christina Perez as Mrs. Hale, Annie Paul-Hitchkock as Mrs. Peters, Noah Trotzke as Sheriff Peters, Greg Johnson as the County Attorney. Photographer: Mick Alderson.

1-3: *Trifles*, by Susan Glaspell, performed at New York University in 2000. Director: Ann MacCormack. Actors: Nina Miller as Mrs. Peters and Shannon Reed as Mrs. Hale. Photographer: Melanie St. James.

Chapter Two

2-1: *Doctor Faustus*, by Christopher Marlowe, performed at Grand Canyon University in 1997. Director and light designer: Claude Pensis; scenic designer: Paul Bridgeman. Actors: Scott Campbell as Faustus and Michael Kary as Mephistophilis. Photographer: Claude Pensis.

2-2: *Death of a Salesman,* by Arthur Miller, performed at the University of Wyoming in 1998. Director: William Missouri Downs; set designer: Ron Steger.

Actors: Kevin Sweeney as Willy, Kathy Kirkaldie as Linda, Rian Jarriel as Biff, Michael Childs as Happy, and Rocky Hopson as Ben. Photographer: Ted C. Brummond.

2-3: *Oleanna*, by David Mamet, performed at Central Washington University in 1994. Director: Wesley Van Tassel. Actors: Duffy Epstein as John and Kerri Van Auken as Carol. Photographer: Leslee Caul.

2-4: *Death of a Salesman*, by Arthur Miller, performed at the University of Wyoming in 1998. Director: William Missouri Downs; set designer: Ron Steger. Actors: Kevin Sweeney as Willy, Kathy Kirkaldie as Linda, Rian Jarriel as Biff, Michael Childs as Happy, and Jason Pasqua as Bernard. Photographer: Ted C. Brummond.

2-5: *The Seagull*, by Anton Chekhov, performed at DePaul University in 1996. Director: Bella Itkin; associate director: Phyllis E. Griffin; set designer: Kevin Hagan; costume designer: Molly Oliver McGrath. Actors: James Driskill as Dorn, Jen Ellison as Masha, Ione Lloyd as the maid, and Carey Peters as Arkadina. Photographer: John Bridges, assistant dean of The Theatre School.

2-6: *Hedda Gabler,* by Henrik Ibsen, performed at Wake Forest University in 1999. Director: J. E. R. Friedenberg; scenic designer: James V. Hilburn, Jr.; costume and hair designer: Lisa M. Weller; lighting designer: Jonathan Christman. Actors: Megan Cramer as Hedda Gabler, Rohom Khonsari as Eilert Lovborg, and Carter MacIntyre as George Tesman. Photographer: Bill Ray III.

Chapter Three

3-1: *Wait Until Dark*, by Frederick Knott, produced by the Castleton State College Theatre Arts Department in 1999. Director: Harry McEnerny. Actors: Frances Binder as Susy Hendrix and Andrew Nystrom as Harry Roat Jr. Photographer: Ennis Duling.

3-2: *The Hairy Ape*, by Eugene O'Neill, produced by the School of Fine and Performing Arts, State University of New York at New Paltz, in 2004. Director: John Wade. Actors: Perry Patton as Yank and members of the "Street" ensemble. Photographer: David Cavallaro.

3-3: *Our Town,* by Thornton Wilder, produced by the Department of Theatre at Louisiana State University in 2003. Director: Jane Drake Brody; scenic designer: F. Nels Anderson; costume designer: Rana Webber; lighting designer: Pat Acampora. Department chair: Michael S. Tick. Actors: Katie Crawford as Emily, and (from left to right in the foreground) Leah Star as Mrs. Gibbs, Gresdna Doty as Mrs. Soames, C. Micajah Burke as Baseball Player/Mr. Carter, Luke Siddall as Former McCarthy, Katie Sills as first Dead Woman, and Blake Williams as Simon Stimson. Photographer: Chipper Hatter.

3-4: *Macbeth,* by William Shakespeare, performed at the University of Wyoming in 1997. Director: Lou Anne Wright; scenic designer: Ronald Steger. Actors: Thomas Martin as Young Siward, Tom Cilek as Macbeth, and Shawn Bunning as Macduff. Photographer: Ted C. Brummond.

3-5: *Trifles* by Susan Glaspell, performed at Messiah College in 2003. Director and costume designer: Kasi L. Krenzer Marshall; set designer: Alexander Libby;

light designer: Melissa Mendez. Actors: Joanna Pfister as Mrs. Hale and Laura A. Sylvester as Mrs. Peters. Photographer: Melissa Engle.

3-6: *Othello,* by William Shakespeare, performed at the University of Kansas, Lawrence, in 2002. Director: Paul Meier; scenic designer: Dennis Christilles; costume designer: Elinor Parker. Actors: Christopher Wheatley as Lodovico, Rita DeLoach as Bianca, Aaron Champion as Cassio, and Tom Picasso as Roderigo. Photographer: Luke Jordan.

3-7: *Othello,* by William Shakespeare, produced by the Department of Theatre, University of Illinois at Urbana-Champaign in 2002. Director: Henson Keys; scenic designer: R. Eric Stone. Head, Department of Theatre: R. B. Graves. Photographer: R. Eric Stone.

3-8: *Waiting for Godot*, by Samuel Beckett, performed at DePaul University in 2003. Director: John Jenkins; scenic designer: Erica Hemminger; costume designer: Nan Cibula-Jenkins; lighting designer: Kathryn Eader. Department chair: John Culbert. Actors: Dan Kerr-Hobert as Estragon and Seth Unger as Vladimir. Photographer: John Bridges. Thanks to Karin McKie and Lara Goetsch for their assistance in obtaining the photos and permission.

Chapter Four

4-1: *Antigone,* by Sophocles, produced by the University of South Carolina Department of Theatre and Dance in 2002. Director: Jay Berkow; set designer: Nic Ularu; costume designer: Rebecca Hadley. Artistic director: Jim O'Connor; director of marketing and public relations: Tim Donahue. Actors: Scott Bellot as Teiresius and Michael Kroeker as Creon. Photographer: Jason Ayer.

4-2: *A Doll's House,* by Henrik Ibsen, produced by the Department of Theatre at Northern State University, Aberdeen, South Dakota, in 2004. Director: Daniel Yurgaitis; set designer: Larry Wild. Actors: Heather Woehlhaff as Nora and Rory K. Behrens as Dr. Rank. Photographer: Larry Wild.

4-3: *A Doll's House,* by Henrik Ibsen, produced by the Department of Theatre and Dance at Minnesota State University, Mankato, in 2002. Director: Nina LeNoir; set designer: Tom Bliese; costume designer: Esther Iverson. Department chair: Paul Hustoles. Actors: Erin J. Drevlow as Nora; Christian D. Bell as Torvald; Trick Danneker as Dr. Rank, and Shannon More as Mrs. Linde. Photographer: Mike Lagerquist.

4-4: *A Doll's House,* by Henrik Ibsen, produced by the Department of Fine Arts and Communications at Tarleton State University in 1999. Director: Mark Holtorf; scenery designer: Carol Stavish; costume designer: Jennifer Harlen. Actors: Summar Cabaniss as Nora and James Brownlee as Torvald. Photographer: Dayle Cox.

4-5: *A Doll's House,* by Henrik Ibsen, produced by the Vanderbilt University Theatre in 2001. Director: John Hallquist; scenic and lighting designer: Phillip Franck; costume designer: Elizabeth Pollard. Directors of the Theatre: Jon and Terryl Hallquist. Actors: Laura Love as Nora and Riley Bryant as Torvald. Photographer: Phillip Franck.

4-6: *A Doll's House,* by Henrik Ibsen, produced by the Department of Theatre and Dance at Minnesota State University, Mankato, in 2002. Director: Nina LeNoir; set designer: Tom Bliese; costume designer: Esther Iverson. Department chair: Paul

Hustoles. Actors: Erin J. Drevlow as Nora and Christian D. Bell as Torvald. Photographer: Mike Lagerquist.

4-7: *The Taming of the Shrew*, adapted from William Shakespeare's play for *Jingju* performance by Hsing-lin Tracy Chung, produced by Denison University Theatre in 2003. Director: Hsing-lin Tracy Chung; scenic and lighting designer: Peter Pauzé; costume designer: Cynthia Turnbull, department chair; hair and makeup designer: Sarah Lentz. Actors: Melinda Hughes as Rouge Tigress and Mark Soloff as Lion Dog. Photographer: Cynthia Turnbull.

Chapter Five

5-1: *Waiting for Godot*, by Samuel Beckett, performed at Belmont University in 2004. Director: Lynn Eastes; set designer: Maddy Rhodes; department chair: Paul Gatrell. Actor: Roxanne Benjamin as Lucky. Photographer: Rick Malkin.

5:2: *A Midsummer Night's Dream*, by William Shakespeare, produced by the Department of Theatre at the University of Alabama at Birmingham in 1999. Director: Karma Ibsen; scenery and lighting designer: Kelly Allison; costume designer: Russell Drummond. Actors: Christopher Reeves as Oberon and Anthony Irons as Puck. Photographer: Kelly Allison. Thanks to department chair, Marc Powers.

5-3: *Mother Courage and Her Children,* by Bertolt Brecht, performed at the State University of New York, Stony Brook, in 2002. Director: Chris Dolman; scenic designer: Kip Marsh; lighting designer: Russ Behrens; costume designer: Peggy Morin. Actors: Will Montolio, Josh Adler, and Grantly Scott. Photographer: Maxine Hicks. Thanks to Steve Marsh, public relations director.

5-4: *The Cherry Orchard* by Anton Chekhov, produced by the Brandeis University Department of Theater Arts in 2004. Director: Liz Terry; costume designer: Suzanne Chesney; scenic designer: Monah Curley-Clay. Actors: Robert Antonelli as Yepikhodov, Shanessa Sweeney as Charlotta, Abigail Milliner Killeen as Ranyevskaya, Mara Radulovic as Dunyasha, Angie Jepson as Anya, and Yaegel Welch as Lopakhin. Photographer: Mike Lovett. Thanks to Alicia Hyland, staff assistant, David Colfer, general manager, and Eric Hill, department chair.

5-5: *Mother Courage and Her Children*, by Bertolt Brecht, performed at the University of Colorado in 2003. Director: Lynn Nichols; scenic designer: Bruce Bergner; costume designer: Anne Murphy. Department chair: Bud Coleman; Publicity coordinator: Margi Purcell. Actors: Tomoko Komura as Kattrin and Courtney Prusse as Mother Courage. Photographer: Steven McDonald.

Chapter Six

6-1: *Oleanna*, by David Mamet. Playbills from the play's opening in New York at the Orpheum Theatre, October 1992. The performance, directed by David Mamet, featured William H. Macy as John and Rebecca Pidgeon as Carol.

6-2: *Trifles* by Susan Glaspell, performed at Messiah College in 2003. Director and costume designer: Kasi L. Krenzer Marshall; set designer: Alexander Libby;

light designer: Melissa Mendez. Actors: Laura A. Sylvester as Mrs. Peters and
Joanna Pfister as Mrs. Hale. Photographer: Melissa Engle.

Handbook

H-1: *Oedipus Rex,* by Sophocles, produced by the Department of Theatre at the
University at Albany, State University of New York in 1990. Director: Jarka Burian;
scenery and costume designer: Paul Tazewell; lighting designer: Andi Lyons. Actor:
Glenn Fleschler as Oedipus. Photographer: Andi Lyons.

H-2: *The Iceman Cometh,* by Eugene O'Neill, performed at Lewis University in
1979. Director and scenic and lighting designer: Harold McCay; costume designer:
Maureen Hunsley. Actors: Dave Fellows as Hickey, Tim Philbin as Harry Hope,
Mark Neal as Don Parritt, Laura Brady as Cora, E. J. Flessor as Larry Slade, Candy
Forsyth as Perl, Dan Walsh as Chuck Morello, Tim Tierney as Ed Mosher, T. Jay
Solon as Willie Oban, Therese Murphy as Margie, Mike Carroll as Rocky Pioggi,
and Rodney McKinney as Jo Mott. Photographer: Harold McCay.

H-3: *A Raisin in the Sun,* by Lorraine Hansberry, produced by the University of
Iowa Department of Theatre Arts in 1999. Director: Harriette M. Pierce; scenic
designer: Margaret Wenk; costume designer: Kaoime Malloy; lighting designer:
Bryon Winn. Department chair: Alan MacVey; marketing director: Judith Moessner.
Actors: Sherri Marina as Mama/Lena Younger, Ruqayya Raheem as Beneatha,
Michael Marina as Travis, Joyce McKinley as Ruth, and Douglas Howington as
Walter Lee. Photographer: Reggie Morrow.

H-4: *Doctor Faustus,* by Christopher Marlowe, performed at Baylor University
in 2003. Director: Steven Pounders; scenic designer: William T. Sherry; costume
designer: Sally Askins. Photographer: Jason Raddin.

Index